The Anza Trail

THE ANZA TRAIL
AND THE
SETTLING OF CALIFORNIA

Vladimir Guerrero

SANTA CLARA UNIVERSITY, SANTA CLARA, CALIFORNIA
HEYDAY BOOKS, BERKELEY, CALIFORNIA

Library of Congress Cataloging-in-Publication Data
Guerrero, Vladimir.
  The Anza Trail and the settling of California / Vladimir Guerrero.
      p. cm. — (A California legacy book)
   ISBN 1-59714-026-0 (pbk. : alk. paper)
   1. California—Discovery and exploration—Spanish. 2. Pacific Coast (Calif.)—Discovery and exploration—Spanish. 3. Anza, Juan Bautista de, 1735-1788—Travel—California. 4. Explorers—California—History—18th century. 5. California—History—To 1846. I. Title. II. Series.
   F864.G844 2006
   979.4—dc22   2006002548

Cover Art: ©Royalty Free/Corbis
Cover Design: Rebecca LeGates
Interior Design/Typesetting: Philip Krayna Design, Berkeley, CA
Maps: Ben Pease, Pease Press
Printing and Binding: McNaughton & Gunn, Saline, MI

Orders, inquiries, and correspondence should be addressed to:
        Heyday Books
        P. O. Box 9145, Berkeley, CA 94709
        (510) 549-3564, Fax (510) 549-1889
        www.heydaybooks.com

Printed in the United States of America
10 9 8 7 6 5 4 3 2 1

Contents

SECOND EXPEDITION

*This book is dedicated to all the living descendants
of the 1776 California settlers, and in particular to
Greg Bernal–Mendoza Smestad and Phil Valdez Jr.,
eighth-generation Californios whose interest in
and extensive knowledge of the Anza expeditions and
routes is surpassed only by their generosity and
willingness to share it with others.*

Acknowledgments

The author would like to acknowledge the generous research grant provided by The Book Club of California, which made possible the acquisition of materials as well as helped defray the cost of travel on the expedition routes. The author would also like to acknowledge the following institutions for copies of manuscript documents: the Newberry Library of Chicago; the Smithsonian, Washington, DC; the John Carter Brown Library of Providence; and the Holt-Atherton Collection of the University of the Pacific. Also helpful was the "Web de Anza" (http://anza.uoregon.edu/), which allowed use of their online archives. And most important, the author would like to thank Meredith Kaplan, former superintendent of the Juan Bautista de Anza National Historic Trail, for her encouragement to write this book, and Lisa K. Manwill of Heyday Books, for her editorial work.

This publication was made possible in part by the Department of the Interior, National Park Service Challenge Cost Share Program. The views and conclusions contained in this document are those of the authors and should not be interpreted as representing the opinions or policies of the U.S. Government. Mention of trades names or commercial products does not constitute their endorsement by the U.S. Government.

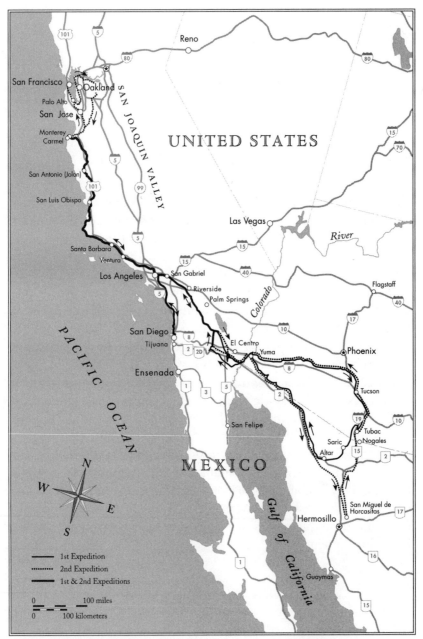

Anza Expedition Routes in Modern Times

Introduction

This is the story of the two expeditions (in 1774 and 1775–1776) that turned the Spanish settlements of Alta California into a unique society. At an individual level, it is also the story of several men of different backgrounds—European and Native American—whose interaction and cooperation made possible bringing the first large group of settlers to the northwestern frontier of New Spain. It is, in short, the story of the migration of a racially diverse and yet integrated group of Spanish subjects who were the genesis of the Californio society, the Pilgrims of the State of California.

The first expedition was exploratory. It left the garrison at Tubac (then a frontier outpost of New Spain, now in present-day Arizona) in January of 1774 and reached the Presidio at Monterey in April of the same year. Since at the time the Spanish settlements in California were only accessible by sea, opening this overland route was an important breakthrough. The second expedition left Tubac in September of 1775 and arrived in Monterey in March of 1776, bringing some fifty families to establish a settlement near San Francisco Bay.

While this text chronicles the exploration of an overland route from Mexico to Alta California and records the events leading up to the colonization of the Bay Area, it is the people who are the heart of the epic. There are four main individuals—one *criollo*, one Spaniard, and two Native Americans—whose interacting roles weave the plot of the story: Juan Bautista de Anza, the commander; Francisco Garcés, the priest-explorer; Sebastián Tarabal, the accidental guide; and Salvador Palma, the chief-facilitator. The background and positions of these men are as interesting as they were different.

Juan Bautista de Anza was a white criollo (an American-born Spaniard). His rank as presidio commander gave him a distinguished position in frontier society. Approaching the peak of his career in his late thirties, by the time of the 1774 expedition, he had earned the trust of his superiors and the respect of his troops.

Anza was accompanied by Father Francisco Garcés, who, like most missionaries, was a Spanish-born white. While he enjoyed his standing as a man of the cloth, his identification with and respect for the Native Americans had won him something he valued more: the friendship of the various tribes he had lived with during the months he has spent trekking solo through the frontier. He combined his religious vocation and love for the land and its people with an absolute loyalty to the crown.

In Anza's service as guide was Sebastián Tarabal, a Native American from Baja California whose education and baptism had earned him the status of a Spanish subject (a "person of reason") and had brought him and his wife north to the mission at San Gabriel (in present-day Los Angeles). While his various skills, including that of interpreter, had earned him recognition by the religious community, it had not earned him the right to choose his place of residence and freely return to his home village; therefore, when he escaped San Gabriel for home, he became a fugitive and, captured by the Yuma, was turned over to the authorities, who eventually sent him to Anza.

The final main character, Salvador Palma, was the chief of the Yuma nation, an agricultural society settled at the junction of the Gila and Colorado Rivers and the dominant power of the region. Palma's acquaintance with Garcés two years before the first Anza expedition had been the turning point of his life. Won over by the priest and his religion, Palma's objective thereafter had been to bring himself and the Yuma into the Spanish political and religious orbit. He thus became an ally to Anza and integral to the success of the expeditions.

Although these four men came from different backgrounds and had different goals, they were all brought together for a common cause: securing strategic Spanish claims. Because English vessels sporadically preyed on galleons returning from the Philippines to Mexico along the California coast, Spain feared England might attempt to establish a permanent settlement there (as Russians trappers had already done further north). If Alta California were to remain Spanish, they would need garrisons in addition to those at San Diego and Monterey, as well as faster communications between those centers of power.

These objectives, however, were no small task. Due to the coastal currents and prevailing winds, to sail north from New Spain to Alta California sometimes took twice to three times as long as crossing the Atlantic. Even the short distance from San Blas on the mainland to La Paz at the tip of Baja California could take two to three weeks. Without a direct trail by land, it was not unusual for communications between Monterey and Mexico (1,500 miles to the southern tip of Baja California, across by sea to San Blas, and a further 500 miles to Mexico City) to take four to six months. By the early 1770s, it was clear that the colonization of Alta California required an overland connection. The more than 2,000-mile distance, already daunting on horseback, would include forging more than 500 miles of unexplored territory between Sonora and the coast of California, an area known to include deserts, the Colorado River, and several potentially hostile native tribes.

The task of exploring an overland route went to Juan Bautista de Anza, captain of the presidio at Tubac, the most northerly garrison in Sonora. Born and bred in the frontier where he had spent his entire life, Anza had the skills and experience to lead such an expedition. His knowledge of the region was unsurpassed and his reputation as a first-class commander well established. In this assignment he would be accompanied by Father Francisco Garcés, a priest from the nearby mission of San Xavier del Bac with extensive knowledge of the region and its people. A more qualified team than Anza and Garcés could hardly be found. The first expedition (detailed in the first half of this book), included 20 veteran soldiers, a second priest, a native guide, servants, and mule drivers—in all totaling 34 men and 140 mounts. Leaving their garrison in January of 1774, they reached Monterey in April and were back at Tubac by May.

The first expedition's success earned Anza a promotion to lieutenant colonel and an even more challenging assignment. King Charles III, having acquired the ability to strengthen Spain's territorial claims, lost no time in ordering the establishment of an additional presidio and mission near the "River of San Francisco." Anza's new task would be recruiting men with families to be soldiers and settlers in Alta California and then leading them there.

Preparations began at the end of the year, and by September of 1775 the second expedition (240 men, women, and children, with over 1,000 animals) was on its way. The second half of this narrative follows the group as it crosses deserts and mountains during the winter to reach Monterey. Having successfully delivered the colonists to the mission in March of 1776, Anza then transferred his charges to Fernando Rivera y Moncada, the governor of California, before returning to Mexico in April. Two months later, in June of 1776, the group was led by Lieutenant Joaquin Moraga to the shores of San Francisco Bay, where they established the planned presidio and mission and thereby secured Spain's position on the coast.

During the last quarter of the eighteenth century, the New World stage had two key players: Spain and England. The former, present in the area for two and a half centuries, controlled most of the land from California to Peru and from the Caribbean to the Pacific, as well as the largest islands of the Antilles. By comparison, the thirteen English colonies, extending inland only a few hundred miles from the coast, were a small and relatively new enclave, even when England's political might, with a navy second to none, was the rising world power, making its strength felt throughout the world. Nevertheless, Spain already administered half and claimed three quarters of the continent.

Within Spain's enormous territory, administered from the capital at Mexico City, there was a population of some four to five million people, of whom 80 percent were Native Americans. Of the other 20 percent, a quarter to a third may have been of European descent, while the rest were mestizo, many in the coastal areas with traces of African blood. Perhaps 25 to 30 percent of the total population, ranging from illiterate peasants to "people of reason," were sufficiently assimilated to participate in the colonial economy and were considered Spanish subjects or, in modern terminology, Spanish citizens.

The peninsular and American-born upper class, making up some 5 to 6 percent of the total population, was predominantly white but, from as early as the mid-sixteenth century, had also included mestizos. The term "criollo," which initially meant a white Spaniard born in America, gradually acquired the implication of racial mixture, eventually becoming interchangeable with "mestizo." Changing over time, the term "mestizo," which had initially designated that a person was racially mixed, acquired the connotation that he or she was of lower social standing relative to a criollo. By the eighteenth century, with a significant presence of mestizos in the colonial aristocracy, the term "Spaniard" eventually came to designate any member of the upper class, regardless of race.

Despite the progressive integration throughout the spectrum of society, the distribution of privilege and power in practice continued to reflect racial biases. While the upper echelons of government bureaucracy, the church, industry, commerce, and the military included mestizos, their numbers were neither proportional to their population nor geographically representative. Their presence in high positions was more frequent in distant outposts than in the metropolis or close to the centers of power, and, by the same token, mestizos and natives dominated labor and service positions throughout the colony and made up the majority of the enlisted ranks in the military.

Although far from equality by present standards, the system did, however, openly enable indigenous participation in the mainstream of the new society. During 250 years of colonization, Spain had transplanted its institutions and traditions while at the same time incorporating indigenous elements to create a hybrid society on the American continent. One example of this integration of cultures was the church's acceptance of the Virgin of Guadalupe, a Native American woman, as one version of the mother of God.

Still, integration was not easy. While cultural and religious differences certainly existed between the many groups of European colonizers in the New World, those paled in comparison with the differences between them and the Native American nations. While European societies shared a Greco-Roman heritage, Christianity in various forms, written (if different) legal systems and languages, and the scientific knowledge that had made their presence in the New World possible, Native American nations, on the other hand, were traditional societies depending on orality rather than literacy for cultural, material, and historical continuity. Coupled with limited technical development and, up to the sixteenth century, lack of horses, most indigenous groups (with the exception of some large societies, including the Aztecs and the Incas) were isolated nations deriving a modest existence from their environment. Lacking a common religion, individual tribes often existed in harmony with the natural environment, seasonal cycles, and animal migrations, all of which they were an integral part.

European nations, however, for the most part failed to understand or appreciate such cultures. The differences in ways of life and material accomplishments, not to mention the challenges they had in communicating with them, created a barrier reflected in their classification of natives as "savage" and themselves as "civilized." Spain, however, approached this barrier differently, due in part to its historical relationship with Christianity.

Spain was forged from the kingdoms of Leon, Castile, Navarre, and Aragon during seven centuries of Moslem, Jewish, and Christian coexistence. After the Moslem conquest of the peninsula in the eighth century, "nationality" was determined by religion; to be Christian was to be "Spanish." The original Moslem invaders had been Arab, and they were followed by North Africans, but over time the majority of the Moslems in the peninsula were descendants of local converts and had for centuries called the region home. The Christians, who referred to their Moslem neighbors as Moors, nevertheless still considered them alien regardless of origin and in spite of their long-established presence in the area.

Converts to Christianity, on the other hand, were considered "Spanish" regardless of ethnicity; in fact, since the end of the fifteenth century, when the various kingdoms came together under Ferdinand and Isabel, baptism was the official stamp of citizenship. This practice was formalized after the reconquest of the last Moslem enclave, Granada, enabled the king and queen to expel from their domains all who refused conversion to Christianity. Since these two events coincided with the discovery of America in 1492, it is easy to understand that the crown viewed the conversion of Native Americans in the same light: Natives who accepted the Christian religion and learned the Spanish language became subjects of the crown; these "gentiles" became "people of reason."

The Anza expeditions of 1774 to 1776 constitute a little-known chapter in American history—the story of an immigrant group that established the character of California as much as the Puritans determined that of New England. Even though these settlers were in the service of the crown, they, like most immigrants, came by their own choosing, motivated by the prospect of a better life for themselves and their families. To achieve that in a distant and unknown land, they had the will and the courage to undertake a voyage as long and difficult as any Atlantic crossing. Whether mestizo, white, indigenous, or black, they were a close-knit society with strong cultural and religious ties. As Spanish subjects relocating within their domains, they remained loyal to their king. It was only seventy-five years later, with Spain and England expelled from the American mainland, that the United States in its westward expansion came to them, and these immigrants—assuming the name of "Californios"—took their place in American history.

Established as a racially mixed Catholic society, Spanish California abruptly found itself the subject of an alien master; the American people were a white, Protestant group of mostly northern European heritage. Primarily the offspring of an English tradition that designated the dominant language, the young nation had little taste for southern European culture or religion, or descendants of African slaves or indigenous people. It is therefore not surprising that the culturally and racially different Spanish settlers did not fit in. Numerically overwhelmed in the 1850s by immigration following the gold rush, the Californios became a minority group in their own land and—as the Anglo majority imposed their language, religion, and legal system—a marginalized underclass. Written history, however, largely reflects the mainstream of American society, and over time cast a romantic veil over the origins of Spanish California. The Californios were incorrectly idealized as Spanish grandees with vast holdings of land and cattle long since vanished, survived only by a few partly indigenous people assumed to have been their servants.

While this book chronologically follows the two expeditions that led to the founding of San Francisco, it will also bring to life the men whose actions made that story possible, and at the same time reveal the origins of an early society that is part of our heritage. With the recent creation of the Juan Bautista de Anza National Historic Trail, which follows the expedition routes, the National Park Service has officially recognized Anza's contribution to American history. It is hoped that this book will not only cast new light on Anza himself and on the society in which he lived but also recognize Salvador Palma and Sebastián Tarabal, two outstanding Native Americans sidelined by history, for their key roles in the settling of California.

Monterey, California
January 2006

THE SOURCES

The reconstruction of this story is based primarily on the journals of three participants: Garcés for the first, Father Pedro Font for the second, and Anza for both. The journals were supplemented by Rivera y Moncada's diary, the relevant correspondence of Father Junípero Serra, and the official records of Palma's visit to Mexico City in 1776. The documents used were photocopies of the longhand originals, textual transcriptions, or, as a last resort, published Spanish editions. All of the translations included in this text are original to the author.

The source materials are heavily biased by each author's agenda and his intended recipient. Anza's journals, for example, are brief and factual, if often overoptimistic progress reports written for the viceroy. They mention few problems, contain precious little about the human side of the settlers or his assistants, and record nothing concerning personnel conflicts. Garcés' writing is equally uncritical, succinct, and laconic. In addition, both authors have such poor command of syntax and grammar that interpreting their texts sometimes required using external sources.

By contrast, Font not only has excellent mastery of the language, but he is also prolific and meticulous in his observation of (sometimes irrelevant) detail. He does not shy away from mentioning problems, giving praise, or criticizing when required. It is because of his openness and his dedication to preparing an extended version of his journal a year after the second expedition that we know so much about it. Having submitted his official and much shorter journal to the authorities, it is unclear who the long version (with its subtle censure of Garcés and open disapproval of Anza) was intended for. Regardless, his text, as told from the perspective of a rigid, intolerant, and Eurocentric priest, is a gold mine of personal detail about the expedition and colonial society.

While Font presents us with a rich human narrative, Garcés and Anza deal only with issues of interest to the authorities: the opening of the route in the first expedition, and the progress of the settlers, the native uprising, and the conflict with Rivera in the second. Once results were achieved, neither paid much attention to how the obstacles were overcome or who was instrumental in the process. With two exceptions—the crossing of the Colorado, where all three diarists recognize Palma's assistance; and the crisis with Rivera, which remained unresolved—credit for each accomplishment implicitly reverts to Anza, most particularly in the commander's own diary. The numerous local guides remain anonymous, and Tarabal's role as guide, interpreter, advisor, and diplomat, although frequently mentioned as a matter of fact, is never openly praised.

FIRST
EXPEDITION

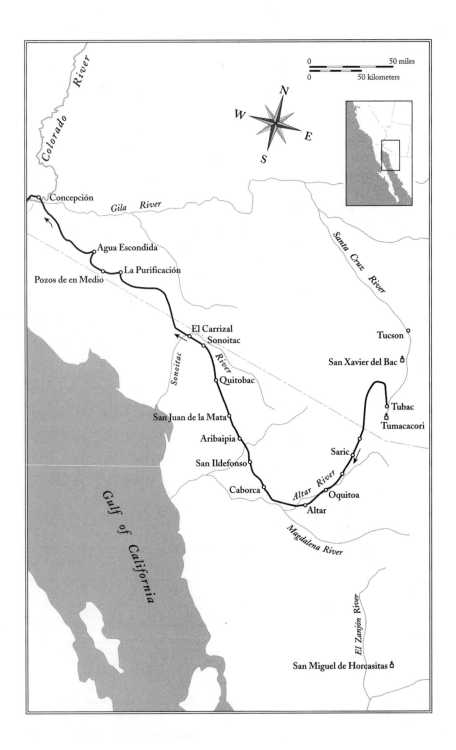

Encounters in the Desert: From Tubac to the Colorado River

January 8 to February 8, 1774

Day 1
Saturday, January 8, 1774

When dawn outlined the hills east of Tubac that winter day, more than three months of preparations had been completed and, in spite of the Apache raid that had taken many of their horses only days before, the expedition was finally getting under way.

Anza had found it necessary to implement some last-minute adjustments, and this had caused friction with Father Garcés, but after considering the priest's opinion, the commander had made his own decision; the expedition was his responsibility, and he had no doubt that the change in route was necessary. Instead of heading northwest, in the direction of their destination, and crossing the Colorado River north of its junction with the Gila River, they would begin their journey by traveling south on the Camino Real, the king's road. The edge of Christendom and, even more significantly, that of effective Spanish control was just a few leagues to the north, beyond the San Xavier and Tucson missions.[1] The Apaches in the area had shown time and again their ability to strike and vanish, leaving death and disaster in their path, and Anza knew that thirty-four men with over a hundred mounts, slowed down by four-score head of cattle, were too tempting and vulnerable a target. And if the expedition were attacked before reaching the Colorado River, the probability of its eventual success would be greatly diminished. Achieving the objective of the expedition—to open an overland route from northern Mexico to Nueva California—would determine Anza's decisions; the priest's reaction mattered little.

It was not at all by chance that Father Francisco Garcés was accompanying Anza. He spoke several dialects, was proficient in sign language, and had traveled over vast areas of the frontier using only local guides. Two years before, he had reached the Colorado River and returned through the same Pima country that they were now to cross. Garcés felt his role in the expedition to be much more than spiritual. Officially in the service of God, he was also and equally in the service of his king, and he saw little difference between army and church as tools to effect evangelization. After all, since the apostle Saint James' (San Yago) appearance fighting Moors during the Reconquest, Spanish clergy had campaigned side by side with the military, sometimes with sword in hand. In the Age of Enlightenment, missionaries no longer bore arms, but that did not preclude Garcés' contributing his skills as an all-around scout and explorer, gathering information on everything from terrain to native politics. In fact, the priest's input had been a significant part of Anza's justification for initially proposing the expedition, and while considering approval, the viceroy had consulted him as well. But this was the military, and Captain Juan Bautista de Anza was the commander, so his word was final.

In age and temperament, Anza and Garcés were very close. The American-born captain was one generation removed from the Basque country, while the priest was a native of Aragón, a neighboring region on the slopes of the Pyrenees. If the Aragonese are reputed to be the most stubborn people in Spain, the Basque are not far behind. Both were in their mid-thirties, and each was recognized by his superiors to be self-reliant, deeply committed to duty, intelligent, and ambitious, and both were well liked by their peers. It was inevitable that these two strong personalities would occasionally clash, in spite of the friendship and mutual respect they had for each other.

From neither of their journals, however, do we gather the depth of their disagreement. It is from a letter written two months later by Father Junípero Serra just after talking with Garcés in San Diego that we learn the priest's opinion. And from Anza it is nearly two years later, in his preparation for the second expedition (in which Garcés also participated), that he emphatically asked Viceroy Bucareli to clearly define and limit the accompanying priests' function to spiritual matters. For the most part, the men were restrained in their writings and cordial in person.

As the sun rose over the Santa Rita Mountains, the presidio was a hive of activity. In the tradition of Spain, no enterprise of exploration was ever set in motion without religious ceremony, and modest in size as this one was, it would be no exception. Fathers Garcés and Diaz, the two priests assigned to the task, were preparing to celebrate a high mass, as solemn and splendid as the limited means of this frontier outpost would permit. For over an hour, all work ceased; soldiers, mule drivers, officers, and indeed every man, woman, and child at the garrison was present. Garcés intoned the opening song; Diaz lifted the crucifix. Behind them the procession slowly crossed the square toward the chapel while the hills echoed their Salve Regina. The music, the candles, the incense, and the ceremony that commemorated Christ's last supper on earth were part of the identity of this nation that saw itself called to bring eternal salvation to all corners of the earth. The two kingdoms, the heavenly one above and that of Charles III in Madrid, could not have been closer. Divine help was requested through the Holy Trinity and protection through Mary, the virgin mother of God in Christ.

When the ceremony was over, the supplies of dried meat, ammunition, tobacco, corn, cooking pots, tools, tents, and weapons were packed and balanced on thirty-five mules. Eventually, the commander mounted his horse. Garcés rode beside him in silence, not bothering to conceal his disapproval, followed by Father Diaz, the corporal, twenty Tubac regulars leading scores of scrawny mounts, the cargo, and, lagging behind the long train, the dust-covered cattle. Accompanying the priests and soldiers were the guide Sebastián Tarabal (a native from a Baja California tribe), five mule drivers, a Pima Indian interpreter, a carpenter, and several servants.[2] At 1:00 in the afternoon, the sun had vanquished the chill. The dusty train

---

[2] The group Anza knew as "Pima" are today called the Akimel O'odham.

moved slowly north, the mule drivers learning to know each other and the animals, and the latter resenting the heavy loads and new ways. They rode north with the Tumacacori Mountains on their left to a trail junction where Anza waited, inspecting the group as it passed. They were not up to military standard. It had taken them several hours to get moving, and it would take them just as long to unload and prepare for the night. They had only been on the march for an hour, but he decided to call it a day. He wanted to set up camp and drill the departure routine before darkness closed the short winter day. The animals were put to pasture; interpreters and guide ate with the soldiers around the fire; the commander and priests, attended by their servants, dined in a small group across from them.

Anza moved with ease among his troops. It was important that all should learn to know and work with each other; in a crisis, trust and teamwork would be the keys to survival. He was determined not to let any grudge fester or even develop. After the meal, he again brought up the reasons for his decision to change the expedition's route. A step-by-step review of the problem would be a way to smooth the situation. Even though he agreed with Garcés on the desirability of traveling in a north and northwesterly direction, both to the Colorado River and beyond, under the present circumstances it was too risky. He again emphasized the higher threat of attack by Apaches north of Tubac. Traveling south, it might be possible to obtain horses at Altar or Caborca or perhaps from the mines at Cieneguilla to replace those they had lost to the Apaches. And once the expedition had crossed the Colorado, he wanted to maximize the benefit of Sebastián Tarabal's experience.

Only weeks before, Tarabal had covered the entire distance between Caborca and Mission San Gabriel—from northern Mexico to present-day Los Angeles—but in the opposite direction, although it could hardly be said that he knew the route. When he had escaped from the mission with his wife and another man, their objective had been to regain their village in Baja California, but fear of capture had driven them east into the desert, where two had perished. Sebastián was rescued from the same fate when he was found, barely alive, by the Yuma.[3] Their chief, Palma, recognizing him for a deserter and hoping to gain favor with the Spaniards, had personally delivered

---

[3] The Yuma people are now known as the Quechan.

him to Altar, the last presidio before the Gulf of California, but instead of being punished, Tarabal benefited from the expedition's need for a guide. Anza took him into his service. Tarabal began to refer to Palma as his savior (*salvador* in Spanish), and the name stuck to the chief, who thereafter was known as Salvador Palma.

On the problem of the horses, Garcés could hardly disagree, but Anza's decision to rely on Tarabal's experience really irked him. Using input from Yumas and his own intuition, Garcés believed that crossing the Colorado farther north of its junction with the Gila and proceeding west at the latitude of San Luis Obispo would take them through easier terrain than the desert. He had experienced the sand dunes of the lower Colorado basin and knew how they would exhaust the animals; there would be little pasture and water would be brackish and hard to find. He felt the alternative could not be worse.

Anza had considered this, weighing the known hardships against the unknown, but Sebastián Tarabal had tipped the balance in favor of the southerly route. The California native had just crossed mountains and desert—and survived. His experience could not have been more relevant, nor his arrival in Altar more perfectly timed; the hand of Providence could be sensed somewhere behind the scenes.

A reasoned conversation helped both men: Garcés may have been stubborn, but he was also generous and recognized Anza's overture of peace. Sentries were posted to watch the horses and guard the perimeter. Below a crystal-clear sea of stars, the fires slowly turned to ash and the camp gradually fell silent.

Day 2
Sunday, January 9, 1774

Packing and loading began at dawn and went smoother than on the first day; the expedition was under way by 8:00, traveling for the first ten days of the journey in the relative comfort and safety of the Camino Real. The royal road marked a vague frontier between the Pima and New Spain. To the west, the Pimería (Land of the Pima) was an arid, mountainous country of dry riverbeds and little vegetation, barely capable of supporting life. The Camino Real traced a northeast-to-southwest route linking the missions between San Xavier at the northern end and Caborca in the south. From Tucson the road paralleled the Santa Cruz River into what is now Sonora, crossing the Pajarito Mountains and following the Altar Valley.

At the time in question, the end of the Camino Real marked the northwest limits of inland Spanish control. The Spanish crown had been present in Alta California since 1769 as far as Monterey, but there was no administrative connection between Alta California and the internal provinces of New Spain. The area beyond Altar was therefore a known and neglected no-man's-land. Only a few Europeans, predominantly Spanish missionaries, had ventured through, the Jesuits establishing two missions there that had not survived. The area extending to the Gulf of California had little to offer, and since the Pima uprising two decades before, Spain had deliberately neglected it. In contrast, the Altar Valley, through which Anza had decided to travel on these first days, included, in addition to the presidio, several villages and missions as well as farming and mining operations. While threatened by Apache raids from the north, it was overall a functioning social and economic province.

Days 3 to 5
Monday, January 10, to Wednesday, January 12, 1774

Monday was uneventful. The clear dawn had given way to scattered clouds as the trail climbed gradually between small sierra on either side. By late afternoon, having covered some seven leagues, the travelers had set up camp where they knew there would be water, a mile west of the Camino Real. Overnight, light rain turned into snow, which by morning had left a wet, white blanket over the hills. Daybreak was dismally gray. Rain and snow alternated sporadically for two days while they waited in camp at Agua Escondida.

Day 6
Thursday, January 13, 1774

During the night the skies cleared, and by early morning the expedition was on the trail, descending along a small river and then southward through the valley. After their enforced rest it was an enjoyable seven-league trek in bright sunshine, and by late afternoon they had set up camp near Saric, a Pima village with a mission church. The surrounding fields could support grazing, and the nearby junction of two streams and a spring could have provided more than enough water for crops to feed a town of two thousand. But according to Anza's journal, due to fear of Apache raids, barely forty families were living there. Slabs of virgin silver had been found on the surface in a mineral-rich area by the name of La Arizona, some eight leagues to the northeast, but this area too remained undeveloped for fear of the Apache.

Days 7 to 9
Friday, January 14, to Sunday, January 16, 1774

The expedition continued on its leisurely pace through the villages of Tubutama, Santa Teresa, San Francisco de Ati, and Oquitoa. These were communities of twenty to thirty families each, mostly Christian Pimas, with Oquitoa also having a dozen families of Spanish subjects.[4]

The Altar Valley was a small wheel in the large mining machinery of New Spain, helping to fill the royal coffers while sustaining itself agriculturally. With laws and enforcement, currency, taxes, a written language, and a Christian church, it was a functioning economy in which both Pimas and Spaniards could participate freely. Farther west, Anza observes in his diary, were the Papago, identical in language and other traditions to the Pima, except for their choice to remain unassimilated, despite official enticements to the contrary.[5]

Still farther west, across the Gulf of California, a different social model was being instituted, motivated not by mineral production but by religion. It combined the objective of spreading Christianity with

---

[4] The term "Spanish subjects" is used here to designate the people that were at the time often called "people of reason," i.e., any white, indigenous, black, or racially mixed Spanish-speaking Christian who was integrated into the economic system of New Spain. The term was roughly equivalent to the modern concept of "citizen."

[5] The Pima were permanently settled on the banks of rivers (particularly the Gila) that could support agriculture. Their crops included corn, beans, squash, "Pima" cotton, and later, wheat. The Tohono O'odham, or "desert people," were of the same tribe and spoke the same language but lived in the desert, away from the rivers. Due to a phonetic misunderstanding, the Spaniards called them the Papago. While the Papago migrated with the seasonal rains between desert and mountain, the Pima remained settled near their fields. Being in a permanent location made it easier for them to interact with the missionaries, accept Christianity, and learn Spanish. The Papago, on the other hand, did not give up their traditional migrations and thus remained unassimilated.

the European certainty of being in possession of a superior civilization; the Spanish believed they were doing the will of God and performing an act of altruism in bringing both the Christian faith and "civilization" to those who had neither. The California mission system was not intended to add bullion to the treasure fleet but rather population and souls to the two kingdoms. To this end, the church and the crown put into practice a completely different social system, more paternalistic and more coercive, than that of the Altar Valley.

As the expedition worked its way past the small villages, the reluctant guide, Sebastián Tarabal, could not help but note the contrast with his experience. A native of the Baja California peninsula, he had voluntarily joined a mission, awed by the priests' knowledge and their generosity in sharing wisdom and food. He had not known that his acceptance implied a commitment that would eventually encompass his entire life. It was not just a question of learning a language, a skill, and a form of worship; it included living in the mission complex and performing the tasks assigned to him according to a schedule of work, rest, and prayer that was incompatible with the way of life he had known before. Many Native people joined this monastic community not entirely aware that they would be forbidden to resign. And in a system where the church and the state were one, it is not surprising that the military was used to capture and return to the fold those who had deserted. To the credit of the religious men running the missions, the great majority of the neophytes felt that the benefits outweighed the costs, and they remained a part of the system. Otherwise, it cannot be explained how a staff of two priests and six soldiers could keep together a community of several hundred natives. Sebastián Tarabal, however, had not seen it that way and had chosen to escape from San Gabriel.

Days 10 and 11
Monday, January 17, and Tuesday, January 18, 1774

After several days of sunshine, dawn was dark and heavy, threatening rain. Fortunately, it was only two leagues to Altar, where Anza expected to halt and obtain some horses. They followed the river downstream and by late morning reached the presidio, commanded by a friend and fellow officer, Captain Bernardo de Urrea. Because its location far south in the valley sheltered it from Apache raids, the presidio had a full complement of quality horses, and the expedition was able to trade a few for some of their most useless mounts. In addition, the soldiers enjoyed the food and hospitality of a post similar to home as well as the company of friends and acquaintances. The rain provided them with an excuse to extend their welcome for a second night.

Days 12 to 14
Wednesday, January 19, to Friday, January 21, 1774

Two more days brought them to Caborca. With some ninety families, it was the largest community in the valley, a center of silver and gold mining operations, and a crossroad, linking the main road to the south, to the Altar Valley, and to the seldom-traveled, undefined trail toward the Colorado River that the expedition was about to follow across the Pima desert. Thus Caborca was the last chance to upgrade the animals or obtain any supplies. By order of Urrea and the provincial governor, the locals offered the expedition two strings of mules, but they were in such dismal condition that Anza, in spite of the need, only accepted three animals. The expedition was detained still another day while a driver went to a nearby town for shoeing iron.

Day 15
Saturday, January 22, 1774

Considering Caborca the official starting point of the expedition, Garcés began his diary on this date. From that point there would be no other Spanish establishment until the San Gabriel mission, five hundred miles to the northwest. Garcés was all too aware that only half of that distance was through known territory. He had traveled as far as the Colorado two years before and met with the Yuma tribe and their chief, Palma.

The chief, a receptive and spiritual man, was impressed with the priest and what he understood of his philosophy. Hampered by cultural differences and language barriers, Garcés customarily made use of visual images and sign language in his travels. He always carried with him a cloth banner with, on one side, a painting of Mary and her newborn child, and on the reverse, a group of men being consumed by fire. The contrast between the peaceful harmony of the one and the pain of the other were universally understood. It must have been the performance of a lifetime to watch this alien and charismatic traveler unroll his banner and, with vibrant sign language, convey through it the rudiments of his faith. His love for the audience obviously protected him because for almost a decade he had wandered alone through vast unexplored areas.

Palma was intrigued by this wanderer who shared not just tobacco and glass beads but also his store of knowledge, and who enjoyed being accepted as a guest. Palma had evidently given thought to the spiritual issues that Garcés presented, because he was immediately won over. At the time, white encroachment in the area was insignificant, although the tribes were aware of a distant Spanish presence around them, as far away as the Pacific coast. It was not that the Yuma either sought or avoided Europeans; they knew from hearsay and sporadic contacts that the Spaniards were materially advanced, enormously powerful, and totally different. But what was not yet formulated in Palma's mind was how the Yuma nation should relate to them. In addition to being a priest, Garcés was also a white Spaniard and had thus favorably predisposed the chief toward the Spaniards, and it was with all this in mind that Palma had taken the extraordinary step of personally delivering Sebastián Tarabal to an authority he barely knew.

On the day that Garcés began to record these latest travels, the expedition left Caborca by noon, moving toward the northwest. It was not the trail Garcés had followed two years before, which was difficult for the animals, but probably the one Tarabal and Palma had recently used. Well after dark, the expedition arrived at San Ildefonso, the first location known to have adequate water and pasture.

Days 16 and 17
Sunday, January 23, and Monday, January 24, 1774

In the arid region between the Colorado and Gila Rivers and the Gulf of California, neither water nor pasture would be easy to find, even in the rainy season. Leaving both behind at San Ildefonso, the expedition moved northwest some eight leagues to a small cluster of sandy wells that supplied three neighboring *rancherías,* or villages, the largest one of twenty-five families. This area was known by the Papago as Aribaipia, meaning "small wells." Due to earlier Jesuit presence, Garcés refers to it as San Eduardo de Aribaipia, and Anza simply as San Eduardo.

The following day brought them to a seasonal pond at San Juan de la Mata with abundant water due to the recent rains. Anza's journal notes that the terrain would lend itself to building a dam that would probably retain water all year. They also encountered four Papago families who were settled there for as long as the water held out.

Days 18 and 19
Tuesday, January 25, and Wednesday, January 26, 1774

Winding their way through a wide valley west of the Sierra Durazno and La Espuma, they covered the eleven leagues to Quitobac in two days. The expedition knew the village as "San Luis Quitobac"—having learned the name from a New Mexico missionary who had once visited—but the locals themselves did not use that name. Spanish influence, however, was evident in the organization of the group of four families that came out to greet them, which included a governor and a justice. "The rest of the villagers are gathering seeds and herbs or have joined the missions," they informed Anza. Typically keeping an eye out for agricultural opportunities, he notes in his journal that "with five small sources of water, and not of the worse quality, this enclave is one of the better sites around. It would be possible to plant at most half a measure of corn, but there is enough pasture to support five hundred animals."

Days 20 and 21
Thursday, January 27, and Friday, January 28, 1774

Snaking north through fourteen leagues of abrupt mountainous terrain for two days brought them to San Marcelo de Sonoitac, where in 1752 the Jesuits had established a mission. During a subsequent Papago revolt, two priests—a Spaniard and a native—had been killed, and the mission was abandoned. Garcés knew the place from his previous trip and notes in his diary that the expedition was then almost directly west of Tubac, their starting point behind the distant mountains. Anza was impressed with the location, surrounded by hills and with a narrow lake bordered by a very moist area, "the largest in this country, about a league and a half long, adequate for planting and, even though lacking in forests, with enough pasture to carry a thousand head of cattle." But Sonoitac was as poor and desolate as Quitobac. "In spite of this site being unquestionably the best in all the Papago country, I saw only six families, the rest being occupied in the same tasks as those of Quitobac." Anza's comments reflect his acquaintance with the region only during the wet season, and also his ignorance of the migratory practices of the Papago. Always conscious of more than the search for an overland route, he had rock samples taken to investigate for precious metals. Even though nothing was found, he notes the mineral potential in his journal.

From Sonoitac to the Colorado River is approximately the same distance as from Caborca to Sonoitac, but the terrain, being essentially desert, was more difficult. Every stage would have to be planned with regard to the location and size of the next water source. Garcés was well aware of these difficulties, which he believed Anza was underestimating. Now that they were about to face these challenges, Garcés' resentment of the route Anza had chosen no doubt surfaced. On his advice, Anza now recruited a Sonoitac native Garcés knew as the most familiar with the trail to accompany them all the way to the Colorado.

Days 22 to 24
Saturday, January 29, to Monday, January 31, 1774

The first day was a nine-league trek to a dry riverbed at El Carrizal, where the water, made drinkable only because there was no alternative, was so brackish that the surrounding pasture was insufficient for the animals. Knowing that the next water source could not supply their total need at one time, Anza split up the expedition. He took the lead with part of the troop, some horses, and the cattle, leaving seven soldiers and the loaded mule train to follow the next day. They left El Carrizal in the afternoon, proceeding north-northwest over a small pass across the mountains, and camped that night without water or pasture. The next day, after five leagues and some sand dunes, they arrived at a bare and stony hillside without a single tree, bush, or blade of grass. By climbing on their hands and knees, they could access a small reservoir known as Aguaje Empinado, "High Water." But because there was not enough water for all, nor a chance of its being replenished for the following group, Anza decided the mule train behind must have it and moved on without watering his own animals. They continued west for three more leagues and, just before nightfall, set up camp in a dry riverbed with some bad pasture, which the animals devoured.

Days 25 to 28
Tuesday, February 1, to Friday, February 4, 1774

After two nights without water, the day's march was mercifully short: only three leagues to some rocky hills where rainwater collected in cavities at a place Anza named La Purificación. The lowest of six reservoirs was easily accessible to the animals and large enough to satisfy all their thirst. Water quality was exceptionally good, and there was even pasture in the vicinity. The higher reservoirs were easily accessible to the men and just as bountiful. Anza observed a species of mountain sheep resembling large deer in size and color but with thick, rounded horns: the borrego. The Papago hunted them by stalking their watering holes. It was a good location for Anza and his men to wait for the others while recovering their strength.

On Wednesday a soldier brought news that the mule train had arrived at Aguaje Empinado in poor condition, and the following day, the expedition was reunited. They enjoyed a day of rest before proceeding five leagues directly west, to camp at the wells known as Pozos de en Medio, "Middle Wells."

Day 29
Saturday, February 5, 1774

Still guided, above all else, by the need to find water, the expedition left Pozos de en Medio before daybreak and traveled eight leagues to a remote source in the hills, known to the Jesuits as Agua Escondida, or "Hidden Water." Unlike the other high reservoirs, fed by rain, this one was supplied by a spring. They were able to water the horses before dark, but because of the difficult access had to postpone bringing the cattle until the following morning.

Remote as the site was, they found there a Christian Papago by the name of Luis traveling from the Colorado to Sonoitac on the lookout for Anza, and, as if that were not enough of a surprise, he carried a message of warning. "Part of the Yuma are waiting to kill us, especially the priests, and take our animals," writes Garcés. "They are determined," echoes Anza, "to prevent my passing [through their lands]…to kill me, the priests, and all our companions [in order] to steal our horses and supplies."[6] Luis further informed them that although Captain Palma had declared "his intention of always favoring [the Spaniards] with his whole nation and his other allies downstream…he has been unable to dissuade the rebels." According to Luis, Palma had taken sides after having tried and failed to convince them that the Spaniards were not coming to wage war; that, as he had personally experienced, they would share their supplies with them; and that if attacked, their firearms would kill many and surely defeat them.

Palma had never forgotten the missionary Garcés, and upon meeting Anza at Altar, he had been equally impressed. In that meeting, Anza had informed the chief of the expedition's plans and told him that Garcés would be participating. As Palma had assumed, delivering the deserter to the Spaniards had borne fruit. He had been received by Urrea, captain of the presidio, as the head of a nation in which Spain had a particular interest, and the coincidence of Sebastián Tarabal's experience with Anza's plans had made his gesture especially welcome. No wonder the Yuma chief had now taken the Spaniards' side and, having failed to defuse the situation, sent Luis to warn Anza. For the second time now, Palma had rendered an important service to the Spaniards, and this one was not by accident.

Anza and Garcés had Luis repeat the message several times, questioning every detail. To engage in combat that would compromise their objective was the last thing Anza wanted. Garcés proposed to go ahead alone and meet separately with the Yumas and rebels, but Anza judged it too dangerous and declined permission. Instead, together they formulated a different plan. While feigning ignorance of the warning, maintaining vigilance, and avoiding the rebels, Anza would meet Palma as soon as possible. The respect Palma had for Anza was

---

[6] The identities of the rebellious Yumas were not known to Anza and Garcés at that time. From the entry for November 27, 1775, in Father Font's diary of the second expedition, we learn that their leader was Captain Pablo, who would cross paths with Anza several times in the future.

mutual, and before risking any action, Anza wanted Palma's opinion.

Days 30 and 31
Sunday, February 6, and Monday, February 7, 1774

Provided with a fresh horse, Luis left early in the morning to arrange a rendezvous with Palma for the following day. The herd was watered and, to the extent possible, fed on the thin pasture. In the afternoon they went south from Agua Escondida, rounding the sierra that lay ahead. Traveling northwest, with mountains on one side of their path and sand dunes as far as the eye could see on the other, they came to rest at a dry creek bed late that night.

Lifting camp just after sunrise, they continued in the same direction and by midday saw the dust from horses in the distance. Anza put his men on alert to meet the approaching strangers, one of whom was armed with a spear, the rest with bows and arrows. It was with relief that they recognized the messenger Luis.

Palma was not in the group—he had been absent from his village—but another Yuma chief accompanied Luis and now announced that they were anxious to welcome the expedition to their houses and share what they had. "Surely you have been made aware of the restlessness," continued the stranger, "which has been resolved by me and Palma, who, upon meeting you later today, will inform you." Anza, pleased with the turn of events, reciprocated with expressions of assurance regarding his intentions and goodwill, and he asked the chief to relay the message ahead with one of his men. But the assurance proved unnecessary, as they soon began to encounter more and more unarmed and obviously welcoming people. Garcés notes in his journal that "the commander behaved toward this Indian with his usual courtesy, liberality, and prudence, while we tried to fulfill our function."

By 3:00, "surrounded by more than two hundred men shouting, laughing, throwing fistfuls of dirt in the air, and otherwise displaying signs of simplicity and friendship," they had reached the Gila River. They set up camp in a pasture where more and more Yuma of both sexes congregated, "marveling at the novelty of our clothing, objects, and doings."

By 5:00, Palma had arrived with sixty of his people. As soon as he dismounted, he asked Anza to embrace him, "which I did with all the appearance of affection. I asked him to sit and we gave him some refreshment, after which he apologized for not having been at his village so that I could have gone there today, and reprimanding his people for not having proposed it to me." He explained that he had been some leagues distant due to the opposition to the expedition's arrival, "of which he assumed I was informed, and [he said] that those who had so acted were not men enough for that, and that they were not of his people but from farther up the river, and that after they took that position, he had expelled them from his nation. And that we should not worry about it because he and his people rejoiced that we were passing through their country. As he had told me at the presidio of Altar, he had gathered his tribe and warned all who were eager to see us that they should not steal anything or pester us." He then told Anza, "Do not take offense at being stared at and touched because, as most of them have never seen Spaniards, they are eager to see how you dress and the things you use, and to understand how you are."

The contrast was indeed striking. Three dozen expedition soldiers in uniform were a small island of color surrounded by hundreds of naked men and barely covered women thrilled with the newcomers. Palma's actions had demonstrated to his people that there was nothing to fear, even though as he spoke he noted the mounted troops holding their weapons ready for action. He pointed this out to Anza, asking that they be put at ease, as there was no danger. Through their body language and conversation, Palma and Anza displayed mutual friendship, and the affection with which many recognized Garcés was just as reassuring. After a quick exchange of glances with the priest, Anza gave the order to dismount. The mainly indigenous and mestizo soldiers were instantly surrounded by the smiling, poking, curious crowd. The Yuma and Spanish leaders had reached out to know each other, and their overture of friendship set the example. If the commander behaved with "his usual courtesy, liberality, and prudence," one could also add that his actions displayed exceptional intuition and no lack of courage or sensitivity.

The Spaniards had encountered a society with a clear cultural identity, a defined territory, and a governing authority. The Yuma, then numbering about three thousand, were permanently settled on the lands around the junction of the Gila and Colorado Rivers. They had learned to live by the cycle of the rivers, profiting from annual floods that left large areas fertile and soft enough to be worked with wooden tools. Every spring they planted corn, beans, cotton, wheat, squash, pumpkins, and melons, regularly harvesting more than their need. Palma had been born into his leadership position, but the respect and affection he commanded were earned. He had successfully waged war against some neighbors and developed alliances with others. The Yuma nation, strategically located and well fed and governed, was the undisputed leader among the neighboring tribes.

But all this was not immediately apparent to the Spanish. The Yuma lacked metal, they had no written language, their dwellings were temporary, and even though they could weave cotton blankets, they felt no need to wear them. To the commander, they were savages; to the priest, heathens. But beneath the meaning of these words, Anza and Garcés felt something that most Europeans did not understand: respect for the Yuma and an actual liking for them as individuals.

As the day passed into evening, the extraordinary encounter continued. Aware that their dialogue was on center stage and eager to respond to Palma's friendship, Anza decided to publicly honor him. "Do you recognize this man as your chief and leader?" he asked the crowd, to which they unanimously replied in the affirmative. "Then, in the name of the King of Spain, who is the owner of everything, I confirm him in the position of chief and grant him the authority to rule with justice. And so that he is recognized as your leader, even by Spaniards, who will respect your laws and privileges, I give him this symbol." So saying, Anza placed around Palma's neck a red ribbon with a silver coin bearing the image of Charles III. The commander and the chief then embraced each other with obvious satisfaction while hundreds of Yumas marveled at the surprising ceremony, admiring the medallion and collectively expressing their joy and pride in the foreigners' recognition of their chief.

Knowing of Palma's religious nature from his contact with Garcés, and sensing the goodwill of the moment, Anza continued privately to address the chief and two of his lieutenants: "There is only one God, who has created us with the sky, the sun, the stars, and everything there is on earth, and one master on earth, the king, himself a subject of God. And all Spaniards, which number more than you can ever imagine, are the subjects of both majesties. God has given the king all these lands and many more that you do not know, and that is why we not only obey him but are eager to follow his orders. The king loves us, and that is why we have such wealth of horses, dress, iron, knives, and all that we possess, which you so admire." On and on he continued, sensing that his every word was being followed with interest. He was neither dogmatic nor condescending; his message not the official party line. He had started out to win Palma over and now found himself sharing his own understanding of the world and the reality by which he lived, communicating it with the directness of everyday language. It was just as if he were explaining himself to a friend. And in spite of their cultural differences, Anza's inability to speak the Yuma language, and Palma's rudimentary Spanish, the message was clearly being understood.

Not long after Anza concluded, Palma asked to borrow his cane. He took it in hand, called for attention and, surrounded by his people, began a harangue that went on for an hour. "As he spoke, I observed the reaction of the audience," writes Anza. "They were enthralled, often opening their mouths wide, which they would then cover with their hands in a sign of admiration. When he concluded, he told me he had repeated to them what he had learned from me, which they had heard with pleasure, and that he would do the same in other villages as far as he would accompany me. And that he would also tell the same to the nations that were his allies."

Day 32
Tuesday, February 8, 1774

Camp was lifted in darkness, and by sunrise, accompanied by a small crowd, the expedition was led along the bank of the Gila to a ford, where the mule train was unloaded. Anza crossed first, placing half the troop on either bank, even though, as he observed, "there was no reason for suspicion." The animals followed, and finally the supplies, carried by hundreds of Yumas with Palma leading them. The crossing, just upstream of the Gila's junction with the Colorado, was completed by 3:00 in the afternoon, too late to attempt to cross the Colorado before dark. By then, between five and six hundred Yuma of both sexes and all ages—again curious, probing, questioning—had gathered. Anza asked them to line up so that glass beads and tobacco could be distributed to all, and having done this, Palma regaled them with a speech as on the evening before. He then asked them to show appreciation for the gifts and leave so that the expedition could rest. While many did so, many remained until dark, which "required of us the greatest patience and tolerance, as little could be done in the midst of the general chaos."

With the help of Palma and his people, the crossing of the Gila had been a success, and with another milestone of the journey now behind them, the camp fell quiet for the night.

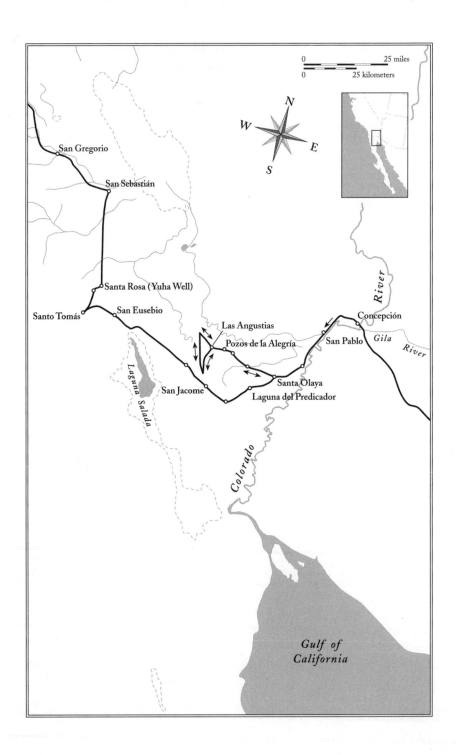

CHAPTER 2

Flirting with Disaster: Ten Days to Nowhere

February 9 to February 19, 1774

Day 33
Wednesday, February 9, 1774

Hampered by the loitering crowd since dawn, the expedition was slow getting to the ford. Ever vigilant, Anza took the same precautions crossing the Colorado as he had the Gila, precautions that again proved unnecessary. The more than six hundred men and women guided the animals through the shallowest waters, three to four feet deep at that time, and across the river's five-hundred-foot width. The mules packed their own cargo, and most men were able to ride across barely getting wet, although Garcés chose to be carried. Continuing downstream, Anza observed that there was no other location where they could have crossed so easily. As they passed fields planted in wheat, corn, and beans, the men, impressed with the quality of agriculture—not to mention thankful for the help they had received—were developing a greater sense of respect for these people who had before seemed merely childish admirers.

Downstream of the junction they camped at a high point on the bank where the river flowed majestically between hills covered with poplars and weeping willows. Anza named it Puerto de la Concepción. It is the same site where the U.S. Army built a fort in the nineteenth century that is now the administrative center of the Fort Yuma-Quechan Nation. The river still flows gently around its base, but agricultural demands in the area have reduced its size and majesty.

That afternoon their escort, numbering more than eight hundred, continued to be a nuisance, but in appreciation for their help Anza set off rockets, had a steer killed, and passed out beads and tobacco; it was, after all, the first time Spanish forces had crossed the Colorado River and was reason for celebration.

From a native he learned that five days west of the river mouth there was a Spanish trail, difficult to reach even in the wet season because of the lack of water. He was referring, of course, to the trail linking the missions in the Baja Peninsula with the new establishments at San Diego.

Days 34 and 35
Thursday, February 10, and Friday, February 11, 1774

The expedition was on the move by early morning, every animal escorted by several natives leading them to the best paths and cleaning debris before them. They traveled six leagues west-northwest past the ranchería of San Pablo to camp by the river with good water and pasture. That day it was brought to Palma's attention that a hatchet and a spear had been stolen from one of the soldiers. Because communal property was so much a part of the native culture, misunderstandings like this frequently became a source of friction, but as was his practice Palma promised to restore the items and punish those responsible.

After the overwhelming attention of the preceding days, by Friday the crowd began to dwindle; the novelty was wearing off and many were now far from home. By late afternoon, when they reached what was the last Yuma village, only Palma and some sixty mostly local natives were with them. Anza was relieved at the relative ease with which they could set up camp, having spent the previous five days surrounded by a crowd twenty times their number. Over that time, however, he had many chances to observe a people who, while appearing to fit common preconceptions about native tribes, were actually quite different from other groups. To what extent this was due to their extraordinary leader he was not sure, but he recorded many of his observations in detail:

"These people are generally very robust, taller than eight hands [about 5'3"], their character the best one finds in Indians; they are festive, affectionate, and liberal. Their color is not as dark as others, nor are they the most stripe marked; they have naturally attractive faces, although they make themselves fierce by painting their bodies and especially their faces. All the men go entirely naked without the slightest sense of shame, considering it masculine; they have told me slightly covering up is considered effeminate. They have good hair, which they arrange in many and different ways with very fine clay on which they spread a shiny powder to make it appear silvery, and so as not to spoil their hairdo, they sleep sitting up.

"They appear to be little inclined toward war and weapons. About a third of them carry five bad arrows and a poor bow, and they seldom have quivers; the other two-thirds only [carry] spears four yards long [used both as weapons and for playing games] or clubs.

Beyond the last Yuma ranchería were two neighboring tribes with whom the Yuma had frequent contact. The Cojat (or Cajuenche) nation then occupied the west bank of the river all the way to the gulf some forty leagues downstream, and the east bank was Quiquima territory.[1] Yumas and Cojats spoke languages of the same origin and could understand each other, but neither could communicate with Quiquimas. The Yuma had previously been at war with each of these groups, but extensive intermarrying had eventually brought them to peaceful terms with each other. On the subject of marriage Anza noted that among the Yuma there was little evidence of polygamy and also that pregnant women and mothers appeared to be older than those he had seen elsewhere. "Most men do not like to marry young girls," he was told, "because they don't know how to work."

"The fields I have seen, from the junction of the rivers to here, are occasionally planted in wheat of such good quality and rich grain that our best irrigated wheat does not compare. Similarly, it can be seen

---

[1] The Cajuenche, also known as the Kohuana, numbered between three thousand and thirty-five hundred at the time of the Anza expeditions. Although they were hunter/farmers and therefore permanently settled, conflicts with other tribes forced them to relocate several times. They eventually joined the Maricopa in Arizona.

where they plant corn, beans, pumpkins, watermelons, and melons in such admirable abundance as to leave us wishing the Indians in our domains could do likewise. The fertility of the upstream and, even better, the downstream land comes from the annual spring flood of the plain due to the melting snows, particularly because it doesn't destroy or carry away the trees but deposits sediment for a half a league or more on either bank. The fertility is similar on both rivers, as is evident from the crops harvested by the nations that inhabit them."

As was his practice, Anza included in his journal recommendations for the land's potential use. "Everything I have seen of these rivers, especially downstream of the junction, seems ideally suited for planting grapevines and fruit trees because they can thrive here without irrigation and because the benign climate (we have hardly been cold at night) will not subject them to freezing. On the hills of the Puerto de la Concepción, if necessary, it would be possible to access permanent water on either side and route it over land as required for planting, but even without irrigation, as we have seen, it is possible to grow excellent crops."

It is amazing to note that two centuries after Anza recognized the potential of the area, modern engineering has achieved his vision on a scale beyond his greatest imaginings. Today the Gila riverbed is dry and the main channel of the Colorado is a shadow of its former self, but the area retains its agricultural richness through a series of modern aqueducts that crisscross land now producing a vast array of crops in bountiful quantities.

Day 36
Saturday, February 12, 1774

The next day's journey took them to a large pasture and a pond, supplied by the river's seasonal flood, that Anza named in honor of the saint of the day, Santa Eulalia or Olaya. En route they were approached by Cojats. Anza halted to distribute beads and tobacco and, as usual, to gather information. Declining an invitation to visit their village, he encouraged them instead to come to the expedition camp. Verbal communication was not as easy as with Yumas, but the message, judging from the hundreds of Cojats that joined them later that day, was understood. The few Yumas who were still with the expedition, including Palma, then served as interpreters in conversations that ranged far and wide:

"I tried to obtain information about this nation as I had done before with the Yuma, to know what kind of government they had and where their leader resided, but they answered me that they lacked both government and a single leader, as the head of each household was the leader of his family."

Palma himself did not consider that system a government at all and made a point of telling Anza that the Cojat, who in no way imitated the Spaniards, were less civilized than the Yuma.

"The Cojat, whose language is distinguished from that of the Yuma mainly by the speed at which it is spoken, are otherwise not very different from their neighbors. They are smaller, slightly darker, and less prone to use dye, but as far as their nakedness, lack of weapons, women's attire, and other habits, they appear very similar. The lands they cultivate are as fertile as those upstream and they have richer pastures. But they do not have as many horses, an asset in which the Yuma surpass them."

Santa Olaya was to be the last camp with Palma. Since defusing the potential confrontation on Anza's arrival, the chief had spared no effort to welcome the Spaniards, and Anza had used his diplomatic skills to reciprocate. Palma had accompanied Anza for six days, during which he had observed the esteem the indigenous troops had for their white commander and the harmonious relations between the white priests and the native and mestizo colonial troops. Anza, in turn, began to know the Yuma and their leader. The expedition, lacking knowledge of the river, would have found crossing it a challenge, but with the help of the Yuma, they accomplished it without mishap. They both recognized the value of this service and Anza could not help but wonder what might have been if the Apache had controlled the area. Anza had generously given glass beads and tobacco to the crowd, but with their chief he and Garcés had shared what Palma most admired: the culture and religion of Spain. The bonds of friendship, trust, and mutual respect were growing stronger between the three men.

Day 37
Sunday, February 13, 1774

As the river flows south toward the gulf, the westbound expedition then had to abandon the secure supply of water and pasture and venture across the most desolate stretch of the journey. Between them and the sierra was an essentially unknown wasteland without permanent inhabitants, recognizable trails, or adequate water. Neither Cojats nor Yumas knew the region well (because for them it led nowhere), and Sebastián Tarabal, who had recently crossed the area, could not, from Santa Olaya, identify his route. For Anza, it was his first time west of the Colorado. Thus it was Garcés who, having traveled the area two years before, was the most knowledgeable. With a vague map in his head, the help of some Cojats and, at the last moment, a Yuma volunteer, they hoped to reach a point from which Tarabal could pick up his own trail.

Palma, having decided to leave the expedition, spoke with Anza about preparations for crossing the river on his return during the spring, when the water level would be very high. He said he would gather wood for building rafts, and apologized for being unable to accompany them any farther. Anza was pleased with the chief's promise of help, which he knew they would need, but he was most touched by the emotion in Palma's eyes when he talked about leaving them.

By 9:00 in the morning, the expedition started west-northwest from Santa Olaya. During the day they passed two streams with water so salty that it could not support pasture. Garcés recognized one as El Rosario and warned that they would not find any better water except perhaps in the vicinity of San Jacome, a ranchería several leagues to the southwest on the San Geronimo sierra. But Anza, relying on the Cojats, whose knowledge Garcés distrusted, continued northwest. By sundown several mules were showing evidence of fatigue and, having covered about seven leagues, they halted by a stream known as El Carrizal with abundant but barely drinkable water.

Day 38
Monday, February 14, 1774

El Carrizal marked a boundary beyond which only two of the Cojats would continue, the rest considering it to be enemy territory. Still, Anza chose to rely on their advice rather than the priest's. The expedition got under way by 9:00 and, approximately one hour to the west, came to a location with tall reeds where it was possible to dig for water. Even though they had only covered one league, after two days of barely potable water the mule train arrived in dismal condition. They dug wells in the streambed that provided clean water and named the location Pozos de en Medio—"Middle Springs."

At that point, the last two Cojats refused to proceed farther into enemy territory and they provided directions to the next water source near the sierra, a day's march on a trail they pointed out. In light of the animals' bad condition, the expedition spent the rest of the day at Pozos de en Medio hoping the animals would recover enough to continue in the morning.

Day 39
Tuesday, February 15, 1774

They started early in the direction indicated by the Cojats. Smoke coming from the area seemed to suggest human presence. After crossing several leagues of sand dunes and no more than a single brackish puddle, they at last reached a small pasture with a deep well of limited but good quality water. The future would bring them back to this waypoint, which they would eventually name the Pozo de las Angustias or "Well of Anguish," but since it was then early in the day, they continued, following the trail until it disappeared in the shifting sand. In spite of the previous day's rest, the mules were still suffering, and the train was falling behind, the drivers warning that the animals could barely carry their loads. Anza realized that if they pressed on without adequate water and pasture, the situation would soon be critical. He divided the group in half:

"Having recognized that the condition of the mules made it impossible to complete the day's journey, it had been necessary to unload half the cargo at the previous well. Upon taking these precautions and providing adequate guards, I announced to the two accompanying priests that it was no longer realistic for the expedition to continue ahead with our full complement and supplies. Therefore I proposed that half of the troops and cargo should return to the Yuma village, where, considering how well we had been received, it would be possible to await our return. The other half could then complete the transit to northern California less encumbered. I emphasized that this plan would lead to success and that

I would be pleased if one of them [Diaz or Garcés] would choose to remain, commanding with his presence the respect among soldiers and natives to ensure that the peace and harmony we had enjoyed through Yuma territory would continue. It would also be necessary for one of them to assist me with his presence. My proposal did not meet the approval I had expected, especially from Father Garcés, who did not believe, as Father Diaz and I did, in the need for splitting up, and also considered the division of our forces very imprudent. I therefore decided to explain clearly what I saw as the inevitable consequences of staying together but refrained from implementing the project against Father Garcés' objections because of his extensive experience. If my judgment was in error I would appear as stubborn and irresponsible."

Unloading half the cargo so the animals could manage, they continued west toward the Sierra de Santa Barbara five leagues away. After struggling through ever more difficult sand dunes, they encountered one that slowed down the horses and stopped the mule train in its tracks. The terrain and the enfeebled animals had brought the expedition to a standstill, and Anza knew that pushing on beyond their limits would probably kill them. His leadership and experience again came into play as together with Garcés he reconsidered their options. Because it was already midday, crossing the dunes to the west had to be abandoned, so the next question was in which direction to head. To the south they could see the dark mountain, Cerro Prieto, in the vicinity of which, according to Garcés, was the village of San Jacome, which, when he knew it two years before, had good water and abundant pasture. "It is important," he emphasized, "that the animals do not return to the reeds and putrid water that had poisoned them."

So it was well into the afternoon when the expedition did an about-turn to the south-southeast and headed toward San Jacome. The horsemen started ahead hoping to reconnoiter in daylight, letting the cattle and mules follow at their own pace. Unfortunately, the sun had set by the time the riders arrived in the area of San Jacome, and they were unable to find a path, trail, or any other sign of human habitation. Some of the soldiers were by that time on foot as the animals were too exhausted to carry them. In the dark and without water, Anza decided to camp on the spot while Garcés and two soldiers continued the search. At one point they perceived a glow in the distance but failed to locate the source. An animal whined and Garcés attributed it to the near presence of water, but they were unable find it. Believing they had made a mistake, the soldiers brought the reluctant priest back to camp, but even then Garcés would not abandon the search.

"Well into the night," writes Anza, "Father Garcés, believing he was within two leagues of San Jacome, decided to make a new attempt to find it, for which purpose I gave him the five soldiers whose horses could still bear them. He rode two leagues and more and returned after midnight without having located it. This failure was not too surprising to me, given the unfamiliar terrain, since the same has been known to happen even along well-known routes."

While the vanguard camped in darkness without water or pasture, the trailing animals did the same some leagues behind. Their inability to locate San Jacome meant that an alternative had to be found without delay. In the cold of the night and aware that the expedition was close to disaster, Anza decided to return at the break of day to the last good well some five leagues north-northeast. Perhaps they could still save the animals.

Day 40
Wednesday, February 16, 1774

Before daylight, the group set in motion toward the well where the cargo had been unloaded the day before. Shortly after dawn they met the supply train resting partly buried in the sand, some of the animals so frail they were unable to rise. With Anza leading them, the reassembled group headed north at a snail's pace. By early afternoon, hungry, thirsty, and exhausted, they finally reached the well. Five animals had died on the way, and the remainder were near death. Believing the expedition had failed, a general feeling of anguish spread among the soldiers, who named the well Pozo de las Angustias. The water supply turned out to be insufficient for their needs, and the group was forced to split again, those that were able continuing to the Pozos de en Medio.

Day 41
Thursday, February 17, 1774

The mood of total failure had begun to dissolve with the brightness of the new day. Rest, pasture, and water had saved most of the animals, although seven more had died since they arrived at the well, and the remaining cattle oozed dark and smelly spittle. The day was spent reuniting the groups at Pozos de en Medio, where water was more plentiful and the pasture better. To rest their horses, many men walked the few leagues from Las Angustias while the mule train carried only partial loads. The difference from yesterday's mood was evident as the soldiers referred to the Pozos de en Medio as the Aguaje de la Alegría (the Pond of Happiness).

Despite this minor reprieve, however, morale continued to decline rapidly. Seeing some soldiers leading their exhausted horses on foot, Anza, conscious of the power of humor, reminded them of the old story about the man, the donkey, and the child.[2] The commander knew both people and humor, but one of the men, too serious to forget their predicament, spoke for the group: "Were we to lose all the animals, we would not hesitate to walk with you as long as needed to reach the goal of our expedition."

Anza nonetheless remained confident, but never forgot that the crisis was far from over. The previous days had shown the terrain could not support such a large herd, especially one made up of ailing animals, and he now knew for sure that success required a smaller and more agile group, as he had proposed earlier and reluctantly recanted. The only logical option was to return to the river junction, where he could leave all but a small part of the group with the Yuma.

---

2 Anza told a version of the traditional Spanish fable that conveys the lesson "No matter what a person does, someone will always disapprove." There are many variants of the tale, but they all follow the same basic storyline: An old man and a child were riding together on a donkey past a group of people. "You are going to kill that poor animal," said one. So the old man, leaving the child to ride alone, got down and walked beside them. But as they entered a village they heard a lady comment, "What has happened to respect for the elders these days when a perfectly healthy child gets to ride while his tired grandfather has to walk?" So, changing places, they continued on, the child barely keeping up. It wasn't long before a passerby asked the old man, "What has he done, your son, that you make him run like that while you ride in comfort?" So, after that, all three walked, the old man leading the animal with one hand and the child with the other until they got home. "What have you bought a donkey for, my husband? To take him out for walks?"

Days 42 and 43
Friday, February 18, and Saturday, February 19, 1774

Friday was spent recovering the cargo left behind and retracing their steps past El Carrizal to the pond at El Rosario. On Saturday the first group, including Anza and Garcés, arrived at Santa Olaya, exactly a week after they had left. It would be two more days before the rest of the expedition made it there.

In the ten days since crossing the Colorado, the overland expedition to Alta California had almost failed, but through the skill of its commander, disaster had been narrowly avoided and the lessons that would lead to success painfully learned. The advice of Garcés, Tarabal, and any other guides would still be considered, but Juan Bautista de Anza had gained the confidence to trust his own judgment above all others.

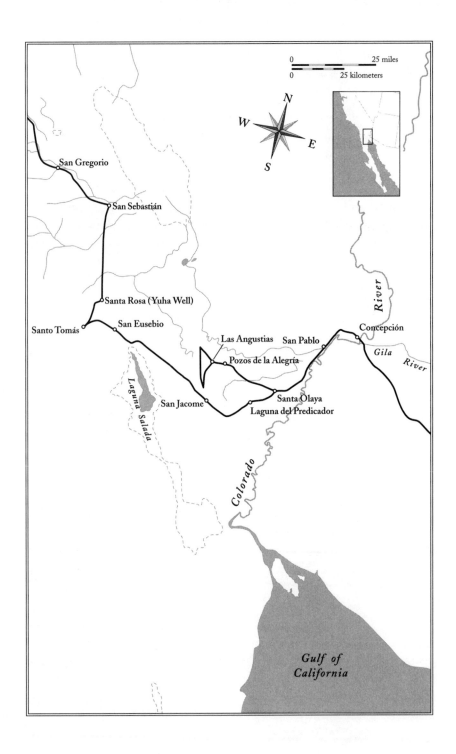

0 25 miles
0 25 kilometers

N
W   E
S

San Gregorio

San Sebastián

River

Santa Rosa (Yuha Well)

Santo Tomás   San Eusebio   Las Angustias   San Pablo   Concepción

Pozos de la Alegría   Gila River

Laguna Salada   San Jacome   Santa Olaya
Laguna del Predicador

Colorado

Gulf of California

CHAPTER 3

Rest and Reorganization at Santa Olaya

February 20 to March 1, 1774

Days 44 and 45
Sunday, February 20, and Monday, February 21, 1774

During the day a good number of Yumas came by, curious about the expedition's unexpected return, but as welcoming as usual. The day before, Anza had sent word through a local Yuma requesting Palma's presence, but Palma being absent from his village, one of his lieutenants came instead to offer his help. Informed about two mules that had gone missing, the young leader took it upon himself to search for them. The next afternoon he returned with one of the missing animals, stating that the other had been killed by the Quiquima, who had presumably stolen them both. Unable to capture the culprit or obtain restitution, he had killed the thief's wife as punishment, now offering Anza the fatal arrow as proof. Instead of the praise and gratitude expected, however, he was met with cold disapproval and a refusal of the trophy. The incident reemphasized for Anza the gap between "civilized" and "savage" that could so easily lead to critical misunderstandings, and, counting as he was at the time on Palma's help for his revised plans, he once again questioned his own judgment. But there was no time to hesitate as Yuma and Spaniard faced each other in an awkward, uncomprehending silence. Seizing the moment, Anza turned his back on the young chief and emphatically addressed all present:

"Both God and the King, of whom I have told you before, order you not to make war or kill. I urge you to seek peace between one nation and another. I will be angry with anyone who hereafter does either kill or pursue war. In the name of God and the King, I ask you to stop all manner of killing."

"To which," Anza laconically adds in his report, "they all answered that they would not fail to do so in the future."

Days 46 to 48
Tuesday, February 22, to Thursday, February 24, 1774

During the next two days the mule train retrieved the cargo from Las Angustias while the surviving horses and cattle recovered their strength at Santa Olaya. On the third day Palma joined them, manifesting the greatest pleasure in seeing Anza and apologizing for having been unable to provide him with directions that would have taken them across the desert. He was most upset at the loss of animals, conscious of the wealth they represented. It was only the third encounter of the two men but it felt as comfortable as a meeting between old friends. During their conversations, while sharing a meal around the evening fire, Anza registered Palma's every gesture and word, trying to discern any reason why he should not trust the chief. That night he came to a conclusion and shared his thoughts:

"Due to the lack of knowledge of the trails, of the location of water, of the quality and limited supply even when found, and of the exhausting dunes, I feel our group is too large and too cumbersome to cross the desert. For this reason I would like to leave part of my men, animals, and supplies with you until my return in about a month."

Palma listened carefully while Anza continued:

"On my return I will be accompanied by more soldiers from California," he added, knowing it wasn't true, "and if, due to my delay, troops from Sonora come searching for us, they should wait for me at the crossing." This he also knew would not happen and only used it as a veiled warning to his audience.

"As we welcomed Father Garcés when he came to us alone two years ago," replied Palma, "and as we treated the California native [Tarabal] that I personally delivered to the Presidio at Altar, so will we treat your men and animals, and you will receive full accountability of everything you leave with us."

Palma was honored by Anza's trust, and his sincerity was beyond question. The commander was leaving troops and materiel under his protection; he had achieved parity with the Spaniards, earned ally status through the respect he had worked so hard to develop. As the men talked, the conversation drifted into detail, and Palma suggested that to spare the animals his men would carry the supplies to the crossing, a proposition Anza only with difficulty convinced him was unnecessary. But again, every sign was positive, and Anza was convinced that he could trust the Yuma chief without reservation.

Since they planned to extend their stay for a few more days at Santa Olaya, tireless Garcés proposed to travel downstream and visit all the rancherías he knew to gather any information that might be helpful to the expedition. Anza agreed to four, maybe five, days of rest and set a deadline for the priest's return.

After Garcés had departed Anza informed the men of the new plan and the arrangements made with Palma. They unanimously approved, considering it the best way to achieve the expedition's goal, even when some expressed concern for the risk to those staying behind. Thinking aloud they quickly reviewed what could happen: The Pima, who had accepted Spanish jurisdiction, were known to be in frequent contact with the Yuma. Were the latter to kill their guests, it would only be a matter of time before the authorities knew of it. Besides, no one felt that their recent experience justified such suspicion. As for the traveling group, moving without cattle and fewer pack animals would enormously increase their mobility and, at the faster pace, a month of supplies would be sufficient to reach the new settlements. Should their horses fail, they could and would continue on foot. It seemed the commander could do no wrong that night. A mood of renewed optimism swept through the camp.

Days 49 to 53
Friday, February 25, to Tuesday, March 1, 1774

For five days the group stayed at Santa Olaya, the animals enjoying the abundant pasture, and the men the rest they could while surrounded by their curious visitors. Yumas, Cojats, and Quiquimas came by the hundreds, attracted this time more by the carnival atmosphere and free handouts than curiosity. Some soldiers played music and taught the women Spanish dances and phrases, rewarding each performance with beads and tobacco. One soldier who played a fiddle became the center attraction. The men were constantly greeted by natives proudly articulating in accented Spanish, *"Viva Dios y el Rey"* ("Long live God and the King") or *"Ave María."* The record does not mention whether after several days and nights of relaxation the men were sad or pleased when the return of Father Garcés signaled their imminent departure.

During the five days after leaving Santa Olaya in the afternoon with three natives and plenty of beads and tobacco, Garcés had traveled toward the mouth of the Colorado, covering three leagues before nightfall. He knew villages where he thought locals might have information about watering holes in the San Geronimo range. The following day near the river he was recognized by an old chief; they shared a meal of beans and in the morning crossed to the east bank on a raft. Stopping at Santa Rosa, a village he had once known, Garcés was as welcomed by the Quiquima as he had been by the Cojat, and he probed them for information at every opportunity. He passed fields of wheat and slept at a large ranchería that night, rafting back across the river to start his return the following day. There were several other friendly encounters and dialogues, but none yielded any useful information. On the first day of March he was back at Santa Olaya.

During his absence, Anza had implemented the decision to leave most of their supplies, cattle, and some horses, as well as nine men, with the Yuma. It was a variation of the plan Garcés had earlier opposed. The smaller group was to follow a southerly route toward the San Geronimo. Confronted upon his return with a decision that had deliberately excluded his input, Garcés was inwardly furious. With no information on available water sources along the San Geronimo, he felt they should follow a more northerly route, as he had always advocated. In addition, he knew that Anza's plan would also preclude a northern alternative on the return since the party's strength and supplies would by then be diminished. But the choice had already been made, and it took the priest's vow of obedience and all his self-discipline to accept Anza's decision graciously.

The group that was to remain with Palma included three soldiers "of patience and good conduct," three mule drivers, one of Anza's servants, and two interpreters. The soldiers put in charge were instructed on how to behave and were ordered to maintain good relations with their hosts, albeit with precautionary instructions in case of trouble. The commander had assured himself that he could trust Palma, but knowing how explosive the abuse of soldiers' power could be, he also wanted to make certain that he could trust his own men. He was relying on those he had chosen for their good character and communicating ability to ensure harmony with their hosts during their stay.

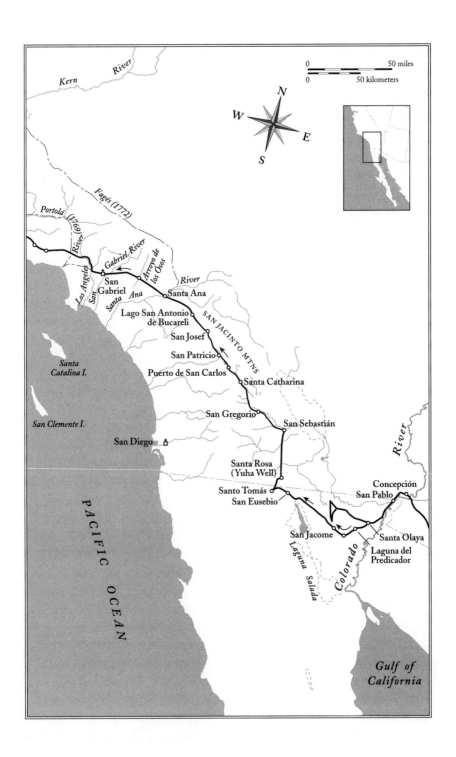

CHAPTER 4

The Breakthrough: Santa Olaya to San Gabriel Mission

March 2 to March 22, 1774

Day 54
Wednesday, March 2, 1774

That day, Palma and his men, together with the nine Spaniards, the cattle, and the mules, started back toward the Colorado River. In the afternoon, Anza and his remaining twenty-four men on their best horses and strongest mules started southwest, accompanied by a Cojat guide who had been living with the Yuma. Even though Garcés had not learned new information about the area, the village of San Jacome, which they had been unable to find in the night, remained their destination. Anza wanted to avoid the dunes that had previously exhausted the animals, hoping to find water near the hills. Moving west from the river, they crossed fertile fields and stands of poplars and willows nurtured by yearly floods. They passed several villages, everywhere asking for information, and that night, having covered four leagues, they camped by a pond near some dry cornfields.

Compared to upriver, the land was just as cultivated and the population as large. Anza was surprised at the similarities between the

Cojat and the Yuma tribes—their physical appearance, their crops, and even their language—and he could not understand why they saw each other as aliens and had frequently fought. As usual, the camp drew a crowd from the neighboring rancherías, and Anza took the opportunity to exhort the Cojat audience to a peaceful coexistence with the Yuma. The event determined the name given to the location, Laguna del Predicador, "Preacher's Pond."

Days 55 to 57
Thursday, March 3, to Saturday, March 5, 1774

Continuing in the same southwesterly direction early the following morning, in three hours they came to a similar pond near a large ranchería. Among the natives, Garcés recognized some from San Jacome who told him that the village had been abandoned after the well had dried up. Asking about two acquaintances, he learned they were "beyond the sierra, near the sea gathering fish." What they called the sea was actually an enormous estuary, the present Laguna Salada, roughly in the direction they were proceeding. The Cojats knew its location, "toward the setting sun," and, of course, the trail. Anza and Garcés knew they wanted to move west and, questioning routes and water sources, they were able to recruit two additional Cojats who, after some hesitation, agreed to guide them the following day. Reaching the estuary was to be the expedition's breakthrough across the desert, but neither the commander nor the priest knew it at the time.

Altering direction toward the west-northwest, they passed a well with good water, then a small village of some twenty individuals, and, late in the afternoon, the abandoned site of San Jacome. They recognized their own still-visible tracks and realized how close they had come the night they went searching for it. Toward dusk they passed a salty pond where the guides proposed to camp but, in the hope of finding better forage, Anza decided to continue. After three futile leagues in the dark they camped without water or pasture, not far from where they had spent the night in similar conditions three weeks before.

Before dawn they were again moving northwest through an increasingly arid country totally different from that near Santa Olaya.

On their left rose the San Geronimo range looming gradually closer; on their right, an endless expanse of dunes. It was ten difficult leagues and as many hours before they came over a small pass to the western slope, down and around dunes to the dry bed of what they believed to be a lake with quantities of dead fish. From the species and size they postulated the "dry lake" to be an estuary open to the sea, but being about ninety miles from the gulf and ignorant of the geography, they could only speculate on the strange phenomenon of the large saltwater fish. Garcés suggested that the lake's saltiness could come from the terrain and took that as the reason why these particular fish would prefer it over the river. "The natives," he observes, "always knew to come here, rather than the river, for the large fish."

They continued the last two leagues on the dry bed to a well on the opposite bank that they named San Eusebio. The guide had brought them through alive but at the cost of near exhaustion—"Hardly what we had been led to believe," comments a disappointed Anza. "The guide was not truthful." Garcés concurs that "it was an extremely difficult journey" but suggests that it could be improved in the future by reopening a dry well they had seen in the sierra. The well at San Eusebio had only a limited amount of freshwater, and before half the herd had been satisfied, it had become so salty that even the thirsty animals wouldn't drink it. The commander's displeasure with their guide must have been evident because, fearing for his life, the Cojat disappeared during the night.

Day 58
Sunday, March 6, 1774

With daylight came the awareness that the Cojat guide was missing; where he had slept they found only his weapons. Also missing were several animals, but no one could be sure if the incidents were connected or if the thirsty animals had wandered off on their own in search of water. Given the salty well at San Eusebio, thirst had become a major problem, and watering the mules and cattle was now the first priority. Another dry and exhausting day would begin killing them. While some looked for the missing animals, another party went in search of the next well the guide had described.

"By two o'clock, I had the whole train moving west-northwest on the tracks of the six scouts and, after three leagues, met two of them sent by the corporal to inform us that a good water supply had been found in the sierra, as well as a young native boy."

Guided by the soldiers, they covered four more leagues detouring toward the southwest, and after dark they rejoined the advanced party at the pond. By that time an adult had come to claim the boy, and the corporal, bearing gifts but instructed to avoid force, had been unable to prevent their departure. The expedition's need for local knowledge notwithstanding, Anza's policy of diplomacy over coercion was strictly observed; experience had taught him that establishing a reputation for violence would do more harm than good.

The pond was fed by five springs, of which one was salt-free. The water was clear and drinkable, the pasture adequate, and Anza named the site for the apostle Santo Tomás, who he believed had protected them. The detour had saved the animals, but it had taken the expedition off its intended course (farther south than Garcés had ever been), and the men were now without a guide in an area about which they were totally ignorant. Far from his own route, Tarabal had not been able to identify any landmarks either. From the natives at Santo Tomás they knew the region was inhabited and water therefore available, but until they knew exactly where, their situation remained precarious.

Day 59
Monday, March 7, 1774

The six scouts were sent north in the morning and again the rest of the group followed their tracks in the afternoon. Four leagues into the march the group spotted them on the horizon with several local natives who, after sharing their water supply, had led the scouts to the source and told them how to reach other wells. When the larger group arrived unannounced, however, the natives became afraid and wanted to flee, and in spite of his skilled diplomacy and enticement with gifts, Anza could not prevent them from leaving, let alone recruit them as guides. Fortunately, the expedition had found water and pasture enough for the present and gathered information about nearby wells to the east. Setting up camp for the night, their long, dark shadows faded into the sand as the sun disappeared over the sierra.

Day 60
Tuesday, March 8, 1774

Leaving shortly after daybreak the expedition located the new wells a long league to the northeast. Because of the excellent and plentiful water, the adequate pasture, and the still poor condition of the animals, Anza decreed a day of rest. The site, which they named Santa Rosa de las Lajas after the large stone slabs in the area, was estimated by dead reckoning to be about eighteen leagues due west of Santa Olaya. "It could have been reached in two days," writes Anza, thinking of future crossings, although they had used seven days in their roundabout route. During the day Garcés recognized having been in the area and Tarabal was able to identify in the distance the pass he had taken from San Gabriel. Certain now of success, Anza laconically records that "this promises us that our expedition will not be frustrated."

Days 61 and 62
Wednesday, March 9, and Thursday, March 10, 1774

In the early afternoon they started almost due north toward a pond known to Tarabal. They covered four or five leagues over easy terrain before stopping for the night near pasture. Continuing at first light in the same direction, they encountered the tail end of some dunes stretching over a league and a half through which most of the men chose to lead their horses on foot. It was not a spontaneous move but a prearranged agreement to preserve the animals whenever possible. By 1:00 in the afternoon they reached a large marshy area with pasture and abundant, if saline, water from a fresh and continuously flowing source. Anza named the site San Sebastián or, alternately, El Peregrino in honor of Tarabal, whose "pilgrimage" had once taken him through the area.

Not far from San Sebastián the expedition came upon a group of natives from a nearby ranchería. Upon seeing the Spaniards, the natives fled, abandoning their belongings. Anza dispatched Tarabal to find them while ensuring nothing was disturbed. Not only was Tarabal himself almost a local to the area, but there was also a chance he might be recognized. He soon returned with a woman whom they reassured with beads and tobacco in order to entice the others back. Two hours later, seven reticent men, including one Tarabal knew as their leader, reappeared and met the expedition, and the chief likewise recognized his former guest with surprise and pleasure.

The ranchería of some four hundred Mountain Cojats was part of a group as numerous as the Yuma. Their way of life, however, was different from that of the Cojats the expedition had encountered on the river delta. Lacking arable land and water this group did not farm but lived from gathering seeds and plants, and hunting. Anza noted that they were not as robust as those along the river, and they appeared less aggressive. They did not own horses and were even scared of the animal's whinnying. They wore their hair short and unadorned, their skin was rather dark, and the men, as usual, went completely naked while the women wore mescal fibers hung from the waist. They considered themselves enemies of the Yuma, with whom they regularly clashed, but Anza, continuing his pacification policy, made the Cojats embrace the two Yumas with him, stating that all the nations he had visited had pledged themselves to peace, a standard that, from then on, would apply to them as well. The locals were obviously pleased as they ostentatiously broke the arrows they were carrying and stated that they would henceforth go to the river only in peace.

Garcés, in the meantime, was gathering information. He also had been recognized by Cojats from San Jacome, and from them he learned that they were not the first whites to have been in the area. Apparently, Spaniards in uniform had preceded them—perhaps deserters or a scouting patrol, he did not know which. Garcés was elated with his discoveries: that there was just one tribe from the delta to the foothills, that Spanish presence was converging from both east and west, and that the receptive native population was ripe for conversion. Making new Christians was his vocation and the indigenous tribes were his favorite people. Charles III would be pleased and Viceroy Bucareli proud of the spiritual and temporal conquest for God and the crown. Although exhilarated with the power and glory of his vision, he did not forget to inquire about the area, and in doing so he learned of two water holes that would enable them to make their return trip from San Sebastián to Santa Olaya in just three days.

Days 63 to 65
Friday, March 11, to Sunday, March 13, 1774

Starting west in the afternoon the expedition was surprised by the difficulty of the wet terrain. Having covered only a league and a half by nightfall, they were forced to camp on marshy land with only mesquite leaves for fodder. As a consequence of the salty feed in San Sebastián, two horses died. From the locals they learned the ocean was only three days away, and in five days they could reach a Spanish settlement. Anza assumed they were referring to San Diego rather than the recently established mission of San Gabriel.

An hour before dawn they were on the move northwest toward the Borrego Mountains, part of the sierra that had been on their left for several days. They climbed gradually, following a creek through dry and easy terrain with increasing vegetation. Having covered six leagues by early afternoon, they stopped in a small, idyllic valley with flowing water and the best pasture they had seen for a long time. The site, near the present-day San Felipe Creek in the Borrego Valley, Anza named San Gregorio. The Cojats informed them they were entering another nation.

As the expedition approached, Tarabal went ahead to meet a group of natives that turned out to be a hunting party speaking the same language as the natives near San Diego. He was escorting them toward Anza when some mules, perhaps sensing the presence of water, brayed loudly. Already on edge in the presence of strangers, the unfamiliar sound caused the natives to scatter and flee. Even though the following day was spent at San Gregorio for the sake of the animals, they were never able to reestablish contact.

Day 66
Monday, March 14, 1774

Leaving camp before dawn, the expedition proceeded west-north-west along the creek, climbing gently toward higher ground. The seasonally green pastures, the vines and abundant vegetation all around—including numerous willow trees in the valley—were in marked contrast to the weeks in the desert. The soil was firm, the terrain was easy on the animals, and finding water was no longer a problem. All signs confirmed that the extreme hardships were over.

Even though they were unable to establish their exact location, they knew they were within days of San Gabriel, and a feeling of pride pervaded the group as the men became conscious that now they could not fail. Using only a compass, a timepiece, and local guides, they had crossed the unknown. From there Tarabal, the only one among them to have been in Alta California before, could guide them to the mission. Covering six leagues for the day, the expedition camped at another excellent site, which they name Santa Catharina.

As usual Anza spared no effort in trying to communicate with the natives and he recorded his observations. Neither he nor Garcés was able to associate these locals with natives of another nation; according to Tarabal, some spoke the language used in San Diego and San Gabriel, but most spoke a different language altogether. Anza noted that these people were smaller and weaker that the Cojat and Yuma and very few had bows and arrows, often hunting instead with symmetrically bent wooden sticks. According to the soldiers, they threw this weapon from a distance to break an animal's legs; few were the hares or rabbits that escaped. Like the Cojats they had encountered a few days previous, these natives were unfamiliar with horses and scared of their neighing.

"In speaking with them," writes Anza, "they repeated what we had learned in San Sebastián [about the presence of other men in uniform], which we later confirmed by horse tracks." He wondered if the Spaniards might have been a search party sent after Tarabal and his companions when they had passed through the area as fugitives.

Day 67
Tuesday, March 15, 1774

After another pre-dawn start, the expedition continued northwest, following the creek upstream. Throughout the day they were accompanied by nearly two hundred natives, some near at hand, others keeping their distance, torn between fear and curiosity. They used an unknown language and their speech was accompanied by extreme movements of their arms and legs, motions so pronounced the Spaniards nicknamed them "dancers." They were described as agile with their hands and feet, and around them objects seemed to disappear without a trace; "Of all the nations encountered, this one seems to be the most prone to stealing," notes Anza, who for this reason chose to withhold his usual gifts.

As the expedition continued along the creek, the valley narrowed into a canyon (present-day Coyote Canyon), and as they climbed Anza correctly guessed the range to be an extension of the Baja California mountains. The ascent was gradual with good footing, and the well-fed animals took it in stride. At one point in the narrow canyon, however, they seemed to have reached an impasse, and when Tarabal hesitated, a corporal was sent to reconnoiter.

The natives, meanwhile, continued to insist there was a way through, and they were correct. The expedition pressed on and soon reached a pass from which the view was crystal clear and magnificent—forests of pines and stands of oaks covered the hills and, in the distance, the snowcapped sierra sparkled. They had reached the point where the waters divided, now flowing toward the "Philippine Sea" instead of back toward the gulf.[1] That night the expedition camped at the pass, which Anza named El Puerto Real de San Carlos (the Royal Pass of San Carlos) in honor of the king.

Days 68 and 69
Wednesday, March 16, and Thursday, March 17, 1774

A mixture of rain and snow fell through the night, delaying the start until early afternoon. From San Carlos they continued northwest, descending into a fertile valley (present-day Terwilliger or Cahuilla Valley), and after three leagues they stopped to camp by a lake, which Anza named, as he had the valley, El Príncipe. That night the rainy snow continued, leading to another late start and short day that took them only to the north end of the valley, where they camped at San Patricio.

During this stretch of the journey, both journals continue to praise the abundant vegetation, the beautiful scenery, and the green winter climate; the first Europeans to reach California from the east had entered the Garden of Eden after weeks wandering through the desert.

---

[1] Spaniards often referred to the Pacific Ocean as the "Philippine Sea" because, at the time, their only Pacific holdings were the Philippine Islands.

Anza and Garcés became the first to record the sense of wonder that would be echoed by overland immigrants for centuries thereafter.

Day 70
Friday, March 18, 1774

Still following the stream northwest through the valley, they entered a narrow canyon overgrown with thick vegetation that made it difficult to advance. Six men were sent ahead with axes, and in the space of one league they had to several times clear branches and fallen trees. Eventually the canyon opened to another wide and bountiful valley abundant with flora and fauna—oaks on the hillside, flowers in the fields, poplars and aspens by the clear stream full of fish, and everywhere "geese whose numbers cannot be counted." Native women were also present, but fearing the strangers, they stayed at a prudent distance. And, as if anything could be missing, Garcés notes that "the men picked up a rock with a visible content of metal." The expedition had entered what is today known as the San Jacinto Valley, which they had named El Valle Ameno de San Josef, the Pleasant Valley of San Josef.

Days 71 and 72
Saturday, March 19, and Sunday, March 20, 1774

Leaving early in the morning, the expedition headed northwest. Throughout the day, they were occasionally approached by some of the more daring natives, among the many who followed with curiosity, but as soon as they were rewarded with gifts, they retired to a safe distance without establishing dialogue. Anza estimated from the tracks in the area that their population must be much larger than it appeared.

As they progressed through the valley, they continued to marvel at the natural paradise around them. Garcés notes the presence of rosemary and sage "of better quality than in Guadalajara," although he also mentions that the same soil that produced such fine herbs was occasionally marshy and impassable, requiring repeated turns and detours "as time-consuming as the hills." Garcés also recognized the area as bear country, although none had been sighted. In the afternoon they arrived at a lake whose surface was "an enormous white field," covered with so many geese that the water was barely visible. Anza named it in honor of the viceroy, San Antonio de Bucareli.

Departure the next day was at 8:30 and the direction was still northwest. The sierra to their right (the San Bernardino Mountains) were covered with snow. Late that morning they entered another magnificent valley, eventually reaching a large river that they named Santa Ana and followed for a league and a half. Unable to find a ford they set up camp at 4:00 in the afternoon and began to build a bridge, which was completed by nightfall. Natives from a nearby ranchería approached the camp and asked Tarabal in the language of San Gabriel if the expedition had come from San Diego. They were incredulous when Anza replied, "We have been traveling for three moons, from the east, where there are many more soldiers than you are aware of."

This thinly veiled threat suggests Anza might have felt vulnerable due to the expedition's limited numbers, but Garcés, who commented only on the handicrafts of the natives, had no such concerns. Entering one of the dwellings he noted baskets similar to those made by the Pima and blankets like those traded by the nations of the Colorado and Gila. "Some of these," writes Garcés, "even reach our missions [in Sonora and present-day Arizona], where we have been always told that they came from these parts." Whereas the captain was vigilant for their immediate safety, Garcés, the amateur anthropologist, speculated on the movement of goods and people across the vast territories.

Days 73 and 74
Monday, March 21, and Tuesday, March 22, 1774

The temporary bridge held steady and by 8:30 all the men and their animals had crossed. It was an easy day over flat and dry terrain in sunny weather with the snowcapped sierra still on their right. Garcés observed a pass north-northwest of their location and noted in his journal, "They say it leads to a valley through which one can reach the mission at San Luis Obispo." They set up camp by a stream bordered by willows, elms, and alders, which Tarabal knew as the San Antonio, but Anza renamed the Arroyo de los Osos or "Stream of the Bears" after the many they had seen that day.

Eager to reach San Gabriel the expedition left by seven the following morning. The terrain, direction, and weather were similar to that of the day before, but because it was both the rainy season and spring thaw in the sierra, the many streams they encountered were exceptionally high. With the mission visible by the afternoon, they spent a long time finding a ford to the San Gabriel River and only managed to arrive by sunset, surprising both the escort and the priests. The mission inhabitants had heard rumors about an overland expedition coming from New Spain, but they considered it unrealistic and seemingly impossible, and thus their extreme joy and excitement at Anza's arrival.

Concerning the presence of Tarabal in the same community from which he had illegally escaped, the journals are conspicuously silent. Because a higher authority had enlisted his service rather than punish him, it seemed his contribution to their success had justified his pardon. Nevertheless, it is curious that the record celebrating the new route and recognizing Anza's accomplishment barely mentions Tarabal's name. Neither his personal feelings upon arriving at San Gabriel nor the reaction of the mission priests were recorded by Anza or Garcés.

The expedition approached the mission hoping not only to rest and relax but also to restock their supplies before continuing north. What they found, however, was a community in need. While each of Alta California's five Spanish settlements had begun to breed animals and plant crops by 1774, the colony as a whole still depended on supplies from New Spain, but due to the small vessels and lengthy voyage, very little arrived and only irregularly. When the expedition showed up in San Gabriel, the missionaries had little of their own to share with their guests, and Anza's troops, in turn having counted on resupplying at the mission, could offer them no assistance. Fortunately for all, the frigate *Nueva Galicia* had recently arrived at San Diego, and Anza thought he could perhaps obtain some supplies from the captain. In spite of these problems, however, the expedition was greeted with tears of happiness and disbelief. Bells tolled, muskets fired, and the occasion was celebrated with a Te Deum.

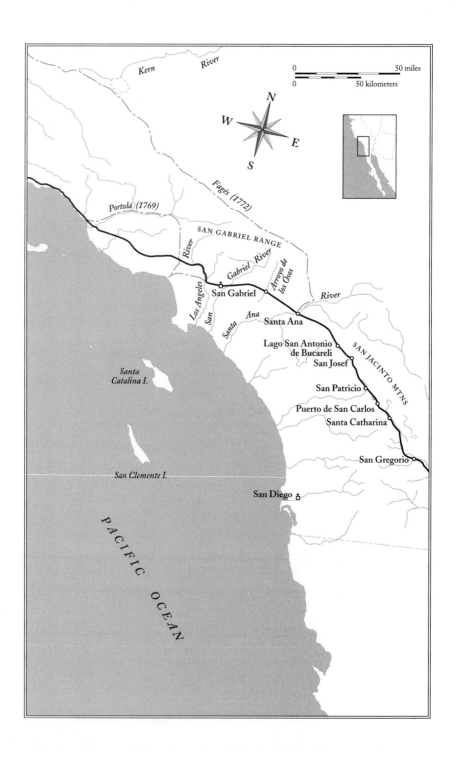

CHAPTER 5

Rest and Reorganization
at San Gabriel

March 23 to April 9, 1774

Days 75 and 76
Wednesday, March 23, and Thursday, March 24, 1774

As in Tubac two months earlier, the first order of the day that spring morning was a solemn high mass offering "thanks to Almighty God for having favored the Forces of His Majesty in this expedition." Prayers were said for "the King Carlos III and his piety in bringing the Catholic Religion to the gentiles in these parts" and for "the Most Excellent Viceroy, who had endeavored to put into practice our sovereign's intentions through the enterprise in question, which will undoubtedly result in the greater glory of both majesties, God and the King of Spain." While bells tolled, candles flickered, and incense burned, the Franciscans, the neophytes, the mission escort, and every member of the expedition joined in the mass. The pomp of the ceremony stood in contrast to the destitution of the outpost, where rations had been reduced to three corn tortillas per day, garnished only with the wild herbs that each could gather. Garcés was embarrassed that the expedition had "brought need to the house of poverty" and had no choice but to impose upon their hosts. The mission could barely feed them as it was, much less furnish their needs to continue to Monterey.

This increased demand meant goods from the supply ship would have to be shared with twenty-four additional men. Anza and Garcés agreed to leave for San Diego the following day to meet the ship's captain and make the request in person. In addition Anza, the optimist, still hoped to obtain fresh mounts from the mission and, if possible, borrow a pilot and sextant from the *Nueva Galicia*. But overnight the river continued to rise and for the next two days it was impossible to ford. The men and the animals took the opportunity for a well-deserved rest while the rain continued.

Days 77 to 83
Friday, March 25, to Thursday, March 31, 1774

On Friday four men and a train of seven mules from the mission were dispatched to San Diego with a letter for both the commander of the presidio and for Don Juan Perez, captain of the *Nueva Galicia*. In it Anza explained the objectives and importance of his expedition and the personal commitment to its success of Viceroy Bucareli, in whose name he was requesting they furnish him with supplies.

With the weather improved two days later on Palm Sunday, Garcés left alone for San Diego. Why Anza chose to stay behind is not explained, but in light of his subsequent actions (i.e., leaving before Garcés returned and deciding to forego exploring a direct route from Monterey to the Colorado-Gila junction), one cannot help but suspect that he did not want to be challenged by the priest. Garcés reached San Diego three days later, on the thirtieth of March. His journal omits details of what he did there, but other sources show he spent some time with Father Junípero Serra, the superior of the California missions just returned in the *Nueva Galicia*. He also met with the presidio commander and the captain, who released supplies for the expedition but could not provide the pilot and sextant Anza had requested, as they were needed for the ship to continue to Monterey. There is no mention in the journals of the mission in San Diego being able to furnish any animals.

On Friday, April 1, the loaded mule train started back toward San Gabriel without the priest. Garcés and Serra were to follow on Monday, the latter planning to complete his voyage to Carmel in the company of the expedition as travel on the Camino Real was safer with a strong escort. As it turned out, the priests were not able to leave San Diego until Wednesday and didn't arrive in San Gabriel until Monday the eleventh, one day after Anza had already left for Monterey.

At this point, Father Serra's voice briefly joins what has so far been a two-man narrative. From him we learn some details about the latent friction between Anza and Garcés. While Anza's journal provides copious information on geography, natives, natural resources, distances, routes, and alternatives, he tends to minimize or ignore difficulties and present a rather optimistic picture. It must be remembered that he was writing for Viceroy Bucareli, the primary supporter of the project, and since Anza's own career depended on its success, it is not surprising that optimism would color his views.

Garcés' official and impersonal journal is equally explicit on practical matters and always respectful of the commander but more cognizant of the often harsh realities of their situations. Since he is never openly critical of Anza, it is only outside sources that can provide details of the true relationship between Anza and Garcés. One such source is a letter from Serra to his superior in Mexico, written after Garcés had spoken with him about the expedition with an openness and sensitivity lacking in his journal. From this letter we know that: during the days before reaching San Gabriel, the expedition had hardly enough to eat and on the last day, the men had eaten nothing at all, arriving at the mission "without as much as a small bar of chocolate." We know that: according to the priest, the influence of the native Sebastián Tarabal as a guide had effectively replaced that of Garcés; "Anza planned his route without taking into account any other information or consulting with Father Garcés, but accepting to go wherever the Indian Sebastián wanted to take them." We know that: in his request for supplies from the garrison and the mission at San Diego, as well as from the ship, Anza had threatened to hold them all responsible for obstructing the expedition's progress should they fail to assist him.

To the image of a determined, confident, and decisive commander beloved by his men and respected by all, this testimony by Garcés, as recorded by Serra, adds dimensions of impetuosity, self-importance, arrogance, and ruthlessness. It also shows Garcés overstepping his spiritual role as priest and missionary when he becomes resentful that his scouting experience and practical knowledge are unwanted. While the friction that is so evident in Serra's letter does not appear in either man's official journal, it is obvious that it must have been simmering just below the surface.

Days 84 to 92
Friday, April 1, to Saturday, April 9, 1774

During the days Garcés traveled to San Diego on his behalf, Anza had remained with his men at San Gabriel. The meager rations and persistent rain made for a period of restful boredom with time for cleaning weapons, repairing gear, washing, and mending. But in spite of their accomplishment so far, their current lack of food meant there was none of the festive mood that had accompanied their stay at Santa Olaya.

On April 5, the mule train returned with all the supplies that San Diego and the frigate could furnish. The staples consisted of nine bushels of corn, a measure of "inedible" dried meat, a measure of flour, and three bushels of beans. Anza estimated it would last sixteen days provided the beans could be cooked at a mission (the expedition did not carry adequate pots), but even then, there was obviously not enough. Furthermore, they knew they could not count on any help from Monterey or Carmel because those settlements were also desperately awaiting the *Nueva Galicia*. In effect, the expedition could not expect to obtain any additional supplies until they returned to Yuma territory, and under the present circumstances, the idea of breaking a direct route from Monterey to the Colorado-Gila junction was unreasonable, especially since they couldn't estimate how long it would take. This was undoubtedly the point Anza did not want to be challenged on and probably the reason he had left San Gabriel before Garcés returned from San Diego.

Father Diaz, far more submissive, was easily convinced in light of the evidence, and it was with his concurrence that Anza proceeded with his new plan. The commander would "ride as light as possible with six men to Monterey and assess the situation there regarding a future direct route to Sonora," which he could not explore then for lack of supplies. Diaz was invited to join him but declined. Anza then ordered that as soon as Garcés returned from San Diego, the two priests and the rest of the men were to immediately retrace their steps to the Colorado. From there, they were to "dispatch two soldiers to the Presidio of Altar with mail for the Viceroy," and wait for Anza's return to the river junction. It was a prudent and conservative plan intended to inform the authorities as soon as possible of their success in reaching and returning from San Gabriel, the trail onward from there to Monterey being already well established.

On Wednesday, April 6, Garcés and Serra left San Diego to rejoin the expedition at San Gabriel as quickly as possible, but with the recent rain, soggy ground, and high rivers it took them five days. When they arrived on Monday, April 11, to discover Anza had already left, Garcés, surprised by the change of plans, was understandably disappointed that they would not be exploring a new northern route as he had hoped; "I am really sorry that it will not be possible to use this opportunity to discover the current of the San Francisco River, which I believe has a connection with the Colorado and both of them with very large lakes, according to what the Gila natives have told me." After learning that he and Diaz had been ordered back to the Colorado with the troops, Garcés proposed to break a new route by returning via San Diego instead, but although compliant Diaz was willing, the soldiers refused to disobey Anza's specific orders to retrace their steps, and the idea was abandoned.

Regarding the vessel's sextant that had been refused by the captain of the *Nueva Galicia*, Garcés informed Diaz that the chaplain, who also had one and would be remaining at San Diego due to illness, might consider lending his. Since establishing latitudes would significantly enhance the description of the route for future users, Diaz agreed to leave the party and travel to San Diego to retrieve the instrument while Garcés led the soldiers east by the same route they had come.

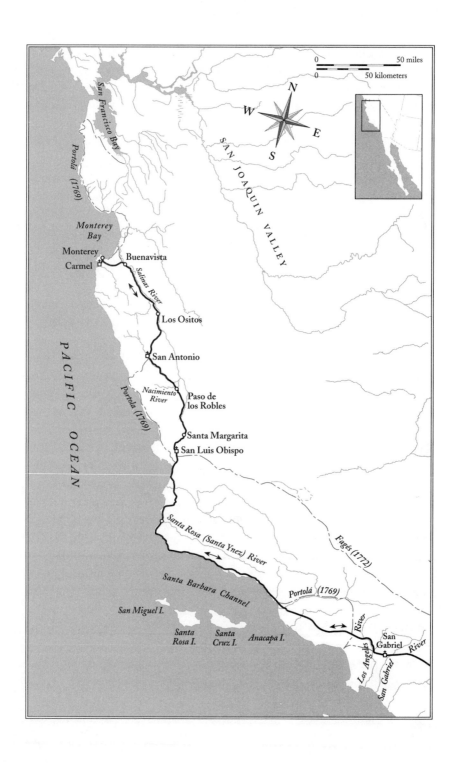

CHAPTER 6

The Camino Real: San Gabriel to Monterey and Back

April 10 to May 1, 1774

Constrained by supplies and sufficient adequate horses, Anza put into practice his alternate plan: to travel as fast as possible with a small party to Monterey while the rest returned to the Yuma nation, where supplies were available, and awaited his return. Consequently, for the rest of April the expedition was split into three groups: Anza and six men going north; Garcés, twelve soldiers, and the mule train heading to the Colorado; and Diaz, with three servants, traveling to San Diego in search of the spare sextant.

Days 93 to 101
Sunday, April 10, to Monday, April 18, 1774
While Fathers Garcés and Serra were still on their way from San Diego, Anza left San Gabriel on Sunday, covering fourteen leagues. The small detachment traveled between fourteen and fifteen leagues per day, covering the three hundred plus miles between San Gabriel and Monterey in eight days. Because the route had been in use since Portolá and Costansó first described it in 1769, Anza recorded

relatively little about it. In his entry for Thursday, April 14, while waiting for low tide to cross the Santa Rosa River (now the Santa Ynez), he summarizes his impressions of the natives settled along the Santa Barbara Channel:

"The entire channel area is well populated, the gentiles being as numerous as on the Colorado River and living, as most natives, naked. They are both strong and large people, armed mostly with small bows and arrows, a sociable group living in hamlets with upward of forty spherical dwellings each. In work and commerce they have no equal among gentiles. Many are occupied building boats and their accessories. The vessels are double bowed, from thirty-six to forty palms [twenty-four to twenty-six feet] in length, and of proportional width. They are built with at least a dozen planks and are so well constructed, joined, and caulked that they are entirely watertight and light enough to be carried by their crews. The tools I saw them using were of stone and, having bought some, I had to admire not only their skill but their patience as well. Each village appears to have between fifteen and twenty usable boats and from seven to ten under construction. Others are engaged in making stone kitchen pots, as well turned as if they had used a wheel, and not only small but in various sizes and styles, some of which I purchased. They also make utensils from sticks and hardwoods such as oak. The women participate in this work and, even more, in the manufacture of tightly woven baskets for various purposes. While straw weaving is common among natives, I have not seen finer baskets…, no doubt due to the local materials, which may not be available elsewhere.

"Most of the day, the sea appears covered with boats fishing. They use hooks made from seashells, as perfect as if they were made of steel. The boats cross to the islands, between four and five leagues to the south. Including those living on the islands as well as those inland from the channel, the group may number between eight and ten thousand. Their land is as fertile and beautiful as that we have seen anywhere, but especially in contrast with the sterile land bordering the Gulf of California, whereas here grass- and flower-covered fields reach out to touch the waters of the ocean."

Crossing the Santa Rosa with low tide at dawn, Anza's group rode north for sixteen leagues to arrive that Thursday night at San Luis Obispo, where the priests and soldiers of the mission greeted them with the same effusion and outburst of emotion they had experienced at San Gabriel. Their stay was brief, and at dawn they rode on to San Antonio, twenty leagues away, arriving there in a day and a morning. Pressed by time, they declined overnight hospitality and continued to camp near the Salinas River at Los Ositos (somewhere between present-day King City and Greenfield) and reached Monterey on Monday, April 18.

Exactly one week before, on April 11, Fathers Garcés and Serra had arrived in San Gabriel and, to their disappointment, discovered they were too late to join Anza. After discussing the commander's orders, the priests decided to revise them, each taking a different task. Leaving Diaz to procure the sextant and Serra waiting for an escort north, Garcés assumed command of the group. With his approval, a young neophyte from the mission joined them, and two days later they began their return.

In accordance with Anza's orders, they retraced their steps, that day going as far as the San Antonio River (their "Stream of the Bears"), where they had camped on March 21. The following morning the soldiers were happy to shoot a bear, adding fresh meat to their diet and a bit of cheer to their mood. The day's march in warm sunshine took them through firm terrain with rolling pastures and stands of elms and willows. The snow was gone from the sierra and the country was colored in shades of green. By early afternoon they had set up camp by the Santa Ana, having covered seven leagues. Garcés does not mention any difficulty crossing the river or the bridge they had built the previous month.

The following day they proceeded by a more southern route toward San Josef (to the east of present-day San Jacinto) than on their outbound journey. Even though no reason is given, this direction would have brought them south of the present Mount Russell, reducing somewhat the distance into the valley. The choice, however, did not save them time as the rains had made some areas impassable, forcing them to detour for a league and a half and, in one instance, requiring them to unload the mules to cross a stream. The natives, more numerous and less fearful than before, came close to the party, one in particular amusing the expedition with his rhythmic singing and dancing.

In the afternoon, the corporal from San Gabriel caught up with Garcés carrying orders to return the neophyte boy that had joined them. The incident cast light on the priest's independent nature as well as on the social hierarchy of a mission: The youth, who Garcés describes as a "Christian boy of gentile parents, who joined us asking me to take him to see other lands, leaving his natural and spiritual parents, as well as his own country, behind" was obviously under parental authority, but because the youth was a Christian, Garcés judged him, despite his age, to be capable of speaking for himself and mature enough to make the request he did. In accepting the boy on his own cognizance, the priest had disregarded parental authority because he considered the youth a "person of reason," whereas his non-Christian parents were considered of inferior standing. In addition, Garcés had deliberately ignored the rules because he knew a neophyte was not free to leave the community without mission approval. In the end, Garcés agreed to return the boy, questioning neither the corporal's orders nor the parents' wishes, but he never admitted any wrongdoing, still believing the boy to be capable of making his own decision.

Proceeding southeast Garcés' party entered the narrow canyon via the trail they had cleared from the other direction, and they set up camp past San Patricio. Communication with the attendant natives, who shared the language of San Gabriel, had become more frequent and relaxed than before, and that night the locals offered the expedition mescal to drink and some food. Later, they engaged in dancing in which "an Indian would shout loudly, moving arms and legs without rhythm, while a woman ran circles around the apparently furious man, gesturing with her hand as if calling him, as our Spanish women do."

Garcés' journal gives no further details of the evening, but the following day's entry (Monday, April 18, 1774) states without explanation that they were only able to start out at 1:00 in the afternoon, and after a short march they reached the Pass of San Carlos by 5:30.

Days 102 to 114
Tuesday, April 19, to Sunday, May 1, 1774
Having arrived in record time from San Gabriel, Anza's group spent a day of rest in Monterey. On Wednesday, April 20, Anza traveled to

---

1 What the journals refer to as San Carlos Mission is Carmel Mission, whose complete name is San Carlos Borromeo de Carmelo.

San Carlos on a courtesy visit to the priests there.[1] The conversation that day revolved around a broken mast that had recently washed ashore. No one could identify the wood used or the design of the strong, two-pointed nails with elongated heads that did not appear to rust. Curious about the origin of the damaged vessel, they decided to send the mast to San Blas in New Spain for examination, hoping to dispel concerns of a foreign power sailing near the coast of California.

After mass the next morning Anza returned to the garrison at Monterey. He suggested to Pedro Fagés, the post commander, that some of his men should learn the new route, and six were assigned to accompany Anza as far as the Colorado River. Eager to be on his way, the group left the presidio in the morning on April 22 and kept up their rapid pace over the next few days, stopping at Los Ositos, San Antonio, the Nacimiento River, and San Luis Obispo. On Tuesday, April 26, they were again near the mouth of the Santa Rosa River.

While Anza's group recovered at Monterey, Garcés was descending from the Pass of San Carlos along Coyote Creek toward the southeast. They continued to be shadowed by numerous natives, both men and women, who no longer feared the Spaniards and mingled easily with the troops. They generously shared "an abundance of mescal" and the soldiers reciprocated with glass beads in a mood of camaraderie. While they celebrated, someone deliberately speared the fattest of their horses and during the night the wounded animal was butchered in such silence that the guards did not discover it until morning. "It seems they had a whim for meat," notes Garcés without further comment, but the incident had made an impression; they would not again be so easily deceived by a friendly crowd.

After camping at San Gregorio they continued through the marshy terrain and late the following night arrived at San Sebastián, where the local natives welcomed them back. Garcés would have preferred to take a day of rest there but was overruled by the soldiers, who were concerned that both the pasture and water in the area were bad for the animals, and their own food supply was very low. Fortunately, from there they would not have to retrace their roundabout route to Santa Olaya but, provided they could get a guide, would cross the desert directly to the lake.

On the afternoon of Friday, April 22, accompanied by two local guides, they started east through a wide-open and desolate plain, the low point of which has since become the Salton Sea. With the mountains in perspective Garcés attempted to reckon his position. He describes two sierra running southeast to northwest, one of which he assumes to originate near the Yuma crossing and the other (the one that had been on their left for days), near the river mouth. He notes an opening on the eastern sierra, guessing it "must provide a more direct route to Monterey." While Garcés does not name the mountains, his geographical observations are essentially accurate and his insistence on there being a more direct route to Monterey east of the coastal ranges is entirely reasonable. It is clear he has not given up his obsession with finding a northern route.

After four leagues, they reached pasture and a small pond that Garcés named San Anselmo. The older guide advised spending the night there, but again the soldiers objected, as they wanted to reduce the distance for the following day. Since the old guide would not budge, the young one, barely a boy, agreed to lead the troops, but he soon lost the trail in the dark, and they were forced to camp in the open without water or pasture. The boy abandoned the group during the night.

Aware of the problem just after daylight, the men were of two opinions about how to continue. Garcés, for the sake of future expeditions, wanted to locate a water source somewhere between San Sebastián and Las Angustias or Pozos de la Alegría, and he therefore proposed to return to San Sebastián to seek another guide. But despite the respect in which he was held, Garcés did not have the authority to command the troops against their own judgment and they would not follow him as they would have followed Anza. From their experience the soldiers knew how vulnerable the animals were in the desert, and after two days already without adequate water and pasture, to turn back would mean another two days of the same. Instead they proposed to head for Santa Olaya, a proven source of good water and only two days ahead by dead reckoning. Garcés was overruled and they started out for the closest well at Las Angustias.

The loss of the guides had cost them another day, but fortunately due to their long rest at San Gabriel the animals were still strong. That afternoon, two scouts left camp to reconnoiter an opening through the dunes, and they returned before dark. The following morning they set out southeast, leaving at 5:30, traveling all morning, resting during the heat of the day, and reaching Las Angustias at 3:00 in the morning, having covered eleven leagues.

The next day they followed their old trail past Pozos de la Alegría, El Carrizal, and El Rosario, and by midnight they had arrived at Santa Olaya. On Monday, April 25, still a day from the river, Garcés noted he was missing both his clock and compass. Even worse, from the locals they heard disturbing news that the companions they had left with the Yuma back in February were no longer there. It was only when they reached the river junction that they learned what had actually happened: some time before, word had reached the Yuma that the expedition had been killed by Mountain Cojats and, based on this information, the men left behind had decided to return to Sonora. Taking only what they required for the trip, they had left the rest of the supplies and cattle with Palma, who now presented the lot to Garcés. Of eighteen animals, two had been slaughtered, but as promised, Palma accounted for the goods even in the absence of Anza's men.

Arriving at the river junction Garcés was confronted with more than the usual welcome; it was a homecoming to the land of plenty. The return of this first party from California, whose survival was now assured, confirmed to all that the expedition had succeeded. On the day Garcés arrived, April 26, 1774, he closed his diary with praise for "the Commander, whose good treatment of the Indians, gentle discipline of his soldiers, and respect and support for the priests had caused Divine Piety to bring about the peaceful and successful conclusion of the expedition." He then dispatched a courier to the viceroy via Altar carrying his just completed journal and a request for supplies from the governor, meanwhile settling in to enjoy the Yuma hospitality and await Anza's return.

That same day, three hundred miles to the northwest, Anza was already at the Santa Rosa River. On April 27, near the Santa Barbara Channel, he crossed Father Serra on his way north. At the priest's request the two spent the rest of the day together, for after having heard Father Garcés' version of the journey, Serra was anxious to hear the commander's.

Four days later Anza was back at San Gabriel. Riding close to forty miles per day with only brief rests in Monterey and San Carlos, he had covered some seven hundred miles in less than three weeks.

His entry for May 1 again states that he has little to add to the reports of Captains Portolá and Costansó concerning the route, but he comments on the gentle nature of the natives and the significant number of Christian converts. According to the missionaries, further conversions are now limited by their inability to provide for more neophytes. "The size of the harvests have been limited up to now," writes Anza, "more by shortage of seed than by the fertility of the land. In both wheat and barley, the size of the grain and the thickness of the stem are larger than anything I have seen in Sonora." The missionaries were sure that if the year's harvest was as bountiful as expected, the number of neophytes would soon double or triple.

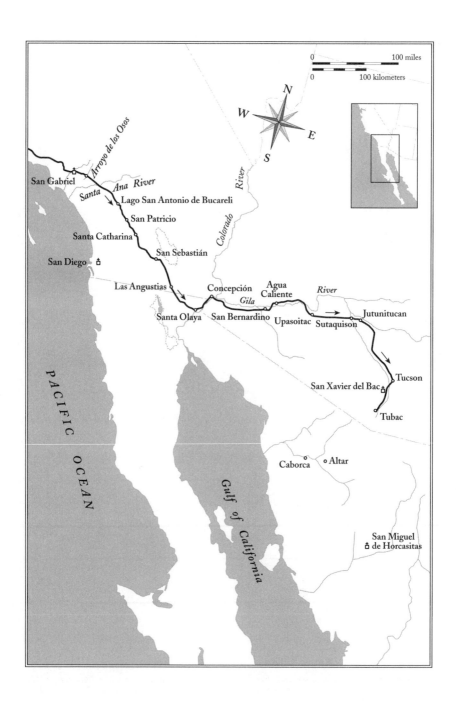

CHAPTER 7

All Is Clear:
San Gabriel to Tubac

May 2 to May 27, 1774

Days 115 to 122
Monday, May 2, to Monday, May 9, 1774

On May 1 Anza arrived back at San Gabriel. In his absence, Father Diaz had been to San Diego, obtained the sextant from the ill chaplain, and returned knowing how to use it. Anza was pleased to include latitudes in his journal, and he gave the reading for San Gabriel as 33°:53' North. Although this measurement was slightly in error, providing latitudes was a major enhancement in describing the route, and from this point on the latitudes recorded are surprisingly accurate. They were, however, still unable to measure longitude, so their east-west positions—measured by time, compass readings, and rate of movement—were only rough approximations.

After a day of rest the group, now numbering seventeen, was on its way again. On May 3 they camped by the stream with the alder trees and the bears, five leagues east of San Gabriel. As Garcés had done three weeks before, Anza attempted to shorten the distance after the Santa Ana River by following a more southerly direction, and with the ground drier this time they had no trouble covering ten leagues to geese-covered Lake Bucareli, which Garcés had missed.

Looking north, Anza noted an opening in the mountains (between the San Gabriel and San Bernardino ranges): "I consider [it] the most appropriate for a direct route coming from Sonora to Mission San Luis Obispo or the Presidio at Monte Rey." On May 5, they continued southeast, following the Pleasant Valley of San Josef, where Diaz took a (correct) reading of 33°:46′ N latitude. They covered nine leagues for the day and camped at San Patricio.

The following day, after the Pass of San Carlos, they were surprised by a volley of arrows, which slightly wounded three horses. Four of the attackers were captured and, after being lashed, were threatened with the death penalty and released. Anza later learned through a conspicuously posted note at Santa Catharina that Garcés had been similarly attacked in the area. The soldiers assigned by Fagés to learn the route recognized some natives from the vicinity of San Diego where, they pointed out, such incidents were not unusual. Evidently, not everyone welcomed the Spanish presence. The discontent that would flare into an uprising the following year was already smoldering.

On Saturday, May 7, after covering eleven leagues, they arrived at San Sebastián. While their pace had slowed since San Gabriel, they were still traveling very fast, spending long hours on the saddle and few at rest. Anticipating a difficult day ahead, they left San Sebastián long before dawn on May 8 and followed Garcés' tracks southeast until these vanished in the dunes. Dead reckoning across the desert, they arrived well into the night at Las Angustias. They had covered an impressive seventeen leagues in as many hours, but the pasture was inadequate and so after only a brief rest they pressed on. Riding five more leagues in the dark they arrived at Santa Olaya by dawn, having covered the more than twenty leagues from San Sebastián in one twenty-four-hour period. Anza, however, realized—as Garcés had—that a mule train or herd of cattle would not be able to do the same. He decided the future route would have to cross the desert (in what is now Imperial County) through Santa Rosa de las Lajas. The latitude recorded at Santa Olaya, 32°:34′N, was only slightly inaccurate.

Resting there most of Sunday, the party set off toward the east in the afternoon. After four leagues, they were surrounded by exuberant Yumas "calling incessantly, 'Captain. Lord. Soldiers. Friends,' which the many who joined them kept repeating throughout the night."

Delayed by the crowd, they set up camp and learned what Garcés had about the men left with the Yuma in February having returned to Sonora on word that Anza was dead. They were also told that Garcés' group had been in the area for two weeks and that Palma was eagerly expecting Anza's arrival.

Day 123
Tuesday, May 10, 1774

At noon Anza arrived at the river junction and was shortly thereafter joined by Palma, whose expressions of affection were as exuberant as those of his subjects. "He treats me with the same satisfaction as if I were of his own nature," writes Anza, "openly expressing his joy at my return." Anza, however, did not quite feel he was "of Palma's own nature." Such a thing would have been rare for a European of this time. Equality in the eyes of God did not erase the racial difference, not for devoted priests like Garcés and Serra, much less for a soldier like Anza, even though he was not a peninsular Spaniard but American-born and possibly of mixed blood.

But did Palma see Anza as a mestizo or as a white Spaniard? Was he impressed by the harmonious relationship between Anza and his native and mestizo soldiers? Or was Anza's conduct such that Palma saw him only as a fellow captain? Whatever the reason may have been, it is clear Palma considered Anza an equal and a friend. Yet, in spite of Anza's respect for the chief, their relationship at this time was not yet reciprocal; Anza's conditional "as if I were of his own nature" has a condescending ring to it.

"Palma told me how saddened he had been by the departure of the soldiers...in his charge and how he had delivered to Father Garcés the supplies and cattle the soldiers had left behind. For all this and the loyalty he has shown in this instance, I thanked this heathen captain and gave him the praise that he deserves." Anza's words seem to suggest that Palma's conduct was extraordinary because, as a heathen captain, he did not inherently share the Spaniards' code of behavior.

As promised on their departure, Palma had ordered a raft built for the expedition, and that afternoon it was ready and waiting. Anza and Diaz got on board and hundreds of Yumas pushed and towed it across six hundred yards of river "with such apparent ease and safety as I have ever experienced." Crossing in groups, it took several trips to bring all the men and animals over, but by late afternoon they had met up with Garcés and his group. This time, however, Anza saw no need for having troops on either bank as a precaution; Palma's loyalty had been amply demonstrated.

Days 124 and 125
Wednesday, May 11, and Thursday, May 12, 1774

It was a day for resting and comparing notes. Unfortunately, Garcés had already sent his journal to Altar, so it does not record his reunion with Anza. The commander was as usual more concerned with facts, and his journal mentions only having rejoined Garcés, making no further comment. If there was any friction between himself and Garcés, Anza was careful to avoid showing it in his journal. He does, however, mention countermanding a request he considered unnecessary. When, shortly after his arrival, Garcés had dispatched a courier to Altar, he had no idea when Anza would join him and by what route they would continue. Therefore he considered it prudent to ask the provincial governor for additional supplies, which, coming from Altar, would follow the southern route to the Colorado. These had not arrived when Anza, anxious to return to Tubac as soon as possible, decided to return by the Gila River instead. Therefore, he dispatched two soldiers to Altar, to turn back the supplies requested by Garcés. While the incident is reported as a matter of fact, it conveys Anza's sense of irritation at having to countermand what he implies was an unnecessary request.

That same day, Fagés' soldiers from the Monterey presidio, "having been informed concerning the directions and trails from here to Sonora, as well as the locations where they could obtain local guides if they so desired," recrossed the Colorado in preparation for their return.

Days 126 to 128
Friday, May 13, to Sunday, May 15, 1774

Just after sunrise on May 13 the expedition got under way along the southern bank of the Gila, Anza staying behind for a last word with

Palma, who had not yet returned from crossing the river the previous day to deliver four steers to Fagés' soldiers. During the morning, the chief arrived together with an old Yuma who claimed that some natives were waiting until Anza had departed to attack the soldiers from Monterey. According to the informer, the rebels believed the soldiers "[came] from the land of their enemies [the Cojat] and therefore [did] not recognize them as relatives, as they did [Anza] and [his] troops." The informer also added that most of the Yumas were not in agreement with the rebels.

The informer's reasons for the hostility appear suspect because (1) the soldiers did not come from the land of the Cojat but from Monterey, far beyond, and because (2) both the Yuma and the Cojat had welcomed Anza's efforts and were at peace with each other. The informer's comment that the rebels did not recognize the soldiers as "relatives," as they did Anza's troops, may provide the key to a more realistic reason for the animosity. Besides the fact that a party of six men with horses and cattle was in itself a tempting target, Fagés' Catalonian Volunteers were light-skinned peninsular Spaniards or white criollos, and to the rebels they looked more foreign and thus more oppressive than Anza's men, who were indigenous or mestizo and much darker. Furthermore, the captain's excellent relationship with his own troops, his standing order to avoid using force with the natives, and his own respectful behavior toward all indigenous people had established his reputation as a "relative," regardless of his own appearance.

"As in such matters one must not ignore any detail," writes Anza, "in spite of the apparent absurdity of the story, I determined immediately to prevent any misfortune by sending Captain Palma with the California native [Tarabal] to help the aforementioned party [Fagés' soldiers] in their predicament, warning them of the situation and providing additional advice in writing to the corporal. They [Palma and Tarabal] were also to inform the potential aggressors that I would be around to witness if they should put into practice their threats, and punish them, and to further emphasize this point I ordered the expedition to turn about, which it did later that day. That afternoon I was informed by a relative of Captain Palma that he had gathered over two hundred chosen Yumas to protect the soldiers in question."

To defuse the situation, which obviously had racial overtones, Anza, rather than imposing his authority, let Captain Palma assume responsibility and, staying in the background himself, sent the native Tarabal as his representative. Within forty-eight hours the situation was resolved. Palma and Tarabal returned on Sunday, May 15, with word from the corporal on his way to Monterey that "up to then they had not been attacked and from that point on he did not expect any problems." The Catalonian corporal also informed Anza (through Tarabal) that on Saturday Palma had returned to him two horses stolen the previous day after punishing those responsible.

Anza records more detail on the Yuma chief's actions:

"Palma had brought with him an axe, previously taken from us and recovered from the same natives, which I let him have. He told me that, discovering these thefts, he would have exacted [the same] justice even if I had not been present, which he would do as long as he lived, during which time he and his nation would not deviate in their friendship for us and their loyalty to the king.

"I repeated to this heathen captain that he should live in peace with neighboring nations (because that was the will of both majesties) and that he should host and deliver to us any 'Spaniard' arriving in his territory, as well as other recommendations, to which he agreed. As a reward for his services to the king I gave him my cane, four heads of cattle, and several articles of clothing, and would have liked to have more available to please this heathen savage that may be one of a kind."

Anza's words of respect and admiration for Palma—perhaps because they were written for the viceroy—do not portray a relationship of equals, but rather one of a commander and his subservient ally. At this time they had only limited knowledge of each other's language and communicated through interpreters such as Tarabal. Remarkable as Palma's services to the crown and his friendship with Anza had been, there still existed a cultural gulf between them. During subsequent encounters over the next two years, however, and particularly during their long sojourn together leading up to Palma's 1777 baptism in Mexico City, their relationship developed into one of true friendship between equals.

Days 129 to 134
Monday, May 16, to Saturday, May 21, 1774

For two days the expedition followed the Gila River upstream in beautiful spring weather, covering nine and eight leagues, respectively. On May 18, they came to a ranchería of some one hundred Cocomaricopas, who received them without any apprehension. Through a Pima living among the tribe as well as through his own interpreter, Anza exhorted the natives to peace with neighboring nations, urging them to approach the Tubac presidio for help in resolving disputes.

They spent the rest of the day at the village, which Anza named San Bernardino and Father Diaz located at latitude 33°:02' N. While there, Anza recorded his observations as usual. In appearance, stature, habits, and language he considered the Cocomaricopa similar to the Yuma, except for having better weapons and covering up "at least their indecent parts," as did the Pima. While some occupied the riverbank, most of the tribe lived in the sierra between the Gila and Colorado, numbering, according to their own estimate, less than the Yuma. Anza notes that "all prior contact of this nation with our troops has been friendly."[1]

The following day they continued along the north bank past a large hot spring known as Agua Caliente, formerly used by the Opa for irrigation of extensive plantings but abandoned at the time because of their wars with the Yuma. The expedition covered eight leagues in ideal weather before camping by a nearby river, flowing with deep, cold water although the country to the south was already parched by the sun.

The next day they crossed to higher ground on the south bank and continued as far as Upasoitac, the last Opa village, near the Gila Bend. From there Anza would have followed a direct route to Tubac, forty leagues southeast as the crow flies, but reports from Pimas flee-

---

[1] The Cocomaricopa, or Opa, tribe was linguistically of the Yuma family. Their language was close enough that they could communicate with the Yuma, but not with the Pima. Like both of their neighbors, with whom they had traditionally been at war, they lived primarily from irrigated farming on the Gila basin. While the Yuma had, through their superior power, been accepted as the regional leaders, the Opa's conflict with the Pima had continued until more recently. At the time of Anza's expeditions, the Opa and Pima tribes were allies.

ing extreme drought made him decide otherwise.

Being within days of the presidio, Garcés considered himself home and his duty to the expedition fulfilled. Therefore, on Saturday, May 21, 1774, accompanied by a servant, he left the group to establish, through the Moqui Province, a route to the Spanish settlement at New Mexico, while Anza continued to follow the river home to Tubac.

Days 135 to 140
Sunday, May 22, to Friday, May 27, 1774

On May 22 the expedition reached Sutaquison on the Gila, a permanent village of two thousand Pimas. As captain of the Tubac presidio, Anza was responsible for overseeing this settlement, appointing its governor and, when necessary, acting as judge. "Two leagues east on the river plain, we stopped for the night at Jutunitucan, or San Juan Capistrano, a larger settlement [than Sutaquison] in every way, where I appointed two brothers, the sons of the former governor, to the positions of mayor and governor, respectively. They command about three thousand people who are united in their defense against the Apaches and successfully cultivate both wheat and corn in fields so big the length of which does not appear to end."

Leaving camp at dawn, they followed the river for two leagues to a pasture where they stopped for feed. Nearby they passed the ruins of a building "known as the Palace of Moctezuma, so large that it can be seen a league away. The design was such that the river had once flowed beneath the building so as to have water readily available. The materials of construction were clay soil mixed with coarse sand or small stones to form a very durable aggregate, judging from its apparent age." Days before in Sutaquison they had seen similar ruins—the remains of a palace built before the Spaniards arrived, and believed to be the work of a nation who had later established their empire in Mexico.

Still in the area were the Apache, who not long before had killed more than sixty people near Sutaquison. Thus, even in the absence of specific signs indicating their presence, Anza was concerned because the soldiers' horses were at that time so worn that some men had resorted to riding mules, which would be useless if attacked. In response to the perceived danger, the expedition, planning to cover as much ground as possible in the least amount of time, left the Gila at 2:00 in the afternoon and rode south until midnight, making only a brief stop before continuing at dawn. "By 11:00 that morning we had reached the water source that supplies Tugson [sic]," writes Anza, "where we stopped to escape the burning sun, and in the afternoon continued until the town of the same name." Tucson also belonged to the Tubac jurisdiction and was home to some eighty Pima families. Since leaving the river to avoid an Apache attack, the expedition had covered twenty-four leagues in less than thirty hours, all without water.

Before dawn on May 26 they were met by six soldiers from Tubac with a message from the assistant inspector of the province, Don Antonio Bonilla, requesting Anza to report to the presidio with minimal delay. The courier sent with Garcés' journal from Yuma to Altar had passed through Tubac, so Anza's arrival was expected. In the company of Diaz and the escort, Anza rode the last twenty leagues that day, passing the Pima village of San Xavier del Bac in the morning and entering Tubac after sunset.

Lifting camp as usual, the expedition followed at its own pace and at noon on Friday, May 27, 1774, it entered the gates of the presidio. The men had been away one hundred and forty days, almost five months.

SECOND
EXPEDITION

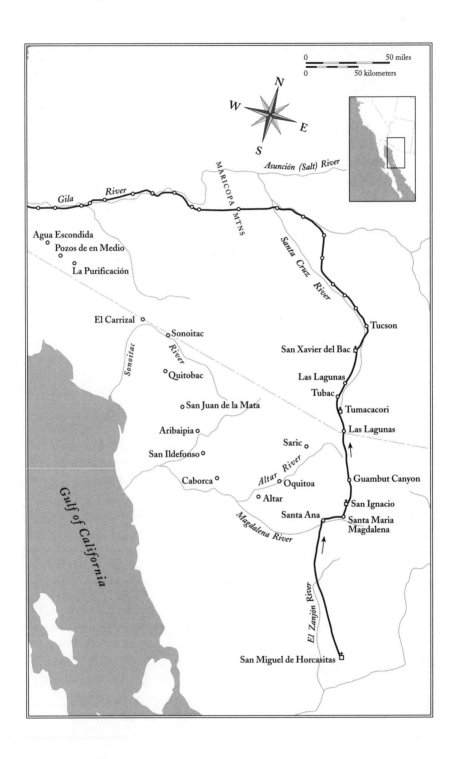

0   50 miles
0   50 kilometers

N
W   E
S

Asunción (Salt) River

Gila   River

MARICOPA MTNS

Santa Cruz River

Agua Escondida
Pozos de en Medio
La Purificación

El Carrizal
Sonoitac

Sonoitac River

Quitobac

San Juan de la Mata

Aribaipia

San Ildefonso

Caborca

Tucson

San Xavier del Bac

Las Lagunas
Tubac
Tumacacori
Las Lagunas

Saric

Altar River
Oquitoa
Altar

Magdalena River

Santa Ana

Guambut Canyon

San Ignacio
Santa Maria
Magdalena

El Zanjón River

San Miguel de Horcasitas

Gulf of California

The Gathering:
From Horcasitas to Tubac

September 29 to October 21, 1775

Whereas the first expedition had taken years to germinate, the second was planned in just fourteen months. After receiving Anza's personal report proving the route feasible, Viceroy Bucareli lost no time in ordering the resettlement of families on a new establishment on the "River of San Francisco." The decree, dated November 24, 1774, put Anza in charge of organizing and leading a group of around three hundred people and some thousand animals overland to Monterey, a then impossible task by sea.

Establishing a Spanish presence in Alta California was being effected in two ways: by the acculturation of Native Americans through the missions and by the permanent relocation of Spanish subjects from Mexico, themselves mostly of indigenous origin. The immigrant population included civilian settlers but consisted mostly of troops whose function in addition to protecting the missions was to confront any foreign power with designs on the coast.

For Anza, recently promoted to lieutenant colonel, the assignment engaged all his skills and energy. In addition to leading the group and organizing the logistics, he was also responsible for recruiting settlers and new troops and selecting from the existing ranks the men most likely to succeed in the new environment.

Ten months after the viceroy's order, the first phase of preparations was complete: gathered in San Miguel de Horcasitas, two hundred miles south of Tubac, thirty-two soldiers and their families were ready to resettle on the northwest frontier of New Spain, about two thousand miles away. From San Miguel they were to proceed to the presidio at Tubac, the final mustering point where supplies, pack animals, livestock, and the escort would all come together.

Father Garcés also took part in the second expedition, but this time his responsibilities were different. Instead of accompanying Anza, he was assigned to explore the Colorado River basin to assess the interest and readiness of the indigenous nations to accept Christianity and become Spanish subjects. Rather than being subordinate to the commander, Garcés was this time a diplomatic envoy reporting directly to the viceroy. That he obtained such a high position so quickly was due as much to his skills as it was to Anza's wish for a chaplain who did not challenge his leadership. While Garcés' journal of 1775-1776 is a fascinating narrative, he only accompanied Anza as far as the Colorado River before departing with Sebastián Tarabal on his own assignment, and thus it is only a minor source for this narrative.

The new expedition chaplain, Pedro Font, was far more intellectual and less of an explorer than Garcés. Intelligent, academic, and intensely devout, he was meticulous in his duties whether taking latitudes or keeping records. His garrulous nature found expression through his excellent command of the written language. With the syntax, vocabulary, and grammar more of a scholar than a frontier priest, he produced a short journal for the official record and an extensive intimate diary in which the full breadth of his personality comes through. Honest in his beliefs and absolute of his superiority, he was self-righteous, inflexible, and dogmatic. His love of God knew no tolerance for human frailty, compassion for weakness, or affection for his fellow man. Unlike Garcés, Font did not even like the natives. The challenger had indeed been replaced by someone incapable of challenging the commander. What Anza didn't know was that the new friar was a keen observer and a gifted narrator. His personal diary, which he begins at Horcasitas, is the most complete record and the main source of information for the second expedition.

Day 1
Friday, September 29, 1775

In the cool of early morning the day of their departure, Font sang a high mass to the expedition and, with all gathered before him, delivered a sermon appropriate to the occasion. Using carefully chosen words, he compared their pilgrimage to the day's gospel and spoke of the difficulties and challenges ahead, the patience that would be required from each, and the example of Christianity their good conduct must be for the "gentiles." For the expedition he requested the protection of the Virgin of Guadalupe, "mother and guardian of the Indians and of this America," a request that was "unanimously and affectionately applauded." For good measure, Saint Michael of Horcasitas and Saint Francis, patron of his order, were also invoked as co-sponsors. The commander's participation gave the seal of approval, and as the Salve Regina was sung, it appeared that unity and harmony reigned between them.

While not yet at its full strength, the group already consisted of 34 officers and men, 106 dependents, 17 civilian settlers, 20 mule drivers, 140 mules, 450 horses, and an unspecified number of cattle. The mules carried expedition supplies, ammunition, tents and equipment, gifts for the natives, and the personal baggage of the commander and officials.

Packing was difficult: everyone was forced to choose at the last minute what was essential and what could be dispensed with; the drivers arranging and weighing cargo; loaded mules waiting and whining irritably; parents gathering their children; everyone excited and not quite sure of what needed doing. It is not surprising that it took all day to get organized. Finally, at 4:30 the waiting was over and the group began to stretch out in a thin procession, the afternoon shadows drifting alongside the lumbering train. Having just reached its full length half an hour later, the train was ordered to dismount and set camp. The first short step of the long journey had been taken.

Days 2 to 9
Saturday, September 30, to Saturday, October 7, 1775

That morning the start-up went much better, although later that day the inexperienced drivers were unable to prevent a string of mules from stampeding and scattering their loads. Efforts to retrieve the cargo and animals continued into the night and into the following day while the expedition remained at camp. Unable to celebrate mass on Sunday (for reasons not given), Font led a group in the rosary and singing the Alabado ("Praise Be to God") in his tent, which also served as the field chapel.

Only a few days into the journey, resentment was already starting to fester between Font and Anza. The friar had asked the commander several times for a servant to handle the daily task of packing, loading, and unloading Font's equipment, but Anza had not yet granted the request. Font's baggage consisted of a tent, poles, books and documents, several boxes of robes, ornaments, and other religious supplies, plus own his clothing, blankets, and a chair, all of which required two mules to transport. While capable of doing everything himself, it was unthinkable for a priest not to have a servant, and Font held Anza responsible for this unnecessary hardship, made worse by the fact that Font, not acclimated to the frontier conditions, was already suffering stomach problems.

In the afternoon, a boy watching over some horses reported that Apaches had taken three mares. The lieutenant and four soldiers were sent to investigate, and the animals were recovered "but not the Apaches," writes Font, "because there hadn't been any." Further investigation showed that "the tracks were old, from when [the Apaches] had passed on their way to San Miguel," and the boy had lied. Driving almost six hundred animals, it was not unusual that some would get sidetracked, fall behind, and get lost, but rather than admit fault it was always tempting to blame others. Two days after the first incident, the rearguard corporal reported six Apaches had taken a mule that strayed. Anza again sent the lieutenant and ten soldiers in pursuit, but they were unable to track the animal, returning after nightfall to report only having met some Pimas that had killed a deer. Still, despite the false alarms, Apache raids were certainly a possibility and their danger not to be taken lightly.

With practice, loading and start-up became smoother and the expedition was soon able to achieve daily stages of five and six leagues. The terrain was not difficult, the early autumn weather was mild and dry, and the men and pack animals were getting to know each other. One day they encountered free-range cattle and the soldiers requested permission for a kill, which was granted by Anza. Over two days they slaughtered a number of steer, providing a feast of fresh meat and salted stores. On Friday they reached Santa Ana, a "Spanish" village devoted to cattle ranching.[1] They remained there the following day while a party was sent after four lost mules, of which only one was recovered.

By order of the viceroy, the second expedition had been provided with a sextant for Font's use. The valuable instrument, however, instead of being delivered to the priest, was kept by Anza, who, not trained in its use, would produce it only when he wanted a measurement taken. Meticulous and responsible as he was, Font resented being deprived of initiative and reduced to the role of a clerk, particularly since he was preparing a map to accompany his official journal. The latitude of Santa Ana, taken at Anza's request, gave 30°:38'N.

Days 10 to 23
Sunday, October 8, to Saturday, October 21, 1775

After an early mass the expedition was moving by 9:30, and by 2:00 it was just outside Santa Maria Magdalena, six leagues northeast. Both the early departure and the distance covered in less than five hours would have been impossible a week before, but the expedition had since become organized and efficient. Font sent word of their arrival to the local priest, and before nightfall Father Zúñiga, a personal friend, came to meet them two leagues from his mission. Anza, who also knew Zúñiga, shared their dinner and conversation. The two priests celebrated the next morning's mass jointly, Font accompanying Zúñiga with an old psaltery (a stringed instrument resembling a zither), "which the commander forced me to bring along," he explains, "for the sake of the natives, especially the Yuma, who are so festive and fond of music."

Moving on, it was a short march to the mission at San Ignacio, where the expedition halted for a day and a half to rearrange and redistribute the cargo. The two friends were able to spend more time together, and during their conversations Zúñiga repeated some comments Anza had made to him about Font. What these were must

---

[1] The designation of the village as "Spanish" probably indicated that its residents were Spanish-speaking Christians, not necessarily white Spaniards.

be inferred from the diary, in which Font reverts to his annoyance at still being without a servant. Anza, with his rough-and-ready frontier personality, not unlike Garcés', was the exact opposite of the punctilious administrator that Font was, and if the priest did not challenge Anza in his command, he certainly irritated him by nitpicking on everything from the custody of the sextant to the prerogatives of his position.

On Wednesday the expedition moved on through the high Pima country, and over the following days they took precautions against surprise Apache raids. On Thursday they halted early to avoid camping in a narrow valley the following night, and when the next day they entered Guambut Canyon, a favorite ambush spot, they ensured the animals did not string out but stayed as close as could be managed.

North of Guambut the terrain became mountainous, making it easier for fast-riding Apaches to attack without warning; "The sierra on the east side extend almost continuously all the way to Tuquison [Tucson] and, on the left side of the trail, widen northwest toward Aribaca" [present-day Arivaca, not far from the Arizona-Sonora line]. On Saturday the expedition crossed what is now the US-Mexico border near Nogales to overnight at Las Lagunas. Still on high alert, Anza requested Font to refrain from saying mass in camp that Sunday and instead proceed with an escort to hold the service at the village of Calabazas, a safer location two leagues away. After mass Font rejoined the group and went with them as far as the Tumacacori mission, where he remained while the expedition continued to the presidio at Tubac.[2] During the week the expedition spent finalizing preparations at Tubac, Font, together with Eixarch, his assistant, and Garcés, were guests of the Tumacacori mission. While the accommodations were crowded with three visitors in addition to the two resident priests, the camaraderie was good and Font undoubtedly compared notes with Garcés while they both enjoyed a little distance from the commander.

On Monday they rejoined Anza at Tubac and for the third time Font repeated his request for a servant. Returning to Tumacacori for the night with Garcés and Eixarch, Font was taken ill and spent the rest of the week confined to bed. On Saturday they received word

---

[2] The Mission at Tumacacori is presently a National Historical Park, and the foundations of the Tubac Presidio are part of an Arizona State Park located four miles to the north. There is a well-maintained trail joining the two sites.

that the expedition was ready for departure and, with Font's new servant reporting for duty, the three priests made their way to Tubac, where they spent the night.

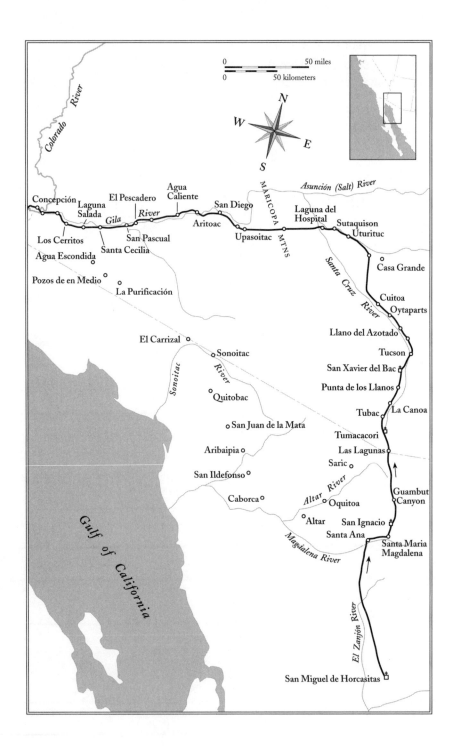

0   50 miles
0   50 kilometers

N
W   *E*
S

Colorado River

Asunción (Salt) River

MARICOPA MTNS

Concepción
Laguna Salada
El Pescadero
Agua Caliente
San Diego
Laguna del Hospital
Sutaquison
Uturituc

Gila River
Aritoac
Upasoitac

Los Cerritos
San Pascual
Santa Cecilia

Agua Escondida

Casa Grande

Pozos de en Medio
La Purificación

Santa Cruz River

Cuitoa
Oytaparts

Llano del Azotado

El Carrizal
Sonoitac

Tucson

Sonoitac River

San Xavier del Bac
Punta de los Llanos

Quitobac

Tubac
La Canoa

San Juan de la Mata

Tumacacori

Aribaipia

Las Lagunas

San Ildefonso

Saric

Guambut Canyon

Caborca

Altar River
Oquitoa
Altar
San Ignacio
Santa Ana

Santa Maria Magdalena

Magdalena River

Gulf of California

El Zanjón River

San Miguel de Horcasitas

A Lumbering Giant: From Tubac to the Colorado

October 22 to November 30, 1775

Day 24
Sunday, October 22, 1775

Through the morning mist, the sun uncovered a tent village surrounding the small garrison. Eleven months of preparations were ending and the presidio village was pulsing with excitement, an anthill of activity. Women carried water, looked after toddlers. Campfires smoked here and there, children played by the river. The men rearranged and packaged the supplies. Cattle, mules, and horses by the hundreds grazed over the Santa Cruz Valley. The priests prepared for the ceremony that would also mark their departure this Sunday. Again, no effort was spared to celebrate a high mass, which was sung by the three priests for the entire community. If Garcés and Diaz, neither a man of words, had inspired the troops when the first expedition left Tubac two years before, Father Font, with his erudition, would do even better. He had, during his convalescence, rehearsed a sermon for the occasion that he considered worthy to be paraphrased in his diary.

As at Horcasitas, he spoke of the importance the expedition's example would set for the natives and of the challenges and difficulties ahead. But this time the exhortation was cast in strict biblical terms: "And making a parallel between the passage of the people of Israel to the Promised Land through the Red Sea and the present expedition to Monterey through the Colorado River, I warned them of the punishments that God would inflict upon them should they abuse or scandalize the gentiles in transit as He had done with the Israelites that engaged in such excesses, or if they should gossip, not pay due respect, or slander the commander or his orders, as had been done to Moses. But I also assured them of God's blessing and the protection of the Virgin of Guadalupe if they conducted themselves as good Christians, and finally, after the many gifts that together with the hardships God would provide them in this life, I promised them the happiness of eternal rest in the glorious nation of the Promised Land."

The ceremony lasted, due to Font's eloquence, until late that morning. The expedition, swollen with additional settlers and dependents, the military escort, cattle drivers, native interpreters, and servants, now totaled 240. The number of mounts also increased to 695 animals and the cattle to a total of 358 heads, according to Font's tally. It is not surprising that preparations were lagging behind and the departure had to be postponed until the following day. Coordinating such a large group required skills that were yet to be acquired.

"At an appropriate hour the mules and horses were brought to camp and each one was responsible to collect his animals. The drivers gathered the mules, and the soldiers and servants [gathered] the horses, for themselves [and their] families, and masters. While this was being done and the animals bridled and saddled, I would say mass; there was enough time. When the mule trains were packed and ready, the commander would call out: 'Begin mounting' and we would all mount our horses. Then the departure would slowly begin in the following order: four soldiers assigned to scout went ahead of the group; the commander would take the lead and I would follow just after him; then the men, women, and children with the escorting soldiers looking after their families. Closing the column was the rearguard under the lieutenant and, behind him, the mule trains. After these came the spare horses and, last of all, the cattle, all together forming an extremely long procession."

This was the routine that they were still rehearsing and that by 11:00 that Monday morning was more or less in motion. As the commander saluted Tubac, Font intoned the Alabado; the soldiers picked up the song and the families joined in, their strong voices carrying across the valley until they met their echo from the Santa Rita hills.

"This was to be our practice every day during the outbound as well as the return…trip," writes Font, "and at the close of the day, having chosen a site and dismounted, the lieutenant would report to the commander if everything had arrived or some animal had strayed behind or was missing, in order to give the necessary orders.

"Once settled down for the night, the people would say the rosary with their families, concluding with the Alabado or the Salve or another song, each in their own style with delightful diversity. Since it was such a large group, each campsite was like a village, the soldiers building shelters with branches and blankets, and especially with the tents, thirteen in all—nine for the troops, one for the lieutenant, one for Fathers Garcés and Eixarch, one for myself, and the largest one, which was round, for the commander."

Days 25 to 29
Monday, October 23, to Friday, October 27, 1775

That October Monday they marched north from Tubac following the Santa Cruz for five leagues. Toward the end of the afternoon, having set up camp at La Canoa, one of the women went into labor and, in the shelter of a tent and with all possible assistance, she gave birth to a boy by 9:00 that night. But it was a difficult birth because the child came breech, and the mother was hemorrhaging. The midwife applied the remedies she knew, and the young woman struggled between life and death for several hours but eventually surrendered before daybreak. Although unable to save her life, her attendants at least had the comfort of providing her with last rites and assuring the survival of her soul and her son.

Outside, with the rain falling through the night, there was little joy for the arrival of a healthy boy (who would live to maturity in Alta California) and much sadness for the high price of his birth. As if nature shared in the somber mood, the rain continued all morning, delaying their departure. It was only by 2:00 in the afternoon that they were finally on the march again, but the joy of the previous day had vanished. It was a funeral procession that followed the river monotonously repeating the rosary for the soul of the departed.

The terrain was not difficult but the mood was somber and, after four leagues, the expedition halted for the day while Garcés and four men continued north to escort the body to San Xavier del Bac, six leagues away. It was well into the night when the small party arrived in the village where Garcés exercised his ministry. Following an early morning mass, just over twenty-four hours after her death, the young mother was given a Christian burial. At about the same time, the rest of the expedition was getting under way at Punta de los Llanos and, after an uneventful march, they arrived at San Xavier in the early afternoon.

San Xavier, the Pima village with the northernmost church in the region, had at one time been larger and more prosperous, but the hostility of the Apache and the poor quality of its water had taken its toll. The water, Font observed, was unpalatable due to its high content of dissolved solids, which a Jesuit had once measured by "taking water from the well and carefully distilling it in a jug." It left behind "two ounces of salts and slag." It says a lot about Font's intellectual curiosity to have found this detail in the mission records and included it in his diary. It was not enough to say that the water was 'extremely brackish'; like the priest who had once done the experiment, Font wanted to quantify the brackishness.

That afternoon in the mission church Father Eixarch baptized the orphan baby, and the following day (Thursday, October 26) Font formalized the marriages of three expedition couples. By 8:30 they were on the march again, traveling four leagues and camping that night just north of "Tuquison." Tucson was a "visit" of San Xavier even though it was larger and had the distinction of being the last Christian village on their route.[1] For these reasons and to better protect the area against the Apache, the Tubac garrison was transferred there the following year and renamed the Presidio de San Agustín del Tuquison.

Tucson being the frontier between Christianity and the "Land of the Gentiles," Font used the opportunity to again remind the group

1 The villages that did not have resident priests but depended on regular visits by priests from nearby missions were called "visits."

of the importance of their good conduct, and Anza proclaimed an order urging all to "act in such a way that the gentiles would not see in the Spaniards a bad example, [and] that they should speak or act in such a way as to cause the least offense, under penalty of severe punishment." Although no hostile natives had been sighted, the Pima villages they passed, decimated by Apache raids, were a constant reminder of a very real threat. Crossing this unmarked border must have made an impression because at least two of the mule drivers decided to hide and return home after the expedition's departure. When their absence was noticed at the end of the day's march, Anza asked some Pimas to track them.

In addition to seeing evidence of Apache attacks on the Pima, Anza had not forgotten the damage Apaches had done to the first expedition prior to its departure. It was for this reason that he constantly maintained a high state of alert. But the fact that the second expedition had not been attacked in the four weeks since leaving Horcasitas was attributed by Font not to the commander's vigilance but to the intervention of the Virgin of Guadalupe, although there was a more obvious reason. The Apaches no doubt valued the expedition's hundreds of horses, but with such a large trophy came a great risk; with over one hundred armed men, many of whom were frontier-hardened soldiers, and a commander who would not be caught unprepared, the expedition was not an easy target.

Leaving Tucson at 1:00 that afternoon they covered five leagues toward the north-northwest, coming to camp in the plain within sight of some hills. The Pima called the area Tutuctac, but the events that day would soon change its name. At 8:00 that night the campfires were already turning to ash when six Pimas rode into camp with one of the captured mule drivers. Anza questioned the man and, having established him guilty of desertion, the expedition was called to witness his punishment: a public lashing and detention. "Lashed" in Spanish is *azotado*, and thereafter the soldiers referred to the location as the Plain of the Lashed or Llano del Azotado. It was a clear lesson to all, which some perhaps pondered that night as the sentries took up watch and the camp settled into a disturbing sleep. It was as if they were at sea and Anza was the captain of their ship.

Days 30 to 34
Saturday, October 28, to Wednesday, November 1, 1775

Leaving the Llano del Azotado shortly after 8:00 toward the west-northwest, they covered almost six leagues through dry and dusty terrain, passing the occasional pond with diminishing water from the rainy season. In the early afternoon they set up camp next to a pond large enough to provide "refreshment for the people, horses, and cattle" next to a Papago village, Oytaparts, which Anza translated as "Old Town." Even though there was still enough water, the seasonal village had been abandoned and there was no sign of crops having been planted. Garcés believed the people had left in fear of the Apache.

Although they had made good progress under ideal conditions, Anza had become withdrawn and was in a foul mood. "I tried to pacify him," writes Font, "but he would not talk to us the entire day." That morning Garcés had requested from Anza some animals assigned to the priest, but the commander had been short-tempered and replied that "he had no animals to give him." Garcés would not accept his refusal and told him so. While this incident is not mentioned in any of the official records, it is part of Font's personal diary and serves to remind us how easily the surface harmony between Anza and Garcés was disturbed.

Sunday morning, four Pimas from Tucson arrived in camp with the second deserter. As before, the driver was punished with twenty-five lashes, and Anza used the public gathering to remind everyone of the regulations and penalties for various infractions. He specifically mentioned "rape of native women and stealing from or threatening natives with force, except in self-defense or under specific orders." He emphasized the importance of "dealing respectfully with the gentiles, whom we are trying to attract to the true religion and dominion of His Majesty," and of "the example we must give by our own conduct and attendance at the religious services during our trip."

He then dispatched four Pimas to give advance warning of the expedition's progress along the Gila. He did not want the surprise appearance of such a large group to be reason for alarm any more than he wanted individuals to damage the reputation he so carefully cultivated for his king. They finally lifted camp late that morning, moving northwest through a flat and spacious valley, and covered some five leagues in as many hours. They passed Cuitoa, a deserted Papago village, and camped just beyond Tacca Mountain (present-day Picacho Peak, just west of I-10 between Tucson and Phoenix). It was a land of little pasture, dusty soil, and scarce water, although that year there remained some seasonal ponds.

After an uneventful night, they lifted camp early Monday for a long trek northwest and north. It was a crystal-clear day; a profile of dark blue peaks marked the horizon. With easy terrain and good conditions, they covered almost eight leagues in less than six hours. But then they encountered an area of thin topsoil that turned to a powder under the animals' hooves and rose to settle on everything—clothing, skin, hair, even eyes. The cattle were covered in whitish dust, the sun was hidden behind a dusty cloud, and the heavy air became hard to breathe.

In the early afternoon, warned in advance, a group of dignitaries—including the governor of the Papago villages of Cuitoa and Aquituni, the governor and mayor of the Pima village of Uturituc, and the governor of Sutaquisan—rode out to meet them. Respectfully dismounting, they greeted the Spaniards and presented them with the scalps of two Apaches killed the previous day. After this welcome, the delegation remounted and guided the expedition to a suitable campsite. By late afternoon, they had reached the Gila, slowly flowing with cold, clear water, its green banks marked by a line of elms.

The warm welcome was as the commander expected: "They display great happiness about our coming through their region..., to which I replied with similar pleasure, which was also true of the entire expedition." Anza's friendship with the Pima and Papago and the reputation he had established with them, however, were news to some of his own group; "Those of the expedition who did not know [the natives] were surprised to discover how gentle and considerate they can be and how attached to us these people are."

"They ask us if we are coming to settle among them and baptize their people," writes Font, "[a happening that] they very much seem to want and have already requested several times. They were happy about our coming and said it would be good if we stayed to live there; that way the soldiers would join them in fighting the Apache."

After the long trek of the previous day Anza declared Tuesday a day of rest for the expedition, but together with Font, Garcés, the governor of Uurituc, and other natives, he set out to visit the ruins of an old structure, Casa Grande, three leagues to the southeast. He was interested in the landmark as a point of reference and wanted Font to record its latitude. At the same time, the large and solid construction was so different from the temporary native dwellings that all were curious about its origin and function.

Located at 33°:3' N, the ground floor revealed a palace with walls 4 to 6 feet thick, three rooms 26 by 10 feet, and two large halls 38 by 12 feet, with 11-foot-high ceilings. The building was surrounded by the remains of a high wall 420 by 260 feet and a collapsed tower in the southwest corner suggesting a defensive enclosure. Both constructions were "rectangular and perfectly lined up with the cardinal winds, east, west, north, and south. The construction was of earth blocks of different sizes and some wood, which appeared to be pine although there was also some mesquite."

Font goes on to describe a channel (five yards wide, according to Anza) eroded beyond repair that once brought water from the distant river. He also postulates the building had three stories and a basement. "No trace of stairs was visible, for which reason we assumed they had used wooden ladders, which disappeared when the Apaches burned the building." Besides the doorways that provided light, there were large, round openings on the walls facing east and west, which, according to legend, "were used by the prince, whom they call the Bitter Man, to greet the sun at sunrise and sunset."

The size and complexity of the ruins were evidence of a degree of technical skill incompatible with the dwellings of the tribes then in the region. Anza comments that "the present inhabitants of the river have only a remote and confused awareness that it was the work of their former masters." On their way to the site, the governor of Uurituc had told them "the traditional history that the Gila Pima believe about the Casa Grande, which amounts to," according to Font, "a lot of nonsense mixed with some confused Catholic dogma." Font nevertheless recorded the story, which was told in the Pima language and simultaneously translated by one of Anza's servants.

Casa Grande and the Origin
of Human Life in the Gila Basin

In very ancient times, an old man known as the Bitter Man on account of his bad temper and harsh rule came to the land. He was accompanied by his young daughter, who was beautiful, and a handsome man unrelated to them, whom he married to his daughter. He also brought with him two servants, Wind and Clouds.

Soon after his arrival the old man began building the Casa Grande and one day sent his son-in-law to fetch wood for the roof. The young man went very far and was away for many days looking for wood, but because he didn't have an axe or another tool to fell the trees with, he returned empty-handed. The old man told him he was good for nothing and said he would show him how to bring wood. So he went to a distant pine-covered sierra and, calling upon God to help him, felled many trees and brought home all the lumber needed for the roof.

When the old man first came to the land there were neither plants nor trees. He had brought with him all the seeds and, with the help of his two servants Wind and Clouds, he planted and reaped large harvests. But in a fit of anger because of his own bad temper, he one day fired the servants, who then left him and went very far away. Unable to harvest without them, and having eaten everything available, the Bitter Man was dying of starvation when he sent his son-in-law to find the servants and bring them back. But in spite of all his efforts the young man couldn't find them and again returned empty-handed. Then the old man went personally and, having found Wind and Clouds, brought them back in his service. With their help one more time he was able to bring in large harvests, which they continued to do for many years. But then one day the family and their servants all left and nothing was ever heard from them again.

Some time after that, another man, by the name of the Drinker, came to the land and, angry with the local people, sent so much rain that the whole country was covered with water. The Drinker went to the mountains visible from Casa Grande known as the Sierra de la Espuma (Mountains of the Foam), taking with him a small dog and a coyote. (They were called the Mountains of the Foam because on one face there's a white horizontal layer near the top that follows a good part of the chain, and the natives say it's the mark left by the foam at the high-water level.) The Drinker climbed to the peak and left the dog behind to warn him as the water rose. (In those days animals could speak.) When the level reached the white layer, the dog warned him and the man took the dog up to the top.

After a few days, the Drinker sent the hummingbird and the coyote to bring him some mud, which they did, and from it he made several men, some of which turned out "good" and some "bad." The men multiplied up- and downstream along the river and spread throughout the land. When some time later the Drinker sent some of his people to see if the upstream men could speak, they found that they did so between themselves but could not be understood by others. Learning this made the Drinker very angry because he had not given them license to speak. Other emissaries sent downstream reported that they had been well received and that even though the downstream people spoke a different language, they could be understood. Then the Drinker told them that the downstream people were them, the Pima—the "good" ones who lived on the river as far downstream as the Opa, who are their friends. The upstream people were the "bad" ones, the Apache, who are their enemies.

On one occasion when the Drinker became very angry with the people he had created, he killed many, turning them into saguaros, and that's why there are so many in that land. Extremely angry with humans on another occasion, he lowered the sun to burn them, but the people, begging forgiveness, asked to be spared. Moved, he agreed to raise the sun, although not as high as it had been originally, warning them that it would be ready to burn them should they again provoke his wrath. And this is the reason why it is so extremely hot in the summer.

While the Pima told the legends of their origin in all seriousness, they were received with smiles and mockery by the Spaniards. Noticing this, the governor interrupted his telling, saying he would continue at another time, but his politeness was only a formality; he was deeply offended by his disrespectful audience, and according to Font, "we never managed to have him tell us another [story]," claiming later that he didn't know any more." Although Europeans of the time could not take seriously a mythology that competed with theirs, it is fortunate that Font had both the curiosity and skill to capture in writing what he could of the Pima oral tradition, even when he considered it "a lot of nonsense."

Back at the camp, mass on the first of November was attended by many Pimas who followed the service in silence, mimicking the gestures and actions of the Christians. After the day of rest, by 10:00 that morning the expedition was on the move west-northwest, following a pleasant trail near the river some four leagues to the first village, Juturitucan, or San Juan Capistrano de Uturituc, a short distance from the Gila.

The large expedition was humbled by the size of the town and the preparations made to receive them. As they entered under a cloudless sky, more than a thousand natives were lined up to greet them, men and women on separate sides. After dismounting, the men approached first, one by one, to shake hands with the commander and the priests. When finished, the women did the same, "all manifesting great joy in seeing us, putting one hand on their chest, and greeting us with the phrase 'God help us' used by the Christian Pimas." It was an impressive, if time-consuming, formality "to which it was necessary to oblige," writes Font.

At one end of the village they had used branches to build for the visitors a five-room shelter with a large cross in front. The guests were provided with food, water, and firewood. Honored by the "Spaniards" and in a festive mood, the natives requested Anza's permission to dance, which they did long into the night with the women linked to each other singing and dancing their way through camp.

These Pimas were eager to become Christians and "some offered their children to be baptized," but the priests were not willing to baptize them without providing adequate instruction. "I have felt great sorrow," writes Garcés, "seeing that we could not satisfy their strong desire to be Christian, but on this occasion the pain was particularly strong seeing so many people together asking us to remain there to baptize them. As the flock is ready to join the fold of the Church may God arrange that which is His will."

Uturituc was a well-organized agricultural society. The fields between the town and the river, fenced with posts and separated into parcels, were normally watered through channels from the river, although at the time of the expedition's visit, the river was so low they had been unable to plant, as the water did not reach the channels. They were, however, planning to dam the river using posts and branches to bring the level up sufficiently. A surprised Font comments that "this shows how applied they are to their work instead of wandering like other nations. Settled in permanent villages with cultivated fields, they have learned how to capture the river. I saw also how they make blankets from cotton they grow, spin, and weave. They also have large rams with good wool and 'Castilian' hens." Besides poultry, according to Garcés, they also bred horses, "some of which they are trading with the soldiers for cloth."

But despite their accomplishments, hospitality, docile nature, and predisposition toward Christianity, Font could not overcome his revulsion at their appearance: "They are powerfully built but very ugly and dark, and even more so the women, perhaps because they eat so much flour ground from the pods of mesquite and other coarse seeds, which gives them, when up close, a rather putrid smell."

Anza's report, on the other hand, mentions with a sense of pride that the tribe had been at peace with their neighbors since he exhorted them in that direction on his return from Monterey in 1774. Impressed with what he saw and the extraordinary welcome they had given the expedition, he was generous with the king's gifts of beads and tobacco.

Days 35 to 40
Thursday, November 2, to Tuesday, November 7, 1775

Starting very early on All Soul's Day, the priests celebrated three masses each, which were attended by the entire expedition and numerous silent Pimas, awed by the ceremony. Departure was delayed into late morning (a number of horses had wandered away during the night and needed to be recovered), but by 11:00 the expedition was on the move, continuing west-northwest following the Gila. They rounded some thick woods and passed two rancherías, advancing four leagues. The nearby river was very low, and the hundreds of animals were followed by a cloud of white dust. A line of small elms marked the banks, and the harvested fields showed evidence of wheat, corn, cotton, and squash. By early afternoon they arrived at Encarnación de Sutaquison, another important Pima village, where the formal reception was as in Uturituc except that the population was smaller (some five hundred according to Font and Garcés; eight hundred according to Anza). The village was in open country at a distance from the river because, the natives claimed, that made it easier to prevent being surprised by as well as to pursue, if necessary, Apache attackers. Anza, looking to the future, noted that there was enough pasture in the area to support a presidio.

That afternoon a single Opa native, his face dyed completely red, arrived at the Spanish camp on a diplomatic mission to the Pima, his visit timed to take advantage of Anza's presence. Located downstream on the Gila before its junction with the Colorado, the Opa had been traditional enemies of both the Yuma and Pima nations, but the envoy brought the news that "the Opa were now friends with the Yuma, having celebrated a peace meeting near Agua Caliente." A Pima interpreter in turn explained to Anza what had happened, and Font recorded the information in his journal: "Palma had offered peace to the Opa, who accepted it, and as a sign of peace they had replied by sending them [Chief Palma and the Yuma] some crosses."

No further comment is given by Font, and, curiously, neither Anza nor Garcés even mentions the incident, although both men were instrumental in the general pacification that followed the first Anza expedition.

As in Uturituc, Garcés used the opportunity to speak to the natives about Christianity. Since the Gila Pima were part of the same nation as those at San Xavier del Bac, he delivered his message in their own language, using his well-known reversible banner of the Virgin of Guadalupe and the condemned souls. Garcés thrived as a religious minstrel, and the audience was receptive, listening attentively, many wrapped in cotton or wool blankets. They, of course, knew the story, having heard him preach before or heard about it from others. Familiarity only enhanced the content as they nodded agreement, admiring the mother and child and abhorring the burning flames. Anza and Garcés had turned the Pima nation into an ally of the Spanish crown; Charles III would have reason to be proud!

Blocked by the Sierra de San Joseph de Cumars (also called the Sierra Estrella) near Sutaquison, the Gila River took an eight-league detour north, where it was joined by the Asunción (today's Salt River) before rounding the hills and turning west at Upasoitac (the

Gila Bend). Rather than follow the detour, however, Anza planned to overnight by a nearby pond (later to be known as "the Hospital") with good pasture and go from there directly west to Upasoitac. The third of November, therefore, was to be a short and easy day.

After distributing glass beads to the women in the morning, they set off by 10:00 but before long were surprised by and soaked to the bone in a downpour that turned the soil into slippery mud, and that was not to be their only surprise. Setting up camp in the afternoon, they left the herd to pasture near the pond.

The following day, Saturday, was the feast of Saint Charles, and Garcés sang a high mass, which Font accompanied with the psaltery. Just as the expedition was ready to lift camp but before the order to march was given, a soldier brought word that his wife was seriously ill. After verifying her condition Anza decided they must halt for the day. Only later did they realize that the woman's sickness was due to the pond. Fortunately, most of the people had drawn their water from the river, but the animals had been drinking the contaminated pond water and many became ill. The site was thereafter named Laguna del Hospital. Coincidentally, it was the feast of San Carlos, the king's saint's day, and therefore reason to distribute a measure of spirits to each man; the alcohol may have prevented further sickness.[2] "The troop," according to Font, "became so drunk that some did not recover until the following day." Many were no doubt relieved when the sick woman could not be moved for a second day and the expedition was forced to remain an extra night.

Another woman fell ill on Sunday, and the stay was extended through Monday when more animals became sick. It was only then they began to suspect the pond water. Font conjectured that the salts that made the soil white were also the reason the water affected some of the outsiders but not, apparently, the local Pimas, "although," cautions Font on the subject, "among the many healthy, well-fed, and strong people that came to meet us, I did not see any old ones." In what was probably an unrelated incident, Font himself became ill at this time with the intermittent fevers that would plague him for the rest of the journey.

Finally, on Tuesday, November 7, after a delay of three days, the

---

2 The spirit mentioned was *aguardiente*, a clear distillate from any number of possible sources. The volume, *un quartillo*, a small quart, was enough to inebriate an adult.

expedition was able to continue. "Forced more by necessity than due to the patients' recovery," writes Anza, "I decided to leave this place because, due to the…water, in the days we have camped by these ponds many horses have taken ill, and many people would have also had we not taken the precaution of going to fetch water from the Gila, three leagues away. They left Laguna del Hospital shortly before 1:00 and, heading generally west, covered some six to seven leagues to camp near a dry creek in the empty quarter between the Pima and the Opa nations. The patients whose three-day convalescence was the cause for the "hospital"stop were still ill, but not to the degree of the two horses that died in convulsions that day.

Days 41 to 45
Wednesday, November 8, to Sunday, November 12, 1775

By 8:00 the expedition was moving west-southwest over the Cocomaricopa Range. In the afternoon they were met in the open by three Opas on horseback who guided them to San Simón y Judas de Upasoitac, where they arrived at 4:00. The herd, enfeebled by the water at Laguna del Hospital, took longer to cover the nine leagues, reaching the village "at the time of evening prayers." Font, still suffering from his recurrent fevers, also had difficulty completing the journey that day. There is no mention of a formal welcome although Garcés comments that about a thousand Opas had gathered to meet them.

Upasoitac was located near the present-day Gila Bend, where the river direction changes from south to west. Having merged with the Asunción (the Salt River), it was at that point a much larger river subject to spring floods after the snowmelt. This affected the local farming practices; instead of irrigating through channels, the Opa relied on the seasonal overflow to provide soil moisture. They planted the same crops as neighboring tribes but obtained larger harvests, due, according to Anza, "to the peace that has been established and that they now enjoy with the Yuma and other nations with whom they were at war." Writing for the viceroy, Anza is not shy in taking credit for the peace initiative, which "has been so beneficial to these docile gentiles, as they have so joyfully conveyed to me, noting that they now have relatives in every direction." And indeed, as Font separately observes, there are a number of Pimas living in Upasoitac, indistinguishable in appearance from the Opas, but identifed (by the interpreters) because of their language. Capitalizing on the acknowl-edgment of the peace dividend that the Opa credit Anza with, the diplomat-commander took the opportunity to remind them that "this benefit is due to the King, who, for this reason, and for the spir-itual benefits that the reverend fathers have foretold, has sent his troops to this region." Later on in his writing Anza comments in passing that Upasoitac is "Apache free, beyond the range of these pirates," but leaves it to his readers to make the connection between that fact and the prosperity of the village.

The herd, in poor condition, arrived late that evening minus several animals—those that were unable to keep up and three that had died. Given the good water and pasture as well as some available corn, Anza decreed a day of rest for the benefit of the cattle, a decision welcomed also by the large group gathered in honor of the visitors. The crowd enjoyed the well-known presentation by Garcés and was rewarded with beads and tobacco. In the meantime, the expedition took time to wash their clothes and themselves in the river. That night an expectant mother had a difficult miscarriage and she, in addition to Font, who continued to be plagued by fevers, brought to five the number of the seriously ill. Unable to move the woman, the expedition remained at Upasoitac a second day.

Early on Saturday under a leaden sky they resumed their march west but, because of the ill, stopped by good pasture near the river after only two hours. A number of shelters in an abandoned ranchería supplemented their tents as a drizzle settled in for the day. Turning later into heavy rain, the downpour continued through the night.

The morning sun was brilliant and, while the river flowed murky, diamonds sparkled on each cactus. After mass they headed out, fol-lowing the Gila west-northwest for five leagues to camp at a village with good crops and pasture nestled between low hills and the river. "Even though when I passed…last year on my way to Upasoitac [the area] had crops and was populated with gentiles," writes Anza, "[the village] has now increased due to the peace they enjoy, which has made the many who were hidden in the bush…, as a precaution against their enemies, come out, as we have seen…from their plant-ings and rancherías." Being the twelfth of November, the feast of San Diego, they named the village in his honor.

Days 46 to 51
Monday, November 13, to Saturday, November 18, 1775

Climbing the hills west of the village while the river flowed north away from them, they rejoined it in the afternoon to camp on the north bank at Aritoac. The water was five to six hands at the deepest, and the animals crossed slowly but without problems. They continued the following morning west-southwest, arriving in the early afternoon at Agua Caliente, a site some distance from the river and so named for its large hot springs. The main spring and some others nearby were ideal for washing clothes, and Anza allowed the expedition a day for this purpose.

A crowd of some two hundred Opas from neighboring areas gathered for Garcés' usual presentation of "The Virgin and the Damned." When afterward the soldiers questioned the natives about their origins, they were treated to a tradition containing many elements in common with that of the Pima. In addition to telling their stories of creation and of a great flood, they said that "their origin was near the ocean, where an old woman had created their ancestors. She still existed but they knew not where. It was also the same [woman] who sent the corals from the sea. After death, [they believed] their hearts went to live somewhere toward the sunset near the ocean, except for some who continued to live as owls." Even as they told these stories, however, they added that "they were not well informed about these things, because those [of their people] who knew their traditions well lived in the sierra beyond the Colorado River."

Aware of the friendly relations their neighbors had established with the Spaniards and of the hierarchy of authority that had been instituted on those nations, the Opa seemed anxious to be granted the same honor. Without a doubt, the respect Captain Palma had been shown by the Spaniards at Altar and during their passage through the Yuma nation had made an impression; since Anza's visit the Opa had been at peace with the Yuma and befriended Palma. At the Opas' request, Anza agreed to recognize a governor and a mayor nominated by them. Acting in the name of the king, he granted the first candidate the title of governor, giving him the name Carlos, while the second one was made mayor and given the name Francisco. They were to rule over the Opa nation, which Garcés estimated at some three thousand souls. As part of their swearing in, "three times the candidates state that they recognize the king as their lord and agree to obey his orders and those of his ministers." Their rule would extend along the river basin from Aritoac to San Bernardino, and all those present vowed to recognize their authority. Anza instructed the officials on their obligations, "overwhelming the new governor to such an extent that for an entire hour he did not stop shaking," but the ceremony concluded happily with the generous distribution of beads and tobacco.

Font, meanwhile, continued in ill health, suffering from an ailment that by then also affected Father Eixarch. Consisting of periods of fever alternating with symptom-free days, the pattern had become so regular they were able to anticipate that on the afternoon of November 16 both would be feverish. In order to be at rest when this occurred, the two priests left early that morning, guided by two soldiers, to arrive at camp before mid-day.

Their destination was San Bernardino, a ranchería four leagues downstream of Agua Caliente. By noon they had not yet reached the settlement and it seemed to Font they must have missed it even though their guide reassured them of the contrary. Trusting the soldier, they continued, but by 2:00, having covered more than twice their expected distance and moving away from the river, Font was certain that they had passed the meeting point. Impatient, feverish, and irritable, he forcefully demanded that they turn back, but the soldier, piqued at his own mistake and not one to suffer the arrogance of the priest, flatly refused.

"Finally," writes Font, "I armed myself and said that I would go no farther because it was impossible that the commander would have planned such a long journey, and so, taking the direction of the river, I rode until we came to the row of elms, dismounted, and said that from there I would go neither forward nor backward."

Eixarch and the two soldiers followed Font without a word. The low river sang around the stones and the elms whispered in gentle motion. The awkward silence of the four men was broken sometime later by three of Anza's scouts returning from their exploration. The two soldiers joined them on their way to rejoin the expedition while the feverish priests remained shivering alone by the river.

Not finding the priests at the expected location, Anza assumed they could not be far ahead and ordered the expedition to continue, expecting to locate them at any moment. "But seeing as the day was ending and there was no sign of us," writes Font, "[Anza] camped at 4:30 at an elm grove by the river and sent the sergeant ahead...to find us." As it turned out, the priests were only a league beyond, and the sergeant left them an escort for the night while he returned to inform Anza of their location.

The incident, so important to Font that he describes it in detail (as if to hold the commander responsible), is not even mentioned in the other journals. Both Garcés and Anza, aware from experience how frequently such things happened, did not see it as significant, and they might even have chuckled learning of Font's reaction. But to the unforgiving (and on that occasion feverish) priest, it was a major irritation and one not soon forgotten.

During the night, the cold built crystals on the puddles and, after a long and lonely evening, the priests welcomed the morning sun. Rejoined by the expedition early in the day, they covered a short two leagues to El Pescadero on the banks of the Gila. On Saturday they continued southwest, crossing the river for a second time and coming to camp at the foot of San Pascual, the last mountain in the sierra of the same name (now the Mohawk). Carlos and Francisco, the recently named Opa officials, together with ten men and four women, joined them there unannounced.

"They have come to the Yuma nation for the purpose of formalizing in my presence," writes Anza, "the peace [treaty] that, due to my admonishment, has been agreed to by both nations. Although both sides have given proof of their intentions, these officials say that they will not be entirely satisfied if I am not a witness to the meeting between them and Captain Palma and to the [ensuing] drinking and dancing with his people, after which I should send couriers to the Opas left behind and [to] their allied nations [to inform them] that a true and perpetual peace [has been ratified]. All of which I have offered to do as well as anything else that may lead to their well-being."

Days 52 to 59
Sunday, November 19, to Sunday, November 26, 1775

Awakened in the early hours by a soldier whose wife was having contractions, Anza mustered the midwife. The starlit silence was broken;

glowing ashes came back to life, water boiled, and candles burned. The hustle of activity resulted in a new member of the expedition, baptized later that morning by Font as Diego Pascual. The mother's condition delayed the group at Cerro de San Pascual (latitude 32°:48' N) until Wednesday.

During the days of rest there was much talk with the Opas. According to Carlos, the governor, "it is only because I am going with you [the Spaniards] that I am happy to go [to the Yuma]; otherwise I fear the loyalty of our enemies because they are evil." Font goes on to add that "the Indians always distrust those that were formerly their enemies," and then he continues with some general impressions: "The Opa nation,…from the Gila Pima [area] upriver to this area, is rather small, judging from the numbers that have come to meet us attracted by curiosity and glass beads. [They are] probably less than three thousand souls, a small number considering the enormous expanse of the territory they occupy with not another nation for fifty leagues in any direction. This shows how poor the soil is, so barren and sterile as to make it almost uninhabitable, and thus the miserable poverty in which they live." Writing for the record he suggests that the tribe could be Christianized with missions located at Upasoitac and Agua Caliente.

With firewood in short supply, subfreezing weather and heavy frosts brought misery to the camp. The infants, the feverish priests, and the convalescent mother suffered the most. Due to their long stay they had to move their thousand horses and cattle about a league away for fresh pasture. But for some it was too late, and by Tuesday six horses had died. While searching for feed some of the men came across a plain of pure salt from which they replenished their own stock.

With the new mother strong enough to travel, the expedition left San Pascual by late morning on Wednesday. The sandy terrain with the occasional dune lacked adequate vegetation as they moved west-southwest. The horses and, in particular, the cattle struggled in the sand. After six leagues they camped near a hill the natives knew as Metate and the Spaniards renamed Santa Cecilia del Metate (Antelope Hill), the first location with any pasture that day.

In the morning, with the mule train loaded and ready to move, word reached the commander that a large number of cattle were missing. Scattered in search of pasture, the animals had wandered far and wide, some into thick undergrowth from where they, "greatly emboldened…, charge[d] us like wild beasts" and were hard to remove. After appraising the situation, Anza ordered the column to return and aborted the march. Recovering the herd took the rest of the day and several more animals died in the process. Scarce feed, fatigue, and the bitter cold were taking their toll.

On the second night at Santa Cecilia (Thursday) another pregnant woman was taken with labor pains that turned out to be premature. Anza notes that "the threatened birth was avoided by means of the medicines administered, which improved her condition through the night." On his entry for the day, Font writes that "a pregnant woman was ill this morning but after the commander helped her with a whim she had, which was a plate of food, she recovered, and for this reason we remained here this day." Although he considers his every discomfort important ("Today my fever was not as intense, perhaps because a soldier's wife gave me a potion day before yesterday"), Font has little tolerance for others' ailments, especially the natives or mestizos.

Leaving Santa Cecilia toward the west, they covered four leagues through a plain where debris marked the high level of annual floods. It was during a slow and cumbersome march through the undergrowth when one of the exhausted horses finally died. En route they met a scout sent by Palma who, anticipating their arrival, had been looking for the expedition for four days. After cordially greeting Anza he started back to inform the Yuma chief of the expedition's approach. They camped that night by a salty lake, Laguna Salada, supplied by the Gila, where they were later met by a group of Jalchedunes. Alerted of the Spaniards' presence they, like the Opas, had come from their tribal lands to meet with the Yumas in Anza's company.

If the previous day's march was difficult, Sunday's, along the same sandy plain, was just as hard. Approaching the hills, they turned toward the northwest for two leagues to camp at a point where the river, at the end of the sierra, narrowed to a deep channel. The only novelty was that in the afternoon some of the men were able to catch a few rather large fish.

Day 60
Monday, November 27, 1775

The following day they continued west of the range where they were met on the way by one of Palma's brothers, who had been looking for them. After covering only three leagues in the morning they set up camp on the foothills at Los Cerritos (the Small Hills), not far from the Gila. Early that afternoon, Palma "with more than thirty of his own, all unarmed," rode into camp. "As soon as he saw me, he embraced me, displaying the greatest joy and happiness for my coming, which he said was shared by his and all the other nations that knew me along the river."

Palma's display of emotion and Anza's warm response reflected a friendship that had not cooled since their last meeting. During the eighteen months the commander had been organizing the second expedition, Palma had continued to pursue his rapprochement with the Spaniards. As leader of a nation that had declared its allegiance to the crown, he had traveled to San Miguel de Horcasitas and met with the governor of Sonora to request the presence of priests and settlers in his country. He had received only vague assurances to that effect but was nevertheless treated with respect. While there he had also learned of Anza's promotion to lieutenant colonel for the success of his overland trip to Monterey, an accomplishment to which Palma had significantly contributed.

"He begged me to tell him if the Spaniards and priests requested from Urrea [the governor of Sonora] were already coming to their land and emphasized that he had been meticulous in complying with all the orders I had given him. He had particularly observed the one about not waging war with any nation, which he had obeyed with one exception only," that of a tribe on the western sierra that had attacked Spanish establishments in Alta California to steal horses and in so doing had killed a soldier.

"[His people] had become related [through marriage] to all the other [tribes] and he had prevented these from fighting among themselves. This he had accomplished through his efforts, on behalf of God and the King, at my request. For this state of affairs to be permanent, he expected Spaniards and missionaries to settle among them, for which he was making all his lands available in the name of the [Yuma] nation. His people had agreed on these objectives and in particular on becoming Christians because they wanted to live by the laws of our religion, as far as they knew them. [Palma], who had dealt with our people in their own villages, felt particularly strong about this. And for these reasons [he hoped] that I and my entire expedition would remain in his lands and so inform the King."

Palma's vision of a Spanish settlement in the Yuma nation was the result of the trust and respect that had developed between three people: Garcés, dedicated to spreading the faith; Anza, a soldier of honor and integrity; and Palma, motivated to bring his tribe the code of conduct that he perceived in these two men and that had been corroborated by his dealings with other Spanish officials.

Unfortunately for Palma, Anza's orders from the viceroy were clear and his answer must have been as difficult to pronounce as it was to hear. "To his statement I responded that I could not do what he was asking me, but that he could be certain that, as His Majesty [the King] and His Excellency the Viceroy were sending me with these troops and families elsewhere to establish the True Religion, it was because it had so been offered to others before [him] and that he and his people would, in due time, achieve the same.

"He reluctantly accepted my reply but added that if, upon my return, the expected settlement in his country had not occurred, he would [personally] come with me to make the request to His Excellency the Viceroy. To which I replied that I would gladly take him with me to [the city of] Mexico provided he had the approval of his whole nation, and that he should so consult with her and also consider the very large distance he would have to travel."

After this dialogue Anza reiterated his endorsement of the Yuma chief and people for the sake of the record: "Since my first meeting with this captain and his nation I have had no doubt that they will gladly embrace our religion and culture as they have given manifest proof of their attachment to both. When they now present their wives [to us] they state with pride that [the woman] is the only wife they have. They have adopted the habit of saying 'Ave Maria' and using other words of our prayers, which they request to be taught. This time we have been surprised to see that they cover their private parts, unlike the total nudity [we observed] on our first visit. And finally, we note the absence of fear resulting from our presence in that almost all ask us to stay and live among them."

In a gesture planned long in advance, Anza presented the chief with the gift of a suit of clothes sent personally by the viceroy, a detail that reflected how clearly Anza had acknowledged Palma's contribution to his success. And in the eyes of his people, "who admired [the suit] with the same exuberance as its owner," it was an additional honor bestowed by the Spaniards upon their chief.

Informed that Fathers Garcés and Eixarch would be remaining to instruct them on religion and that Garcés would undertake certain explorations from there, Palma replied that "in his house and nation he [himself] will answer for their safety and for anything else that [Anza] should leave in his care."

Font, who was meeting the Yuma chief for the first time, describes the encounter from a fresh perspective: "Salvador Palma arrived, accompanied by another captain (to whom we gave the name of Pablo) and several members of his tribe. They all greeted us with effusive demonstrations of joy, particularly Captain Palma, who embraced each one of us and presented the commander with a gift. In the afternoon Anza took him through camp so that he could meet the people, and in doing so he embraced each man, woman, and child as a sign of goodwill. This Captain Palma is the present leader of the whole Yuma nation, which he dominates because of his courage and verbosity (as is often the case among Indians) and more so because of the prestige bestowed upon him by the Spaniards, lately by Captain Anza and earlier by Captain Urrea.[3] [This is why] he is recognized as chief by the other captain [Pablo]."

About Pablo, Font goes on to explain: "We gave him that name because he is the leader of the rancherías located near the hill Garcés named Cerro de San Pablo [presently Pilot Knob near Andrade, California], but during the first expedition he was known as Capitán Feo [Captain Ugly] on account of his physical appearance. The population of Pablo's rancherías is larger, and his personality as strong if not stronger, but he is subordinate to Palma. Pablo is a powerful speaker with a resounding voice and [is] rumored to be a wizard. Tonight he gave a long and rambling harangue that boiled

---

3 Captain Bernardo de Urrea, commander of the presidio at Altar and provincial governor of Sonora, had met with Palma when he delivered Sebastián Tarabal to Altar in 1773 and again when Palma made a request for priests and settlers at San Miguel de Horcasitas in 1774.

down to telling his people that they should not steal from or hurt the Spaniards because we did no wrong and were friends."

If Font's first impression of Palma was not particularly warm, his initial reaction to Pablo was one of suspicion and dislike. Immediately following the above introduction, he paraphrases an anecdote Anza had shared with him: "The commander told me that during his first expedition, Captain Pablo counted the number of soldiers and, seeing they were not many, began telling his people that it would be easy to kill them all and take their horses and supplies, which was his intention. Informed of this, Anza told him that if he wanted war he should gather all his people and more, and he would see what defense they could muster. This cooled him down [then] and now he appears friendly and compliant, when at the time he was opposed to the expedition crossing the Colorado."[4]

Days 61 to 63
Tuesday, November 28, to Thursday, November 30, 1775

In the company of their hosts, the expedition left Los Cerritos at 9:30 in the morning toward the west-northwest. Under the eyes of the Yuma leaders, the convoy, led by Anza, Font, and Garcés, intoned the Alabado with more than the usual vigor as they picked up the march. Anza knew how to display pageantry, and the sight must have warmed Palma's heart; behind his two friends—the commander and the priest—rode settlers, women, children, colorfully uniformed soldiers, and horses, mules, and cattle by the hundreds. It was the might of an unrivaled power leading Spaniards and Spanish-speaking natives in Christian harmony toward a new frontier. Was this not his own vision for the Yuma nation?

They traveled four leagues, fording the Gila easily before it joined the Colorado. In the early afternoon they arrived at a village between the rivers where the tribe had built for them out of branches a "four-by eight-yard shelter." There they were introduced to Palma's wife and family as well as other prominent individuals. A large crowd had

---

4 For Anza and Garcés' notes of this incident, see the entries for February 5 through 8, 1774. The identity of the rebellious leader was not then known and is therefore not mentioned in the 1774 journals, however, subsequent information must have established Pablo's connection to the event.

gathered, including the Opas Carlos and Francisco, as well as their group. Anza ordered a squad of soldiers in formation to fire a volley into the air. "It was our way of responding to the exuberance displayed by the crowd for our arrival, to which they reacted with much shouting and excitement," writes Font. The stage was set for more ceremony.

Governor Carlos of the Opa, on horseback, addressed Chief Palma while the gathering listened. His dialect could be understood by the Yumas (but not by the expedition), and his voice, masking any insecurity, dominated the crowd. Speaking to an audience who was on foot, the governor, on a horse that was prancing from side to side, appeared threatening. "This bothered Captain Palma," writes Font, "who made him understand that if he was coming with a good heart to confirm peace, he should speak to them on foot, as he [himself] was, and not riding in front of everybody the way he was doing. After hearing this, Carlos dismounted and both he and Palma with their batons sat on the ground, where they continued talking. Then Captain Pablo, standing up in the middle of the group, delivered a long sermon, the message of which was that [the Opa] no longer wanted war because that was the way we (and saying this he pointed to the commander, me, and the priests who were present) ordered it. He then pointed to the four winds, repeating in each direction in a loud voice with body movements and facial expressions that they now wanted, with all nations and people, to be related and in friendship, or *queyé*, which means 'of the same country.' To conclude, the commander ordered the captains, Palma and Carlos, to embrace, which they did, and following their example, the rest did the same."

The peace movement was originally promoted by Garcés and reinforced by Anza during the first expedition with assurances that it was the king's wish and that Spanish soldiers would be available to prevent one nation from abusing another. But it was also the result, according to Font, of the trade the nations had begun. "Last year there was hardly a [Yuma] Indian with a blanket, and now we see some with cotton blankets made by the Opa and some black woolen blankets made by the Moqui and traded by the Jalchedune."

Governor Carlos and the entire Opa delegation as well as the expedition members were invited to eat with Palma as part of the celebration. Anza comments on the abundance of food, which included "more than three thousand melons" and a large quantity of beans, seeds, grain, and corn provided as gifts to the expedition and to the Opas for their return trip. "They remained until late that night," writes Font, "and I stayed with them for a while, Yumas and Opas on the ground around the fire, half buried in the sand and laying on top of each other like pigs as is their habit, singing their dismal songs and playing the drum."

Font, who had just met Palma for the first time and felt the need to personally verify what Anza and Garcés already knew, took the chief aside with an interpreter that night and had a long conversation with him. "To my question regarding his wish that I and other priests should come and live with them he answered that both he and his people would welcome it. I then continued by telling him that for this to happen it was necessary that they would want to learn doctrine to become Christians, that they would also have to learn to be masons, carpenters, farmers, laborers, etc., and settle to live in town instead of spread out all over as they did now, and that a house would have to be built for the priest as well as a church. To this Palma replied that they would be pleased to do all that I was saying and that, even though his head was already a little hard for learning, he would prefer that it would happen immediately and that we didn't have to leave them. To build a town, he said, there was on the other side of the river a hill or plateau where the floods never reach, and he had already planned that we should live there. This was Concepción [presently the Fort Yuma-Quechan Reservation administration]. I told him that I would report his wishes to the King, and that since he and his people wanted to be Christians and have good relations with the Spaniards, undoubtedly the following year the King would grant that we would return to live with them. And, I added, that if I were to come myself, I would teach him to work and also to sing. He was so pleased to hear this that he began to sing the Alabado with me. In departing he embraced me several times with much pleasure, saying that he was already Spanish and I, Yuma and queyé. All of this was witnessed by Captain Pablo, who appeared to agree completely with Palma's vision." While Font's corroboration of the chief's intentions appears to be an unnecessary duplication of Anza and Garcés' assessment, it must be remembered that Font's responsibilities included looking at the frontier with new eyes and preparing an independent report, a task he was meticulous in executing.

That day, four soldiers sent to scout possible routes across the desert rejoined the expedition after six strenuous days of exploration. Along the direct route used in their return from San Sebastián they had found neither water nor human or animal tracks, but they had located the wells they knew along the longer southerly route and found these in the same condition as during their first passage. They also reported having had to swim quite a long stretch across a very cold Colorado River, which they found too high to ford. This confirmed local knowledge about the river's condition, which had recently changed course, making it impossible to ford where they had before. The possibility of using rafts was considered but ruled out as too time-consuming, difficult, and risky for such a large group. Exploring the east bank through heavy vegetation, they located a possible crossing over three wide but shallow channels, and that afternoon the mule drivers cleared a path through the brush to reach it.

In the shelter, adorned by Garcés' banner of the Virgin, Font said mass in the early morning of November 30, 1775, with the whole Opa delegation in attendance. After the ceremony Carlos "made a speech saying his heart was very happy for the peace that had been achieved," and the Opas then started on their way home, taking with them letters and reports from the expedition that they would carry all the way back to the presidio at Tubac. At about the same time— around 7:00 in the morning—the expedition was getting under way.

Moving through the newly cleared and narrow path it took them two hours to reach the ford. At the "Beach of the Colorado," cargo was unloaded and rearranged while the women and children began to cross on the strongest horses, surrounded by men walking beside them in the water. The current ran cold and clear "between four and six hands deep, and the three channels, if they were one, [would be] at least 240 yards wide," according to Anza. Font notes that there was a location in one of the channels where the horses lost footing, but in all, "everybody crossed without mishap, although there could have been, because in climbing out..., the animals had to swim and one...sank entirely, so that a blanket and some baskets were taken by the water, and one man almost lost a child he was holding. But the Virgin wanted that we should come across with no more damage than getting a little wet. The water reached the chest of even the large horses, as mine was, so the water came up to my knees."

After the settlers, the mule trains crossed with lightened loads, followed by the spare horses and finally the cattle. "It was only the load that included the holy oils and vestments that got wet," writes Font, "because, as they pay such little attention to...what I say, even though I specifically asked the drivers and even the commander to give special attention [to it] so that it shouldn't get wet, it was the load that was most neglected.

"Father Garcés was carried across faceup as a dead body, on the shoulders of three Yumas, two at his head and one at his feet. I crossed on horseback and, as I was feeling ill and faint, [I was] accompanied by three naked servants, one in front leading the horse and one on either side holding me so that I wouldn't fall. Due to the size of our train it took over three hours for all to cross. From what I have said about the ford one can imagine how monstrous the river is when it is high since this is the season when it is lowest and we crossed before it is joined by the Gila."

While Anza writes that the breadth of the Colorado that day was "at least 240 yards," Font estimates it at "3 to 400 yards" and Garcés "is of the opinion that it is some 400 yards" wide. Whatever the exact dimension may have been, it was one of the main obstacles on the route to California, and on that last day of November 1775, it had been successfully overcome.

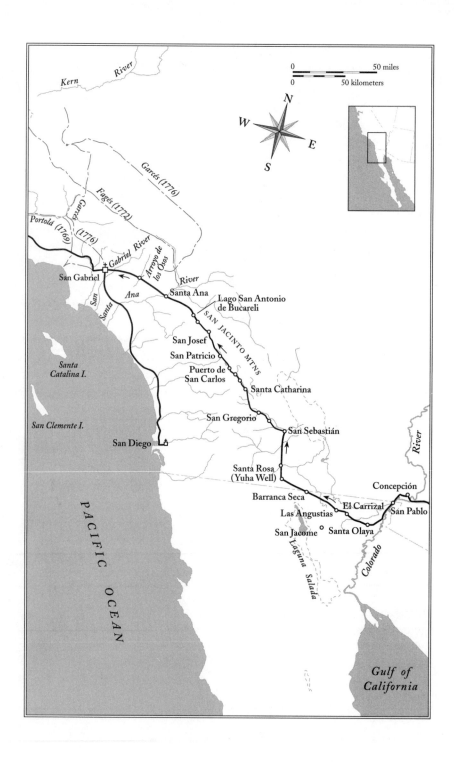

CHAPTER 10

Over the Top:
From the Colorado
to San Gabriel

November 30, 1775, to January 4, 1776

Days 63 to 66
Thursday, November 30, to Sunday, December 3, 1775

Cognizant of having reached an important milestone, Anza, Garcés, and Eixarch proceeded to Palma's village to select a location for the hut that would house the priests during their stay. In the meantime, the expedition set up camp on the riverbank west of the ford. That afternoon a delegation of Jalchedunes (four women and a man) arrived at camp. Aware of Anza's presence, they had come, according to Garcés, "in the name of their nation determined to establish peace with the Yuma."[1] In the evening, Palma joined the Spanish camp wearing his new officer's dress uniform, complete with long stockings, shirt, yellow vest, blue jacket, and a black velvet cape decorated with stones. In spite of Palma's presence in the camp that night, none of the diaries comments on his response, if any, to the Jalchedune

---

[1] This incident is mentioned by both Garcés and Font, but only Garcés notes (without comment) that the delegation is composed "of four women and one man," indicating the matriarchal nature of the tribe, a major cultural difference Europeans consistently failed to understand.

peace initiative.

Although the camp location was not ideal, the expedition remained in place Friday while Anza led a group to construct the priests' hut. "It is a heavy day," writes Font, who remained at camp, "because from dawn a northeaster, so strong that we could hardly keep the tents in place, began to blow, lifting the layers of fine, sandy soil the river leaves behind. The dirty, sticky dust covered our clothes and made it difficult to breathe or see and continued [to blow] until sunset." As many as ten expedition members were sick at the time, according to Anza—some having been ill since Tubac—but on this day two were near death. They were given the sacraments and, unable to be moved, held up the expedition on the flood plain for a second day.

Always probing for information, Garcés elicited a story from the Jalchedunes regarding a man who had come from one of the California missions. As he traveled east together with a viper, he had presumably been killed and cremated repeatedly by the nations through which he passed, but he had the ability to turn himself into a whirlwind and be reincarnated. The narrator and the rest of the delegation considered him a wizard who killed Jalchedunes, and they were in absolute fear of his power. While respectfully listening to the story in public, Garcés dismisses it in his diary as "humorous," meaning, of course, that it was not to be taken seriously. He notes that the commander, "even having the large store of patience that he has with the Indians (which is worthy of imitation by all those devoted to these undertakings), is actually irritated" by the tale. He then concludes without further comment on the incident, writing "I asked him [Anza] for some beads and made them a present."

This anecdote is significant for the positive light Garcés casts on Anza's character, especially because, on the same day, Font severely criticizes him on several counts. Claiming Anza had presented the viceroy's gift to Palma on his own, without even informing the others, he writes: "He is in the habit of usurping such actions to gain personal praise, which he does not want to share [with us] or accept that anyone around him be the center of attention, a position he considers exclusively his own. Even though it would be expected that His Majesty's gifts of beads and tobacco be distributed [to the natives] by the three priests of the expedition to gain their goodwill, since, after all, it is they who will minister to the Indians, and these [people] recognize and favor those who give, even so, the commander always did the distribution by his own hand and never wanted us to do it. During the entire trip I didn't have a single string of beads to offer at my discretion except on one occasion at the San Luis [Obispo] Mission on our way back, when I specifically asked and was given some."

At the Colorado River ford "I suggested to the commander that the latitude should be taken, but because he didn't want any observations to be made under my name or even that I should be mentioned in connection with them, he was always present [when taking a reading], as if he were making the observation himself. This is why he never released the quadrant provided by the viceroy. And today because he was busy with the building of the hut, he said that [the measurement] would be taken another day, at Concepción, and so I was unable to take the latitude I wanted.

"Since the day he came to my mission at San Joseph de Pimas he insisted that I should take with me the psaltery, which, he said, would be very useful in attracting the Indians, especially the Yuma, who are so fond of celebration. Even though I objected for fear of losing it on such a long trip, I gave in under pressure and took it along. In spite of the inconvenience, he has not once mentioned it nor suggested I should play it. He personally does not like to hear it or have people gather in my tent, so the wretched thing has served no useful purpose, for the Yuma or anybody else.

"The commander wanted to finish building the hut in one day," continues Font, "but it wasn't possible, so that night after dinner, in reply to my question, he told me we wouldn't be leaving the following day, as he had said that morning. So, in order to avoid the hardship of our location, where the wind and the dust made it almost impossible even to cook, I asked him, as long as we had to stay another day, to move our camp to where the hut was being built, but he flatly refused. Yet the following day, without [my] asking him [again], he did so, having had us endure an uncomfortable extra day for no reason.

"I asked him because I was concerned about the conditions in which Fathers Garcés and Eixarch were remaining by the river and about why he was leaving them among the gentiles without an escort. He reacted aggressively, saying that it was not my business to question him; that he did not have to explain his decisions to me; that he was already doing more than his duty by building a hut, which was not part of his orders; that he was not responsible for how the two priests would stay there; and that, since they had volunteered for the assignment (which was not an order from the Viceroy), they should well know themselves how they remained there."

Font goes on to take issue with Anza as to whether or not they had been pressured to volunteer, revealing in so doing his superficial knowledge of Garcés, who not only thrived on his own among the natives but actually had orchestrated the whole assignment. While their task was both to instruct the Yumas and to explore the disposition of neighboring tribes, Garcés chose to leave the instruction to Eixarch and do the exploration himself. His loose interpretation of "neighboring" furthermore enabled him to wander as far west as the Central Valley of California and through the Grand Canyon to the upper reaches of the Colorado on the east, a five-month trek covering parts of present-day California, Nevada, and most of northern Arizona.

An annoyed Font continues his criticism of Anza: "The commander finally agreed to let the priests have their two servants, the three interpreters, and two mule drivers. The so-called interpreters were three worthless Indians whose little knowledge of Castilian made them useless at their task. Of the two drivers, one was Sebastián Tarabal, who accompanied Father Garcés in his travels, as he explains in his diary; the other was a youth that had come with a soldier and wished to remain. This one had neither an animal nor the means to continue [in the expedition] and, even though he served Father Thomas [Eixarch] well (indeed, he was the only one that was any use), he was not paid or rewarded in any way because the commander said he had not come in his charge and was not his responsibility. Of the two servants, the useless one, who offered to remain with Father Garcés and was not given anything, soon deserted to return to Sonora, while the other one was [only] a child who had come with Father Thomas to look after his horses and serve as a page.

"I record all this so that what frequently happens with the commanders of expeditions is not ignored and [conditions] are firmly established from the beginning and [one is not misled] by fancy words and oral promises as Father Garcés was when he discovered that the reality did not match the promises. Because the masters that command such expeditions and those who govern these remote outposts do not have an overseer to check them, they are absolute lords and one must be extremely patient in dealing with them. Even the best of them cause a lot of suffering, as our Venerable Father Antonio… knew from experience and would say in his maxim: *'A militibus libera nos Domine,'*" [sic] (From soldiery deliver us, Lord).

What prompted Font's outburst of criticism on this particular day is hard to say. Perhaps it was his sickness aggravated by accumulated fatigue and the dismal camp location. It does show, however, how isolated he was both from the rank and file and from the leaders of the expedition. The erudite priest, who knew the Old Testament, could quote Latin, and wrote perfect Spanish, was not in the leader's confidence. The misguided concern he manifests for Garcés and his considering Sebastián Tarabal (who skills as scout, diplomat, and interpreter had often been demonstrated) as no more than a mule driver show how little Font knew of them. The sense of his own importance to the expedition—manifested as attempts to emulate the conduct of frontier-savvy Garcés—could not have been more inappropriate. Time and again Font overstepped his responsibility and ability, unable to understand why Anza should lose patience with him. And yet, ironically, he is the sensitive, independent, and skilful narrator that has left us the most complete record of the expedition.

Building the hut continued Saturday as Yumas and mule drivers worked under Anza and Garcés' supervision, while Font, again taken with fever, spent the day at camp. On Sunday the hut was complete and the expedition was relocated to Palma's village. Supplies were then transferred for the priests and their helpers: "a third [measure] of tobacco, two boxes of glass beads, an *arroba* [twenty-five pounds] of chocolate, the same of sugar and lard, five heads of cattle, three thirds of dried beef, a load of beans, a load of ground flour (some not ground), a measure of chickpeas, a box of biscuits, three hams, six cheeses, a frying pan, a flat earthenware pan [for cooking maize cake], an axe, twelve bars of soap, twelve wax candles, and a container of wine [so foul that it neither looked nor tasted as wine and could not be used for saying mass, thus forcing them to send to Caborca for more]. The supplies were adequate but only just, considering they were for nine people and had to last until our return."

"That night," continues Font, "I had Captain Palma and Captain Pablo...come to my tent, and by means of the interpreter I urged them to care for and look after the priests who were remaining [and told them] that if they did so, upon my return I would go to the King and inform him of everything so they would be recognized and then the Spaniards would finally come and settle down with them. To all this they replied with reassurances that Palma, [originally] with the baton and now with the suit of clothes from the Viceroy, remained as the representative of Captain Don Juan [de Anza] and that he would look after the priests as I myself would, punishing anyone wanting to hurt them or causing disturbances. Captain Pablo added that he would kill anyone who tried to hurt them or steal something. To this I replied that neither I nor God approved of killing, that he should punish them by tying them up and lashing them. He liked this so much that he spread himself out on the ground and, stretching arms and legs enthusiastically, cried: '*Ajót, ajót!*' which means, 'Good, good!' While I was in this conversation, the commander sent for Captain Palma, only to get him out of my tent because he did not approve of anybody else talking to the Indians, especially the chiefs, and giving them instructions. Later on, as entertainment, [the Yumas] danced in the light of the fire in front of Anza's tent and I had no further chance to speak to them."

Days 67 to 69
Monday, December 4, to Wednesday, December 6, 1775

After hearing the first mass celebrated in the priests' new shelter, the expedition left Palma's village along the flood plain as Garcés and Font waved their good-byes. Moving slowly through thick vegetation they came to a branch of the river, which they crossed, and by mid-morning they reached the Puerto de la Concepción, "a narrow passage between two small hills through which flows the Colorado after its junction with the Gila." From the hill on the north side they could see the large plain and some boundary landmarks: "about ten leagues northeast, Giant's Head [now Castle Dome Peak], which the Indians call the Bauquiburi, a large spherical mound on a rugged sierra between the Colorado and the Gila; three to four leagues north, the

Bell [Picacho Peak], towering above another equally rugged chain; and [directly west] the Cerro de San Pablo [Pilot Knob], below which flows the river." By mid-afternoon they came to Captain Pablo's village, where they stopped for the night. The captain, however, was not present as he had relocated to Palma's village to be near the priests.

There was a heavy frost during the night and among the animals camped a league behind them "a mule and a horse are found dead from a cold...so extreme...that the urine in the pot inside my tent was frozen," writes Font. And Anza, blaming the weather, notes that eleven of the settlers were then sick. The next morning, they lifted camp and were on the march by 10:00 with the animals following still a league behind at a slower pace. The terrain with thick vegetation and abundant streams continued to be difficult but "only half as much as yesterday," according to Font. Moving almost directly south toward Cojat territory, they passed good agricultural lands and the last Yuma villages, "where the people, coming out on the road to greet us, rejoice at our presence and all want to take us to their houses.

"Among the natives that from time to time accompany us, today a half-Yuma, half-Pima Indian insisted on guiding us on foot. His father was a prestigious Yuma captain and the leader of the nation until his death, at which time Palma assumed power. His mother was a Pima Indian, whose status [as the chief's widow] is still recognized by the Yuma. For this reason, as the commander later told me, during the first expedition he [himself] had named the Pima woman the Queen, and the young man the Prince." The reason for the playful titles was that the Jesuits ("so given to exaggeration"), on reporting the first Spanish contact with the Yuma, had stated that these natives had neither a chief nor a captain but a king, "which was none other than this young man's father."

Because of his knowledge of the Pima and Yuma languages, the Prince had, during the first expedition, served as an interpreter for Anza (who did not speak Yuma) and they had come to know each other. "Yesterday night, he came to the commander's tent, but his face was so made up that...he was not recognized until he began to speak, at which point one of his servants proficient in the Pima language said to the commander: 'Sir, it's the Prince.'"

They camped that night by one of the seasonal ponds on the boundary between Yuma and Cojat countries, and "a large number of natives [came] to trade squash, beans, and other seeds for beads, which the commander distributed to the soldiers for that purpose." A steer was slaughtered for the expedition's needs, as was the practice every six days, while Anza and Font were irritated by the large number of curious natives pressing tightly around them.

"They were so filthy, so close, and so foul smelling with their constant passing of wind," writes Font, "that it was impossible to breathe or even get some breathing space. I stood up and asked one of them for the stick he was holding, about ten hands long, [of the type they] often play with, and smiling, politely, gently probed them to move, [giving ourselves some room]. But one of the Indians became very angry and, pushing the stick aside, moved close again while others followed his example. The owner then grabbed the stick from my hand and the one who had become angered gave me a severe and haughty look, which he maintained until I withdrew to my tent. From this [incident] I felt that their friendliness, due more to the gifts of beads than to their docile nature, might turn to pride when one tries to subject them to Christianity and to our control, especially if we should attempt to change their habits and way of life." The evening so inauspiciously begun did not improve that night as a noisy and disorderly crowd continued to loiter, and a sword, a clay dish (later recovered), and some clothing were stolen. Also, one of the expedition's sick was close to death and given last rites.

Still accompanied by the Prince, they were on the move by 10:00 the next morning and with the cattle following at their pace they reached Santa Olaya in the early afternoon, the coastal ranges clearly visible across the winter desert. The narrow lake at Santa Olaya, about a league long and roughly parallel to the Colorado, was not connected with the river almost four leagues to the east. Using nets, the Cojat caught over a thousand fish in less than an hour, including, according to Anza, several saltwater species. Garcés, already on his way to contact tribes on the southern delta, arrived and remained with them for the evening.

Days 70 and 71
Thursday, December 7, and Friday, December 8, 1775
"Because here we will leave the river and for three days will have no

pasture and only limited water," writes Anza, "I decided to give the animals two days of rest and the patients time to recover somewhat so that they can cope with the…difficult days ahead. It will be necessary to march in separate groups [on subsequent] days so that the water will be enough for all. The cattle will have to cover in two days and without drinking the distances we will cover in three as, unlike the horses, these animals are unable to drink from the elevated cisterns."

Not only the cattle but the horses and mules also arrived at Santa Olaya in poor condition. Conscious of the first expedition's near disaster across the desert, this time Anza was meticulous in his planning. With a group eight times larger, he had to know exactly where they were going and how much water would be available at every stop. This is why, after the scouts' reconnoitering, he decided to cross the desert from Santa Olaya to Santa Rosa (Yuha Well) using the Cerro del Imposible (Signal Mountain) as a beacon.

At Santa Olaya, the Cojats also came in large numbers to trade the usual produce as well as some Moqui blankets. Given the good location for rest and recuperation, and cognizant of the soldier's accumulated fatigue, that afternoon Anza issued brandy to the expedition. The consequences were soon felt: both he and Font missed dinner because their servant was unable to cook and "there was that night among the rabble a rather loud and excessively drunken feast," which Font severely disapproved of. "In the morning…I went to see the commander in his tent and said, 'Sir, it appears there were some drunks this night,' to which he replied that 'there had been something.'" But Font's attempt to hold Anza responsible ("Your Lordship does not ignore the intemperance of these people when given brandy") is met with "no sign of repentance." Anza, patiently aware that Font is incapable of understanding, chooses to change the subject: "Would Your Reverence like to take a reading at this location?" The latitude at the Lake of Santa Olaya is found to be 32°:33'N.

As he had done with the Pima, Opa, and Yuma, Garcés made the same religious presentation to the Cojat. After distributing beads and tobacco, he displayed the large banner with the Virgin holding the child, a move that was met with "great joy and cries of approval and, according to the interpreters, the statement [by many] that they wanted to become Christians to be as white and beautiful as the Virgin, and that they would gladly receive baptism. To this it was explained to them that for the time being they could not be baptized but that in due time they would be." The display of the sinner condemned to the flames of hell on the reverse side of the banner was received with the customary horror.

"It is obvious," continues Font, "that the people are well predisposed to joining the Holy Church provided the means are made available to them. They do not object to becoming subject to the laws of God and our King and they say that they would be pleased to have Spaniards and priests settle among them. It seems to me a great number could be converted to Christianity but, given the fickleness of the Indians, I believe that a strong garrison would also be necessary so that respect for weaponry would prevent any attempt at rebellion once they have become subjected."

After spending two days at Santa Olaya, Garcés was ready to go south, but his interpreters, warned that they would be killed (even when the priest would not), were afraid and refused to continue. "When Father Garcés explained the situation to me," writes Font, "I advised him that…he should not go alone for there was little to be gained from revisiting nations he already knew, especially since the object of assessing their receptiveness to Christianity could not be achieved without the interpreters. I told him that the best thing would be to return to Father Thomas and after Christmas visit the Jalchedune to assess their receptiveness and that of the adjacent nations. The nations downriver could [always] be converted once a mission and garrison were established at the river junction."

Garcés appeared convinced by this argument when a messenger arrived informing him that Palma and Pablo with a few mounted men would be proceeding south on the east bank of the river to observe secretly how the natives received the priest. Distrustful of the Cojat, Palma was letting Garcés know that he was taking measures to protect him if necessary. But the priests, fearing such an action might be misinterpreted as aggression and lead to dangerous consequences for Garcés, reacted negatively. In order to prevent the unwelcome assistance, Garcés, together with a relative of Palma's (the one who met the expedition on November 25) decided to send the chief "a message to keep him from leaving his ranchería." In addition, Palma's relative proposed to "send ahead of Garcés two women (either slaves held by the Cojat or women from that nation married to Cojats) to announce that the priest who had visited them before was on his way to see them again; that he was bringing presents and was going to mediate a peace agreement with the Yuma." This new plan restored the confidence of the interpreters, who agreed to proceed as originally arranged.

"Father Garcés is so adept at understanding and being among Indians that he appears to be almost one of them," writes Font. "He sits with them in a circle. He spits constantly, as the Indians. At night around the fire, legs crossed, he can spend two or three hours or longer dumbfounded, forgetting everything, calmly, phlegmatically speaking with them. Their...meals, as dirty and disgusting as the Indians are filthy, Garcés eats with great pleasure, saying they are healthy and very tasty. As far as I can see, God has made him ideally suited to serve these unhappy, ignorant, and primitive people."

"The Cojat nation," writes Anza, "which received...gifts of beads and tobacco like the previous ones, has provided us from their harvests much more than the others: corn, beans, squash, and over two thousand enormous watermelons, many of which will be wasted because we cannot carry them all, and they have also continued to bring us fish [during the two days we have been here at Santa Olaya]."

Days 72 to 76
Saturday, December 9, to Wednesday, December 13, 1775

What is today a fertile basin southeast from the Salton Sea across the Mexican border to the Colorado River delta was, in the eighteenth century, a barren and formidable barrier. The Cojats near the river had so little contact with their kin in the hills to the west that the Spaniards believed the Mountain Cojat were a separate tribe. The oval-shaped area, one hundred miles long and fifty wide, partly crisscrossed with sand dunes, had little vegetation and only a few meager sources of water; the desert that had almost defeated Anza's first expedition now presented an even more difficult obstacle to the larger group. The crossing from Santa Olaya to San Sebastián (through what is now the well-irrigated Imperial Valley) would have to be planned in detail.

To ensure enough water at each stop, Anza divided the expedition into four groups staggered over three days. The first, consisting of himself, Font, a mule train, and twelve soldiers with their families and horses, would leave on December 9. The second and third groups, each consisting of a mule train and twelve soldiers with their families and horses, were led respectively by Sergeant Grijalba and Lieutenant Moraga; they were to follow from Santa Olaya at twenty-four-hour intervals to water sources at El Carrizal, Las Angustias, and Santa Rosa (Yuha Well) before turning north to San Sebastián. The last group, consisting only of cowboys and the remaining soldiers, was to drive the cattle (some 350 heads) directly from Santa Olaya northwest to San Sebastián. While the southern route—chosen for the first three groups—had access to water at Santa Rosa, the shortcut between Las Angustias and San Sebastián—the route for the fourth group—was expected to be a two- or three-day stretch without water for the animals. It was planned that the four parties would rendezvous at Santa Catharina (at the southern end of Coyote Canyon in the present Anza-Borrego State Park).

The first group left Santa Olaya on Saturday at 9:30 at the same time Garcés and his interpreters departed for the south. The land was flat, sandy, and salty, with only scant brushwood and prickly bushes for vegetation. They passed the brackish pond and wells at El Rosario and by 3:30 arrived at El Carrizal. "It is an awful place, with some reedgrass for the only pasture and permanent but very salty water," writes Font about the wells, the Pozos de la Alegría, which had once saved the first expedition. To improve the site, they "dug a [second] well, which filled with slightly better and somewhat more drinkable water." At this point they were in the middle of nowhere, 47 days and 120 leagues from Tubac, on a cold gray day under heavy clouds. "Some fifteen leagues to the south we can see the long and rugged sierra Father Garcés named San Geronimo [the Cocopah Mountains] on the other side of San Jacome [Cerro Prieto], and beyond that, the Sierra Madre de California....Very far to the northeast is the Sierra de San Sebastián [the Chocolate Mountains] and directly north, beyond the sand dunes, in the distance, the rugged mountain chain, which, coming from La Campana [Castle Dome Peak] goes to join the Sierra Madre." Careful to leave fuel for the subsequent groups, the fires were allowed to die out shortly after dark, leaving the small camp shivering in the empty desert.

After Font said mass and the animals were watered, Anza gave the order to march. The notes of the Alabado followed the processions, six leagues from each other and starting west at about the same time from El Carrizal and from Santa Olaya. The terrain was similar to the day before and the sporadic sun brought little warmth. The ground was intermittently soft sand, which slowed down the horses. In the early afternoon they passed the wells at Pozos de la Alegría and after that they came upon an occasional wash where rivers once flowed. They identified tracks left by the first expedition before passing the last, and now almost depleted, well at Las Angustias.

Having covered some seven leagues, they set up camp at 5:30 in a broad, sandy crevice without pasture or a hint of moisture. Font names the area Barranca Seca (Dry Canyon). The site provided an abundance of prickly bushes that some gathered in the fading light to fuel their fires. Others passed out rations of corn, forage, and water carried all the way from Santa Olaya for the animals. The December night was long and, according to Anza, "extremely cold." Unable to sleep, at 3:00 a.m. he dispatched an advance party (some of the same scouts who had explored the route in November) to prepare the wells at Santa Rosa. The camp stirred, the animals were fed their rations, and by daybreak the group was moving west again.

The terrain alternated between sandy dunes and hard, whitish flats scattered with ancient marine debris. As daylight barely relieved the chill, the groups beyond the horizon also started moving, two following the first party's tracks, and the fourth one herding the reluctant cattle northwest. Yesterday's scattered clouds were now heavier and thicker with only the rare spot of sunshine breaking through. Fortunately, the animals' thirst was mitigated by the cloud cover and the low temperatures.

The day's monotony was evident in the journals' records. While both men agreed they marched for eleven hours, Anza estimated they covered ten leagues whereas Font put the distance at fourteen. In the fading light they reached Santa Rosa de las Lajas for evening prayers.

The advanced party had been digging wells for some time. "At first we were worried," writes Font, "because there was no water, but they worked hard in deepening the wells and it was the wish of the Most Holy Virgin of Guadalupe, our Patroness, that water should appear. Had it not been for that, the expedition ran the risk of perishing on her feast day, which is tomorrow, for lack of water."

Using wicker baskets to bring water to the animals was a slow process, but by 10:00 p.m. most of them had drunk. A total of six wells were dug, widened, and made deeper, and the water gradually refilled them. With temperatures dropping and little firewood at hand, they spent a cold and miserable night at Santa Rosa. At 2:00 a.m., by the light of the moon, the men still working the wells, Anza returned to watering the horses, beginning with those that had not had any. The effort continued all night and through the morning, life-giving water enabling the animals to feed on the forage they had carried with them. The clouds touched the sierra while a gusting wind kept the temperature around the freezing point.

With the well work completed, Anza was satisfied that the groups following would have adequate water upon their arrival. "The sources are now flowing so well," he writes, "that as long as they are kept clean, they can supply, with a small delay, enough for more than three hundred animals. And if they were made permanent they would be even better for in that case they would be deepened still another yard beyond what they now are."

They left Santa Rosa shortly after noon (at 12:30 according to Anza; at 1:45 by Font's clock), moving almost directly north. Covering four leagues through mostly flat and hard ground they came to camp on a dry creek bed chosen for its "abundance of firewood and some pasture," writes Anza, "but especially the former, desperately needed to repair the bitter cold and...the rain that is threatening on the horizon."

"Toward noon a cold, stiff wind began to blow from the west," records Font, "coming from the dark, cloud-covered Sierra Madre..., where it appeared to be raining. It picked up in the afternoon and continued through the night almost as strong until dawn. The...wind, which must be frequent in these plains, is responsible for the various shapes of dunes, large mounds of sand resulting from the whipping of very small grains (as I was able to observe today in the distance) into thick...clouds [that move] close to the ground."

The camp awoke the next morning to not rain but blowing snowflakes and a biting wind from the sierra, where it was snowing heavily. Lifting camp by 9:00 they covered the seven leagues to San Sebastián in the same number of hours. Although the terrain was not difficult, an occasional soft spot in the ground caused the odd animal to trip, often while carrying women or children bundled in blankets.

The low-lying ranchería of a few Mountain Cojats beside a stagnant marsh could not have been a more dismal place. At its source "the water is not bad, but the soil is so salty in this depression that at times it is as white as flour." Due to the salinity, there were only reeds, poor pasture, and some small mesquite trees usable for firewood.

"As far as I can see," writes Font, "only a few mountain Indians… live here, perhaps twenty or thirty miserable, skinny, puny, and hungry souls. Coming out to meet us, they scattered at the sight of the first soldier, until he reassured them. It is a marvelous thing to see these Indians totally naked, as cold as it is here, and bathing, unperturbed, at the source, first thing in the morning….They have bows with a few poor-quality arrows and a wooden weapon made of thin hardwood shaped like a moon, three fingers wide and two feet long, which they use for hunting hares and rabbits by throwing it in a certain way so as to break their legs. They also catch them with nets made from fine threaded rope so soft it feels like hemp, although I couldn't find out what it was for lack of an interpreter. Their language, different from the Yuma, seemed to me similar to the Cojat. They eat the occasional hare, although there aren't many, sometimes maguey, which they gather in the sierra, but mostly the seeds and pods of mesquite and the reeds that grow in the marsh, which make their few remaining teeth filthy. They are so hungry they quickly ate, together with a bit of soil, some grains of corn the mules left on the ground. These Indians…seemed to me the poorest and most unfortunate of all I have seen."

Anza had the group gather as much firewood as possible "to cope with the cold and the wind, which returned forcefully at five, foreshadowing rain and snow…for the night."

Days 77 to 80
Thursday, December 14, to Sunday, December 17, 1775

A cold wind blew through the night, and morning brought a blizzard that kept the expedition fixed in place. Font took refuge by the fire in Anza's tent, where he spent the day. The changing conditions, however, difficult as they were, at least solved the shortage of water; they no longer needed to stagger the access to San Gregorio, their next source, or delay their rendezvous until Santa Catharina. They expected Sergeant Grijalba, following on their heels with the second group, to appear that day, but the storm had also stopped them somewhere. Instead, they spotted the slow-moving cattle of the fourth group coming toward them through the snow that afternoon. They had left Santa Olaya on December 10 and since Las Angustias had driven without feed or pasture.

The cold, dismal weather had been a blessing for the animals, although Font failed to understand or recognize this. From his journal it appears he did not personally witness their arrival and that, barely on speaking terms with Anza, he did not even get an accurate description of it from anyone else.

"The cattle," writes Anza, "which, as mentioned, came...by a different route than the rest of the expedition, arrived at noon. Ten animals were lost [along the way] due to exhaustion, but the rest, which had not drunk in four days, had so little thirst, due to the present climate, that after driving them to the edge of the water, most chose to feed rather than drink." Font's version, on the other hand, states: "While it was still snowing, the cattle, which had left Santa Olaya on the tenth,...arrived and, because it had not had anything to drink at all during those days, threw itself in the water like lightning. Eleven animals were lost along the way." By his own words, however, Font does admit that he had "spent most of day in the commander's tent," and therefore did not experience the arrival firsthand.

Font's inaccurate picture was probably inferred from what happened the following day, where discrepancies again point to the poor communication between Anza and Font. The commander writes that "during the night six heads of cattle and a mule died as a consequence of the extremely cold temperature, which actually froze the snow," whereas Font puts the number at "eight steers and a mule" and attributes the deaths to a combination of the animals' "gorging themselves with water because they arrived so thirsty" and the very cold night.

After the snow, which had plagued them all day Thursday, stopped, a bitterly cold night followed. Morning brought a vision of endless snow-covered mountains dissolving into fog in the low areas. Grijalba and his group arrived Friday at noon "dying with cold, having suffered the cruel previous day on the road." Caught in the open north of Santa Rosa and unable to make it to San Sebastián in spite of their efforts, several people had frostbite, one so badly "it had taken four campfires around the heavily bundled body to save his life." They had also lost five horses on account of the weather, even though locating the wells and finding them full had made their passage easier than for the first group.

In the afternoon a layer of fog descended from the Sierra Nevada with the renewed threat of snow and rain, but in the overcast day that followed, the temperatures softened. During the night, however, three horses disappeared, and the sentry, following their tracks until his mule gave out, reported that they had been taken by "the natives that came to visit us in the afternoon." Anza dispatched the sergeant and four soldiers to track the thieves "today…and tomorrow if necessary" and, once found, to "ask them [up to] three times to return the stolen animals, warning them that another infraction would be punished with the force of our arms." The soldiers were told to impress upon the natives "fear and respect" but refrain from using weapons "except if met with resistance." The party returned after nightfall having recovered the animals from two rancherías in the hills (the Superstition Mountains), where the natives had left the animals and fled.

When the third expedition group failed to appear that Saturday, on Sunday morning Anza sent two soldiers with twenty horses to find them. At 3:30 that afternoon, Lieutenant Moraga's group finally rode into camp, in the worst shape of all. The first day out of Santa Olaya they had been caught by the storm. Ill-equipped, without warm clothing or blankets, they had spent two nights in the open with little firewood. Several people were partly frozen and, neglecting his own care, the lieutenant had developed a severe earache that left him temporarily deaf in both ears. All survived, but by the time they reached Santa Rosa on the third day, they had lost fifteen animals and were, in spite of the cold, badly dehydrated. Moraga determined they needed a day of rest at San Sebastián before moving on.

"In the midst of the misfortune of the loss of so many animals that the snowstorm has caused us," writes Anza, "it seems [the weather] may have improved the health of our people. Nine days ago, fifteen were ill, three of them in danger; today not even five are sick and none seriously. This sudden well-being, which we had not seen since the start of the march, can also be attributed to the many watermelons [and fresh produce] that were consumed at Santa Olaya."

Also, in spite of some losses, a majority of the cattle had survived; only two heads had perished that day out of the more than three hundred that had made it across the desert. Without fully developing his argument, Anza was in effect comparing the present situation to the time the first expedition had spent at San Sebastián, when the brackish water had sickened many of the animals. He credited the better water quality on this second visit to the dilution resulting from the storm.

The improvement in the temperature and the arrival of the last remaining group brought the expedition a mood of happiness and relief. "That night," writes Font, "with the joy of all being reunited, a raucous party broke out among them and a rather wild widow sang some bawdy verses to the loud approval and applause of the riffraff. This bothered the man with whom she was living, [and he] punished her." Font does not elaborate on what form the punishment took but, from what followed, it was obviously enough to interrupt the festivities: "Hearing [the noise], the commander came out of his tent and reprimanded the man who was punishing her." At this point, according to his journal, Font intervened, telling Anza that the man was correct in his action, to which Anza replied: "No Father, I cannot tolerate these excesses in my presence." But Font, in powerless disagreement, concludes: "He restrained that particular excess but did nothing to restrain the excess of the party, which lasted until quite late."

Days 81 to 85
Monday, December 18, to Friday, December 22, 1775

Font was still upset the next day. "I said mass and with it I couldn't help but say a few words condemning the raucous party of the previous night because, rather than giving thanks to God for having come through alive when they could have perished painfully as the animals, they seemed to be thanking the devil with such parties. It didn't seem to sit very well with the commander because he didn't speak to me all morning, but that happened to me many times. As a matter of fact, [he didn't speak to me] during most of the trip; he was so touchy and haughty he would take offense at any little thing [I said], making a mountain out of a molehill. Sometimes he would spend two or three days or longer…addressing me only the odd word and cutting short any attempt at conversation. Together with the illness that afflicted me constantly, this situation served as my cross to bear. Thanks be to God!"

The morning following the party, reality came rushing back to the camp. Two more heads of cattle had died that night and five others were unfit to continue. They were slaughtered and their meat salted, but its appearance, smell, and taste were so poor that Anza questioned whether it would be usable. Preparations for departure continued all morning. The forage carried from Santa Olaya was dumped to make some twenty mules available so adults and children didn't have to ride on the same animal.

After a cloudy week the sun was back in the sky and the general mood, Font notwithstanding, was positive. By 1:30 the long procession had left San Sebastián, moving west-northwest. Near and far, the mountains sparkled in their brilliant cover, particularly the sierra toward which they were moving. The flat road was sandy and firm, marine debris ground into flour over millions of years. After three and a half leagues they halted in a wide canyon with adequate pasture and firewood.

Leaving camp at 9:30 the next morning they covered four leagues in as many hours to reach the well at San Gregorio (near the present-day Borrego Springs). They advanced slowly and conditions were not difficult, but still three horses and four steers didn't live through the day. "The animals are so dried up and thin they bear no resemblance to the ones that began the march," writes Anza, "especially those that weren't used to the cold, which is most of them. Of the ones from the presidios, which [actually] do twice the work, we haven't lost any." The water at San Gregorio was good but the source gave out before half the herd had been watered. Working into the night they dug several new wells, but still the supply was not enough for all.

The temperature dropped again and with it the animals, "three horses and five steers during a night so cold that, busy stoking the fires, hardly anyone slept." Some animals, thirsty and restless in the darkness, broke loose in a stampede, retracing their steps. A detachment was sent in pursuit at first light, but without water at camp, the expedition couldn't wait for their return. Moving northwest they began a gradual ascent following the canyon toward Santa Catharina (Coyote Canyon). They covered four leagues before reaching a point where the stream was actually flowing with clean water and there was good pasture. Some women gathering seeds in the area were frightened at the expedition's arrival, and they fled, leaving behind their baskets, a bow, and some skins. Attempts at coaxing them back failed, so their possessions were placed in evidence to be recovered by their owners.

The next afternoon, "four 'gentiles' came to camp, so skinny and withered that they looked more dead than alive," writes Anza. "As they were extremely uneasy I tried to reassure them with the usual welcome and presents, giving them food and returning the objects the women had left behind, part of which they took with them. Soon after, another six came, not as unhealthy looking, and recovered the rest of the items. These came under the impression that, because we had not hurt the first group, they would not be hurt either, a practice common among Indians, who often put only their weak and useless at risk to test our intentions."

Without word from the detachment, Anza, concerned with the loss of animals and uncertain how many would be recovered, sent two additional soldiers with extra horses to help with the roundup; "I gave orders that they should drive the cattle as slowly as possible to minimize losses." He also sent soldiers to recover the other animals that, too weak to continue, had been left behind the previous day. As it turned out, most of the escaped herd had returned to San Sebastián, where some fifty animals had perished in the swamp, but by late Friday the sergeant had returned with the survivors.

The losses were a significant setback that Anza tried to explain as an accident: "The stampede was not due to any lack of attention or care…as from the beginning I have provided seven men for this purpose, to guard, watch, and drive the herd, advancing or delaying their pace as required, and no effort has been spared to prevent any misfortune. Yet, the aforementioned has occurred, as painful as it is irreparable."

Font, however, attributed responsibility for the incident to the commander: "Since the mule trains were so long (at forty cargoes each) and overloaded when we left San Miguel [de Horcasitas] and the drivers so inexperienced that only one knew his trade well, the others learning on the road, the mules were badly abused. And thus for not spending money on good drivers, we were now paying the price in lost mules and horses, besides the fact that we would not stay where the animals could rest and recover but had to stop in dismal locations. Perhaps it was these losses and delays that had the commander in such a foul mood. He spent the day in his tent and I in mine without speaking or seeing each other except at mealtime."

The heavy clouds settling over the hills seemed to reflect their mood. With the mountains under a blanket of snow, the tents in the canyon dripped silently through the night while the stream sang softly to the sleeping camp.

Days 86 to 89
Saturday, December 23, to Tuesday, December 26, 1775

With the detachment back at camp, unable to recover any more animals, Anza gave the order to march under an overcast sky, and by 12:30 they were following the canyon northwest in a light drizzle. They passed the willow where Garcés had once warned about the natives spearing a horse and, after covering only a league and a half, set up camp by the source of the Santa Catharina stream. "We saw several Indians between the rocks high in the hills," writes Font, "dark, wretched, small-bodied, totally naked, and reticent as stags. Shortly after we arrived, the commander went to visit their ranchería, and when they saw that we did not hurt them, two came with some firewood and a head of mescal, which they offered to the commander. I tried it and it tasted very good. This being the season [for mescal] perhaps explains why there are now more Indians in the area than the last time. But they are so distrustful that [most of them] remained hidden behind the high rocks and not one woman let herself be seen."

The miserable weather continued, but by 9:30 on December 24, the expedition was again moving along the canyon. "The surrounding hills are rocky or piled with stones of all sizes such as found in rivers, with some sandy or arid soil [in between] and not a tree or anything useful on them." They passed natives who mostly kept their distance on the ridges, except for only one woman courageous enough to approach them, who was rewarded with a string of beads.Following the rain, a thick fog descended upon the train, reducing visibility and slowing their progress to a crawl. They were near a ranchería when one of the women's labor pains forced the expedition to halt after only three leagues. In spite of the two easy days and improved feed and water, the cattle were still extremely weak, and five animals died.

That afternoon Font approached Anza: "Sir, even though my opinion is worth little and I don't play any role here, I cannot help but inform you that I am aware that there will be drinking tonight."

"There will be," answered the commander.

"Well, sir," continued Font, "it does not seem to me appropriate to celebrate the birth of the child Jesus by getting drunk."

"Father, I do not give them [brandy] to get drunk."

"That is as it should be, because that would be an even greater wrong, but if you know that they will get drunk, don't give it to them."

"The King authorizes it and it is issued to me for the troops."

"That is well and good," replied Font, "but it's understood [to be for use] in case of necessity."

"Father, to get drunk is a lesser evil than doing something else."

"Sir, drunkenness is a sin, and the one who cooperates [by making it possible] is also guilty…; thus, if you know that it takes so much for one to get drunk, give him less or don't give him any at all."

"[Anza] didn't answer another word," writes Font, "and I retreated to my tent unable to prevent [the coming] disorder because he had already decided to issue…a measure of brandy to each one. But when it was [being] distributed he did announce in a loud voice: 'Make sure you don't get drunk, because if I find you drunk outside your quarters, I will apply the penalty.' With this he satisfied his conscience and, that night under the influence…, the people celebrated, singing and dancing without a thought for the dark sierra, the rains, the delay of the animals, or the exhausted and dying cattle."

The woman whose condition had halted the expedition that afternoon had exactly a month before at the Colorado River also suffered labor pains. Fearing the worst, Font was called to her side while the camp celebrated, but this time the pains served their purpose and before midnight another baby was welcomed as a new member of the expedition.

Christmas morning was cold, damp, and foggy, the sun making a feeble appearance in the afternoon. Font celebrated three masses, baptized the newborn with the name of the savior, Salvador Ignacio, and delivered a sermon on the intemperance of the previous night, which "did not sit well with the commander judging from the dryness and lack of courtesy he showed me all day." Orthodox and inflexible, Font was disturbed that the Noche Buena, the "Good Night" of Christ's birth, had been profaned into one of excess—eating, drinking, dancing, and debauchery. "Oh World, World that everything turns upside down," he writes. "The most sacred days become the most profane!"

Because there was not enough water for the cattle, the herd was sent ahead along the canyon while the expedition spent Christmas Day resting. That night, either ill or spiteful, Font was absent from dinner, and after the meal Anza (perhaps to avoid another clash) sent the comptroller to him with a message: "The commander wishes to know if Your Reverence has any word for San Gabriel." A puzzled Font replies: "How for San Gabriel?"

"He then told me that after the next day's journey, Anza was dispatching an advance party to that mission. I would write, I told him, but how am I to do so at this late hour? The fact is that he had decided to send that courier long before. He had made the decision at the Colorado River to send it from [the Pass of] San Carlos but did not tell me [then] and only lets me know at the last minute."

"Well Sir," concluded Font curtly, "you may tell [the commander] that I will write when we arrive tomorrow and that if [the letter] cannot be sent, I shall bear it with patience."

Dawn on Tuesday, December 26, was cold and clear; the early morning sun suggested the weather might finally be changing. Having ensured that the newborn and his mother were capable of moving, Anza gave the orders to lift camp after Font celebrated mass. The mules were packed and with the caravan ready by 9:00 a chorus of voices again intoned the marching hymn. As they moved northwest on the tracks of the cattle, the sunshine vanished behind a fine drizzle. It was a slow and gradual climb along the canyon, over a small hill and into a widening high valley. The drizzle was mixed with a light snow and the vegetation was richer—small oaks on the green slopes, pines at higher elevations. Font and Anza rode in silence.

They passed a ranchería where the ashes were still warm and the tracks fresh; invisible eyes watched them from a distance, and now and then a human figure was profiled on the ridge. After four hours they had covered less than three leagues, and by 2:00 they had set up camp under a drizzling sky near the Pass of San Carlos. "Toward sunset," writes Anza, "we heard a strong, distant thunder that was followed by an earthquake lasting four minutes." Font mentions feeling a mild aftershock shortly after, but he had other things on his mind:

"When I was getting ready for bed late that night, the comptroller came to my tent and said: 'Father, the letter?' 'What letter?' I answered. 'For San Gabriel,' said he."

"Your Lordship," said Font, "enter and listen. How was I to know that there would be time to write?…Neither you nor the commander have told me anything, nor has he mentioned a word on the subject all day, and since our arrival this afternoon at 2:00, the courier could already well be four or five leagues on his way.…Not being informed about this—I am never told anything; the servants, the boys even know what decisions are taken before I do—I assumed that the courier was on his way."

"Well, no, Your Reverence," answered the comptroller, "the courier will leave at dawn tomorrow."

"In that case I will write a note to the fathers," Font said, "even at this late hour."

"So I wrote my letter and took it to the commander who, aware of my conversation with the comptroller, was even more unpleasant than usual, and giving it to him I returned to my tent without exchanging…a single word."

Days 90 to 94
Wednesday, December 27, to Sunday, December 31, 1775

Three soldiers made up the courier carrying letters not only to San Gabriel but also to San Luis Obispo, San Antonio, and Monterey. "Given the poor condition of the herds," writes Anza, "and the difficulty in going directly from this area to the Presidio at Monte Rey…as I have always wished, and up to recently intended to do, I have been forced to change plans for fear of the large losses we are certain to experience. Instead, to minimize the loss of animals, [I plan to follow the familiar route] and obtain the cooperation of the missions along the way. Therefore, I have sent advanced warning…of the approximate date of our arrival [to each mission] and requested the commander Don Fernando Rivera y Moncada to make arrangements for the supplies we will need at each location to supplement our own."

The slight distortion of the truth in this entry (intended for the viceroy) is an example of Anza's pragmatism and diplomacy. Obviously under pressure to explore a possible shorter Sonora-to-Monterey connection along the corridor favored by Garcés, Anza used the excuse of the exhausted animals to do what he had always intended to do. In both expeditions, the commander had been unwilling to take risks that would endanger his principal objective, which, in the present case, was to deliver the families to Monterey with their goods and cattle. What he would not attempt with a handful of soldiers in the first expedition he certainly would not consider with a group including so many women and children, but he portrayed himself for the record as exercising good field judgment in the face of changing circumstances.

In the letter to Rivera y Moncada, Anza also dealt with the plans for founding the new settlement, which would require the commander's cooperation. "I also requested the commander to make the necessary preparations so that upon my arrival at the garrison we could proceed without delay, together with the captain of the vessel, if present, to explore the River of San Francisco."

Leaving San Carlos at 9:45 toward the northwest, the expedition entered an area of rich pasture and vegetation fed by the moisture trapped by the San Jacinto and Santa Rosa Mountains. The ranges, in front and to their right, were at that moment so covered with snow that they "inspired horror to most of our people,…coming as they did from a warmer climate." Recalling how they had suffered cold and lost animals when there was only a little snow on the ground, women wondered in tears how they were going to cope where the snow was so abundant. "But to these concerns," writes Anza, "I explained that by going near the coast, as I had decided to do, the climate would be as in their country, and that in the missions located along the way we would be able to rest and obtain the assistance we needed." By 2:30, having covered six leagues, they camped near the source of a stream. They were in the Valley of the Prince (Terwilliger Valley) when Font observed "the terrain is completely different since crossing the pass of San Carlos."

That night, the woman recovering from childbirth was in extreme pain, and the expedition took a day of rest while the cattle went on ahead. On the morning of December 29, they resumed the march from San Patricio, following the stream (the Bautista Creek) until it opened into the Valley of San Josef and became the San Jacinto River. It was a long day's march covering six leagues in seven hours, during which they were forced to constantly cross and re-cross the stream in a narrow canyon. They passed some huts hastily abandoned, and toward dusk they saw the natives, always following at a safe distance, before they disappeared into the night.

December 30 was "not as cold as we had expected in spite of our being so close to the snow-covered sierra, and I felt much relief from my ailments," writes Font. "No sooner had we crossed the Pass of San Carlos than I began to experience improvement. The beautifully crystalline waters of the stream, flowing from the Sierra Nevada through a canyon so luxuriant we named it Paradise Canyon, agreed well with me."

It was a satisfying march of five hours through the wide valley to camp between a hill and the lake of San Antonio Bucareli, again covered with thousands of geese. After mass the following morning, the expedition traveled one league directly west (to avoid Mount Russell) before marching west-northwest for the rest of the day. Covering seven or eight leagues in seven and a half hours, they came to camp on the banks of the Santa Ana. "We walked a league through flat terrain followed by three more through a wide and fertile valley, which communicates with that of San Josef before crossing a gentle pass over some hills and descending into a canyon that led into the Valley of Santa Ana. But it was still another three…to the river. The land is moist and the hills have an abundance of rosemary and herbs, sunflowers in bloom, vines as plentiful as a vineyard and requiring only little cultivation to yield good grapes. In short, the land appears very good and if only it had some trees one could not ask for more.

"The Santa Ana River runs in a deep channel and carries a lot of water. It is only four to five, at the most six, yards wide at this location but so deep it had very few and difficult fords due to the strength of the current….The beautifully clear water originates in the Sierra Nevada and flows from the northeast to the southwest between hills. A few elms grow on the banks, the only trees in the lowland, although in the sierra there are pines and perhaps other [trees] not visible from this distance." Now that availability of pasture and water were no longer a problem, it was the supply of firewood in the continuing cold spell that had become their main preoccupation, and thus Font's frequent references to the lack of trees.

Days 95 to 98
Monday, January 1, to Thursday, January 4, 1776

The current of the Santa Ana was so strong it upset the animals and Anza considered it too risky for the people to cross mounted. Instead, they rehabilitated the bridge of the previous expedition and prepared an access for the animals to ford alone. The work took all of Monday morning and by noon, one by one, they were carrying their irreplaceable goods across the fragile bridge while the animals forded with minimum loads. In spite of all precautions, a bull and a horse were swept by the current and drowned, the only losses in the three-hour operation. Because the day was so advanced and there was wood available in the area, the expedition camped on the west bank but again sent the cattle and some of the horses ahead.

"About the time we had finished that afternoon, the three soldiers I sent on December 27 to San Gabriel arrived with the mission corporal and seventeen fresh horses," writes Anza. "He brought me the sad news that days earlier [in November], some 'gentiles' together with neophytes from the San Diego mission had rebelled, killing one priest and two servants and wounding the entire mission escort, after which they had set fire to the few buildings in the settlement. He added that they believed the Indians in the vicinity of San Gabriel were gathering forces to do the same there and, for this reason, had not forwarded my letter to Commander Rivera y Moncada [at Monterey], as news of the uprising had been sent [to him] the month before and they were now expecting him to appear [at San Gabriel] to take charge of the situation."

Early the next morning a return courier was sent to San Gabriel announcing Anza's arrival within two days, and the expedition train, with a new sense of urgency, started out from the Santa Ana by 8:30. The terrain was mostly flat with only the occasional gentle slope, everything covered in shades of green pasture. There was tender wild lettuce (which delighted Font) and "the constant long and soft song of birds similar to but somewhat larger than sparrows." Only the weather continued to be miserable with a persistent drizzle that soaked to the bone. They covered six leagues in six hours on the trail of the first expedition and came to camp by the Arroyo de los Osos, at the same location where they had stopped two years before. Camp was pitched in the rain, which, mixed with snow, continued well into the night. On a tree where Anza had in 1774 engraved the letters IHS (the Latin initials of Jesus, Man, and Savior) with a cross above the "H," Font carved *Año 1776, Vino la Expedicion de San Francisco* (In the year of 1776 came the San Francisco Expedition).

Despite the tempering effect of the ocean and the fires left smoking through the night, the soaked expedition still suffered in the cold. Daylight came through a heavy fog, which later lifted just enough to cling to the mountains, and by 8:45 Font and Anza had taken their place at the head of the reluctant procession. The landscape was similar to that of the previous day—bountiful and beautiful even in the absence of sunshine—but the waterlogged soil slowed the animals and they were unable to reach the mission that day. After covering five leagues, they camped by a creek two leagues short of their destination. They arrived at San Gabriel the morning of January 4. The priests together with the commander from Monterey, Rivera y Moncada, rode out to meet them while the church bells tolled and the soldiers fired a welcoming volley. The "Expedition of San Francisco" had reached Nueva California.

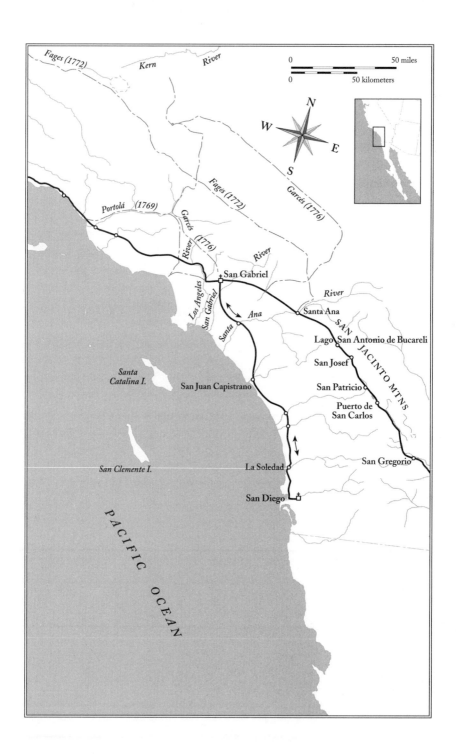

CHAPTER II

Unexpected Delay: The Native Uprising at San Diego Mission

January 5 to February 20, 1776

Days 99 to 104
Friday, January 5, to Wednesday, January 10, 1776

Commander Rivera y Moncada, a large and powerful man in his fifties, was a mestizo with a long and distinguished military career in the service of Spain. The son of a rural bureaucrat, he had enlisted after his father's death and risen through the ranks. Commissioned captain at age twenty-seven, he was given command of the Presidio of Loreto in Baja California. With a paternal concern for his troops, whose loyalty and respect for him bordered on worship, his reputation as a deeply religious person and a family man was supplemented by an excellent thirty-year service record in both Californias. The climax of his career had come in 1774, just after Anza's visit to Monterey, when he had been appointed military governor of Alta California, a remarkable achievement for an officer without family connections and of average intelligence, limited education, and a mixed racial background.

The celebration of Anza's arrival was soon followed by an exchange of views between the two men concerning the uprising and its consequences. Rivera's plan was to proceed to San Diego, where he would remain as long as necessary to capture and punish those responsible. The problem was that the rebels, according to survivors, numbered over six hundred and, after supplying escorts for the other missions, Rivera had only a dozen soldiers available. Regarding the expedition, he was of the opinion that his absence from Monterey would necessarily delay the establishment of San Francisco, which required assistance from his troops. At the same time, Mission San Gabriel itself feared the unrest could spread to their neophytes. Anza listened carefully as Rivera requested to assume command of his troops. "Having considered the given circumstances and judging that the Viceroy would approve my granting the commander help toward the important ends in question, I offered him not only the men under my command, but to participate myself personally if it should be necessary. To this end we agreed to notify His Excellency the Viceroy of our joint effort for whatever may be required in the service of both majesties."

The Mission of San Gabriel had reason for concern. At the beginning of 1776 it was a far cry from the starving outpost Anza had visited two years before. Relocated close to a spring almost a league to the north, it consisted then of three thatch-roofed wood and adobe structures (a combined priest's room and storage warehouse, the church, and the soldiers' living quarters) and a large number of huts for the five hundred natives that made up the community. An aqueduct between the main buildings and the neophyte village brought an ample supply of water. Surrounding the complex were open fields, both in grain and in pasture "of such quality that one cannot find any better," writes Font. "The cows are well fed and provide rich and abundant milk with which they make excellent cheese and butter. They breed chickens, pigs, and sheep, of which they killed three or four animals to celebrate our arrival, and I cannot remember ever having tasted more delicious mutton. They have abundant oak and other trees both for building and for use as firewood.

"Near the water source they have celery, lettuce, cabbage, watercress (of which I ate my fill), as well as other herbs. No wonder Father Paterna says [the place] is like the Promised Land even though the beginnings were far from easy and during the first two years they endured great penury, lacking almost everything.

"The priests do not believe in forcing Christianity but accept [for conversion] only those who voluntarily seek it. This they practice as follows: Because the Indians normally wander like animals over the land and mountains, they are [first] informed that to become Christian they must settle permanently in the mission and give up living in the wild. Should they [after joining] run away from the mission ranchería, they [are advised that they] will be found, caught, and punished. The priests then begin instructing those who have accepted these conditions and voluntarily joined, teaching them the sign of the cross and everything else and, if they persevere with the catechism for two or three months with the same interest, having completed their indoctrination, they are baptized.

"The day's routine is the following: Mass is normally said at sunrise. After, or instead of the service if no mass is said that day, the Indians assemble together and the priest leads them in prayer concluding with the singing of the Alabado. The same version of this hymn is sung at all the missions and, for uniformity, in the same tone, even when the priest may not have a good voice. A breakfast of corn porridge is then served before beginning the day's work....The Indians are taught their tasks by the priests, who also monitor and encourage each with his own example. At noon they are served *pozole*, a dish of boiled barley, beans, and meat, before returning to work for the rest of the day. Toward sunset there is religious instruction, prayer, and the Alabado. The baptized [Christians] and the gentiles are distinguished by their clothing or lack thereof, according to the usage of the country. While only Christians are entitled to the ration of pozole, the gentiles also regularly receive something from the leftovers.

"When an Indian requests permission to visit relatives in the hills or gather acorns, he is given leave for a number of days. For the most part, they do not fail to return, sometimes even with a relative who chooses to remain for the catechism, following the others' example or attracted by the pozole, which appeals to them more than the weeds and seeds they eat in the wild, which is why they are caught through the mouth.

"Religious instruction...is strictly according to Father Castañi's book, to which no one is allowed to change or add a single word.

It is taught in Castilian even when the priests may know the native language as in Mission San Antonio, where Father Sitjar…has translated the whole to the local dialect. Yet because the First Mexican Council has decreed that Indians should be taught in Castilian, they only hold one daily prayer in the native language, with everything else being in Spanish. [In this way] they are to be encouraged to learn Castilian because [their] languages are so primitive and have such a limited vocabulary.

"It is the policy of the missions that unmarried maidens live in separate quarters, and at San Luis Mission…the wife of the…foreman has the job of looking after them (which is a load off the father's mind). The young women look upon her as their mistress. During the day she teaches them sewing and other skills and at night confines them to a dormitory where 'they are safe from insults,' for which reason they are known as 'the nuns.' This seems to me a very good thing.

"Overall," writes Font, "the entire organization of the new missions seemed to me excellent, and I note that what is practiced at one is done at the others, except for San Diego, the poorest mission, where the location is inadequate for public or private plots, there are no native dwellings on site, and no communal serving of pozole. Instead, the Indians live in their own rancherías and are required only to attend mass on Sundays, as is done in Baja California."

Such is Font's vision of the communes where the faith, knowledge, and values of Europe are bestowed upon the indigenous people. And if such people had risen in anger against the institution in nearby San Diego, why wouldn't the same also happen in San Gabriel?

On Sunday, January 7, Rivera, Anza, Font, and thirty soldiers started for San Diego with the best horses and a mule train, leaving the lieutenant in command at San Gabriel. It was a clear day with a strong northwest wind, and without women and children, the small party covered ten leagues in seven hours to reach the Santa Ana River. The trail, in use since the Portolá expedition of 1769, was well known and documented, with the important landmarks already named. Anza therefore did not record any details of the route.

Picking up the pace, they covered fourteen leagues on each of the following two days in spite of the many hills and streams. They passed the site of a mission (San Juan Capistrano) whose construction had been interrupted by the uprising and then came to camp by a river of the same name at the end of the day.

Riding twelve difficult leagues on Wednesday, January 10, they reached the Ranchería de la Soledad, a Christian hamlet of the San Diego Mission. Greeting them, the village chief displayed three arrow wounds ostensibly received from the rebels during the uprising. "As I later learned," writes Font, "they were not arrow but bullet wounds suffered while fighting with the rebels. He talked to us [only] for a short time while some Indians brought firewood, because Captain Rivera was suspicious [of him] and made it very obvious. After dinner, [some] fishermen were [selling their catch], crying 'cassau, cassau' and brought to our tent the largest and most beautiful sardines, just out of the water, the size of [what] they call herring in Spain. I took a few and in spite of the [late] hour, cleaned them and [cooked them]. I ate three fried and one roasted on the coals. Anza only ate part of one because it was so late."

Day 105
Thursday, January 11, 1776

They left La Soledad at 7:30 and, covering four leagues in three hours with a strong north wind behind them, arrived that morning in San Diego. In the shadow of the nearby hills, the presidio sat on a small, uneven plateau at the foot of which flowed a river— occasionally a torrent, but most of the time a dry, sandy trail. It was located a league downstream from the mission and two from the sea, with the dry riverbed serving as a connecting trail. But since the night of November 6, when the thatch-and-wooden mission had burned, the survivors had been living at the presidio. Isolated and fearing another attack before help could arrive, the small community received Rivera and the troops with great joy and relief.

Because of the ease with which the attack was carried out, the priests suspected the rebels were helped by the neophytes, although the latter pretended to have been surprised in their sleep and forcibly held in place. Proclaiming innocence, they attributed full responsibility to the sierra natives who had refused to accept Christianity. "It cannot be denied," writes Anza, "that responsibility also lies with the [four-man] mission escort allowing itself to be surprised and only recognizing they were under attack when the buildings were already on fire." Unprepared, two soldiers were immediately put out of action, but in the chaos of the flame-lit night, the smith, the carpenter, and a priest, Father Fuster, managed to join the others in the palisade and resist. While arrows and embers rained upon them they held the attackers at bay through the night although the smith and the carpenter were eventually killed. The other priest, Father Jaume, captured by the rebels, was found dead the following morning, his body speared and his face disfigured beyond recognition.

"The mission natives claim," writes Anza, "that as soon as they were free they turned against the aggressors [in the dark] and chased them back to the sierra. But this counterattack of which they are so proud was undertaken without alerting or coordinating with our people, who only learned of it days after the fact, when they discovered some neophytes had bullet wounds." It was fortunate, however, that only the mission was destroyed. "The presidio," according to Anza, "would have suffered the same fate...if they had succeeded [with their plan]." They had intended to coordinate actions: one group surprising the stronger garrison first, with a second, surrounding the mission, ready to attack after the presidio was on fire. But the group coming to the presidio took too long to reach it, and the others unleashed their assault prematurely. Seeing the glow of the burning mission, the former assumed they had lost the element of surprise and, instead of proceeding as planned, returned to join the fight at the mission. As fate would have it, the sentry on duty at the presidio had attributed the distant glow to the full moon and did not raise an alarm. It was only when the wounded arrived the following morning that they first became aware of the attack on the mission.

From captured prisoners they learned that as many as forty rancherías had taken part in the assault. Because the neophytes in San Diego did not live in the mission ("even after they are baptized...they live in their villages together with the gentiles, who are a majority"), the Spaniards suspected they were also with the rebels. This suspicion was reinforced by the fact that the attackers had intended to capture the two cannons at the presidio. "That objective," writes Anza, "could not come from the sierra natives, who are ignorant of the use of even small weapons, but must have been instigated by the Christian neophytes, who have such knowledge."

"The result of the uprising has been a great loss to Christianity," writes Font. "According to Father Fuster, there were some five hundred converts living in the rancherías that, even though they deny it, we believe took part in the rebellion. But after the failed uprising they [all] fear punishment, keep their distance, and refrain from coming to the mission for instruction. The priest who was killed in the attack [Father Jaume] was fluent in the local language…, and his absence is also a great loss."

Days 106 to 113
Friday, January 12, to Friday, January 19, 1776

More than two months after the attack (which took place on November 5, 1775) and four weeks after receiving the news in Monterey, the military governor of Alta California was finally in place and ready to impart justice. In spite of their negligence on duty, he considered the sentries innocent of any wrongdoing whereas Lieutenant Ortega, the presidio commander, was held responsible for allowing to develop the conditions that led to the rebellion. According to Font, Rivera's judgment was colored by his protective attitude toward the soldiers and his dislike for the lieutenant, who was held in high esteem by the priests. While the root of the problem was cultural conflict (which the lieutenant could not be held responsible for), the visible culprits were, of course, the heathen and Christian natives Rivera intended to punish. Five presumed ringleaders held in the presidio had been questioned, but Rivera did not consider the information reliable. In fact, the investigation, according to his diary, was hampered by two problems: "First, that I have not found a single Indian I can trust…, and second, that we lack adequate mounts, Anza's horses being so…exhausted it was necessary to borrow animals from the mission."

On January 15, two neophytes were caught presumably on their way to join the rebels and, suspected of plotting a new attack, were lashed, both for information and as punishment. The lashing, in the heightened tension of the presidio, was so severe that one of them died. The other one, gravely wounded, was instead of being locked up nursed by one of the priests. "But the ungrateful Indian," writes Font, "finding himself somewhat better today, disappeared. They say he went to his ranchería."

In the stressful conditions of the crowded, "miserable, and unhappy presidio," a rift developed within the group. On one side, Font and the missionaries (Fuster, Lasuen, and Amurrio) tended to put into practice their Christian beliefs of charity and forgiveness toward the rebels. On the other, the military governor advocated the most severe punishments. It was a tense environment.

Alerted that several ringleaders were nearby, Rivera ordered a search party to prepare in secrecy. In the late afternoon, smoke signals rose over the surrounding hills. Under cover of darkness, the sergeant, an interpreter, and fifteen soldiers left the garrison in complete silence; only the commanders knew their destination. Stagnant days followed each other like the calm before a storm. Font was again very ill and, with boils in his mouth, had trouble speaking. Rumor spread that a whale had beached. A cold fog rolled in from the sea.

In the evening of Friday, December 19, the search party returned with four captives "welcomed [to the presidio] with fifty lashes each." Two were heathen captains whose rancherías had participated in the attack. According to them, the ringleaders were two Christians, one baptized Carlos (ironically, after the King) and the other, Francisco (after the founder of the Franciscan order). They were known to have escaped "with the religious images and other booty to the abrupt heights of the sierra from where it will be very difficult to extract them."

Days 114 to 119
Saturday, January 20, to Thursday, January 25, 1776

"In the afternoon," writes Font, "I was able to experience a live example of what the…mission fire must have been like, when a medium…structure…used as a forge caught on fire and could not be extinguished in spite of the efforts of all who came to help, which was everyone. I saw [in practice] what I already knew [in theory]: how extremely dangerous the branch, thatch, and grass constructions really are."

At the commander's request Anza questioned the new prisoners alone the following day to check their information. Afterward, Rivera released those considered innocent "to warn the tribe to maintain the peace and reject the troublemakers…, lest it bring about their own destruction." According to Anza, "Rivera assured [the messengers] that [any unrest] would be immediately suppressed and warned them that unless they delivered the two presumed ringleaders...or these gave themselves up, he would go after them with the troops."

In spite of the warning, a stalemate settled over San Diego. During the cold and rainy days that followed, smoldering boredom fanned the flames of tension. While drizzle, damp and foggy nights, and low clouds hid the surrounding hills, Anza waited to set a deadline for his departure. "Should it go beyond the present month," he told Rivera, "I believe it will prevent the timely execution of my orders. I would leave [you] ten of my soldiers to assist with the ongoing operations and continue [myself] with the other seven to deliver the expedition to Monte Rey. From there, in spite of the rains, I would proceed to reconnoiter the port of San Francisco and report my findings to His Excellency.

"To this the commander replied that, at the present moment..., nothing was more important to...God and the King than the total pacification of this important port, lest the rebellion should spread to all of Alta California. For this reason," continued Anza, "he requested me to refrain from removing any of the men under my command and not to consider going on to establish the [new] garrison and mission at San Francisco until this [area] had been entirely pacified. But such pacification appears to me to be a very long-term project, especially if it is to be followed by some exemplary punishment, which we are not in a position to deliver until after the rains end and the horses have recovered their strength.

"However, not wishing to oppose the will of he who is in charge of this frontier, it seems to me that my best service to the King consists of complying with Rivera's request to remain available until the return of the search party that he intends to dispatch to the sierra very soon. If the intelligence gathered by this party does not result in a campaign requiring my participation and troops, which is the reason for my being here, I will then return to [San Gabriel] to fulfill my orders. It is understood that Commander Rivera will not be available in Monte Rey...to receive the expedition and will take responsibility for that with His Excellency. I believe that my conduct would be reprehensible if I were to remain idle here for the months that the commander expects his pacification efforts to take instead of doing what I have [been sent] to do without jeopardizing his efforts."

A light drizzle continued to dampen the presidio, where the troops were kept busy improving the palisades and repairing buildings. Another beached whale was reported and, with Font's condition improving, he trekked down to see it. "But we made the trip, two long leagues, in vain, because what was stranded was not a whale but a large fish, about three yards long…, of which only the bones and ribs remained, the Indians having taken all the flesh. But I did see on this occasion the water spouts that the whales, which are abundant in those waters, cast up."

After dark and in total secrecy on January 25, the sergeant and sixteen men left the presidio guided by one of the captured heathens to surprise the two presumed ringleaders at the Ranchería de San Luis before dawn.

Days 120 to 125
Friday, January 26, to Wednesday, January 31, 1776

The following evening the party returned with nine captives including one of the village headmen and a woman recently escaped from the garrison. Still, the principal leaders remained at large. Two of the captives were found to be Christian, and a piece of church canopy and some vestments were recovered. After being lashed and questioned, two were held in chains and the rest released with a warning that "they would lose their lives if they helped or hid any of the rebellion leaders."

Without time to rest, the search party was sent out again for a second night. Carlos, who had been stalking the Spanish movements, was believed to be at La Soledad, and the soldiers intended to capture him before daybreak. "Although the captain of the ranchería denied it," writes Anza, "the sergeant learned from others that Carlos had indeed been at La Soledad and left the day before. The sergeant then had the man lashed and warned that if on another occasion he did not give us warning, he would be considered an enemy and treated as such."

In the absence of new intelligence, no patrols were sent out for three days. Concerned with their inactivity, on January 28 Font writes: "Tonight I asked Captain Anza what he was planning, given the fact that we remained in the presidio without undertaking any action to finalize the question of the rebels and that, in addition to consuming what little the priests had (which disturbed me), the days were passing and we were still so far from Monte Rey. To this Anza replied that Captain Rivera had not yet made plans for a campaign and that unless something changed, he [Anza] was planning to leave San Diego the following Sunday, eight days from today."

Days 126 to 129
Thursday, February 1, to Sunday, February 4, 1776

On February 1, a courier was sent via the California peninsula to the viceroy in Mexico with reports on the rebellion and its aftermath, and Rivera's plans, Anza's update on the expedition, and Font's letters to his superiors. The soldiers were to deliver the post to the northernmost mission, Velicata, provided it could be immediately relayed onward. If not, they were to continue to the next mission or as far south as necessary for the reports to be passed on without delay.

That Saturday five soldiers arrived from San Gabriel with news from Lieutenant Moraga. After providing for their two hundred guests during the month of January, the mission had been forced to cut their rations by half and could continue to supply them for only eight more days, as otherwise they would not be able to feed their own neophytes. The troops were, to say the least, "very unhappy with the situation as even the full [San Gabriel] rations were less than their normal military entitlement."

"Having conveyed this information to Commander Rivera," writes Anza, "we were both equally disturbed, because it will affect the plans we had made [and submitted to the viceroy] for the pacification of the Indian rebels. In light of the circumstances, we agreed, first, to send to the troops [in San Gabriel] a load of corn and beans from here, and second, that the twenty soldiers there should proceed [as soon as possible] to Monte Rey with their families, while the families of the soldiers on duty with us...should remain in place. We also agreed that I should escort the group past the Santa Barbara Channel, given the large Indian population there and the fact that last year they attacked our people, even if without major consequences. Beyond that point they should be able to make the necessary rest stops in the [San Luis Obispo and San Antonio] missions, which are now well established. In order to gain time, I will in the meantime go on to reconnoiter the San Francisco Bay Area provided the rivers are low enough to be passable.

"Although these decisions are contrary to the plans just communicated to His Excellency, the reasons for the change are obvious and motivated by the need to achieve…the pacification of this presidio, where Commander Rivera will remain, while I proceed with the preparations required for the establishment of San Francisco."

After Sunday mass, the mule train left San Diego with "mostly worm-eaten corn," according to Font, "for the people that had remained at the [San Gabriel] mission….It was [also] decided that we should leave the following day, although I was not informed of that decision…nor was anything said to me."

Days 130 to 137
Monday, February 5, to Monday, February 12, 1776

The plan agreed upon was the result of the continuing tension between the two officers. As military governor, Rivera was of the opinion that the men under his command were insufficient for the task of protecting Alta California, making him feel that, for reasons beyond his control, he was in a position in which he could not perform his duties adequately. For a commander with an impeccable career record, this possibility was very disturbing. To make things worse, the Franciscans were pressing to establish additional missions, and the viceroy wanted a Spanish settlement in the San Francisco area. Both facilities would further dilute his already limited resources. The rebellion had confirmed Rivera's worst fears: it was bad enough that the attack had happened at all, but unless he was able bring it under control, it would be on his record as a personal failure. Whatever reasons were behind the uprising, they were probably present elsewhere and, given the overwhelming numbers of the indigenous population, a simultaneous rebellion in all four missions could well mean the end of Spanish rule in Alta California.

From Anza's perspective, his task, as commander of the expedition, was to bring about the new settlement in the San Francisco Bay Area. He saw Rivera as overreacting to an emergency that, he felt, had merely provided the governor with the perfect excuse to obstruct any new establishment. Equally conscious of his career and reputation, Anza was as determined to press ahead with his orders. Thus, while Rivera would stay in San Diego as long as necessary to stamp out dissent once and for all, Anza would take the settlers on to Monterey and reconnoiter the Bay Area. The two officers agreed to eventually rendezvous at San Gabriel upon Anza's return to finalize any remaining business between them.

Although cordially negotiated, the new plans barely masked their conflicting objectives and would eventually result in a permanent rift between them. What Anza ignored at the time was the extent to which Rivera had already committed his prestige (in an earlier report to the viceroy) against a new settlement at the mouth of San Francisco Bay. "From that night on," writes Font, "Captain Anza was forever out of grace with Captain Rivera, so strongly opposed was he to that new establishment and, as Anza's companion, I also became the object of his hatred."

With the new plan reluctantly accepted by Rivera, Anza's departure was set for Monday, but constant rains and strong winds delayed it for four days. On Friday, in spite of the high streams, "six hands deep next to this presidio and the rest as high as rivers," they left San Diego. In two days they reached the Santa Ana River, where they caught up with the mule train, which had been struggling for a week on a trip that should have taken three days. By early afternoon on Monday, Anza's group entered San Gabriel, followed that night by the loaded mules. Meticulous Font records having climbed more than 125 hills on the way from San Diego.

Days 137 and 138
Monday, February 12, to Wednesday, February 13, 1776

Since dispatching the courier, the morale at San Gabriel had deteriorated. With supplies from the mission no longer available, the expedition was scrounging for food and going hungry. Anza's absence, six weeks of inactivity, lack of information about their departure and, as of late, insufficient food, had taken their toll. The captain's return and the thirty loads of corn and beans couldn't be more welcome, although it was almost too little too late. The troops, openly disgruntled, held the commander responsible. "We found the soldiers of the expedition," writes Font, "extremely unhappy, saying they had been deceived by Captain Anza and questioning [even] whether to continue. They claimed that having enlisted for a salary of 365 pesos and rations, they were now without rations and going hungry, had not yet received the cattle promised when they joined, and [instead of money] the salary was paid in goods charged at 150 percent of their value."

The depth of the dissatisfaction came as a complete surprise to Anza, who was even more disturbed by the events of the previous night. Five men (a soldier, three mule drivers, and a servant) had deserted, stealing twenty-five horses and a supply of glass beads, tobacco, and chocolate, as well as two firearms, a saddle, and other minor items. Their absence discovered during the night, Lieutenant Moraga lost no time in organizing a search party, but since the fugitives had taken five of the best horses per man and had several hours of lead time, they were at a significant advantage over their pursuers.

"I have investigated as much as possible," writes Anza, "to determine whether the mood of desertion exists among the soldiers and individuals that have come to settle in these lands. This I have found not to be the case, which agrees with the fact that none of them was among the fugitives. The soldier [from the Monterey presidio] believed to have been the instigator [of the escape] and to have enlisted the others is a daring and desperate man who already once before attempted to desert from Baja California on a reed raft."

Reassuring as Anza's theory may have been, the incident had again changed their plans and complicated their logistical problems. Given the flooded streams and soggy terrain after a week of rain, all of the soldiers were needed to help move their families. Therefore, the expedition's departure would have to wait until Moraga and the ten men returned, with or without the fugitives. But as conditions at San Gabriel were precarious and the additional supplies from San Diego were inadequate, they could not wait very long.

Days 139 to 145
Wednesday, February 14, to Tuesday, February 20, 1776
An impatient stillness settled over the group. The days continued overcast and threatening still more rain. Font accompanied the head

of the mission on his daily tasks, which that day included opening a new field to be planted in wheat. "I was pleased to see the recently converted Indians applying themselves to the plowing and other chores, taking on the labor of the priests, who teach them by example, and Father Paterna personally handling the plow." When the neophytes gathered for the afternoon prayer, Font played his psaltery to their delight.

That night two of the soldiers from the search party, their animals too worn out to continue, returned. "The lieutenant is following [the deserters] on their fresh tracks," they reported, "determined to capture them." But the fugitives, with better horses and stopping only to change mounts, were no easy prey. Moraga figured that sooner or later they would make a mistake, but he couldn't predict how long it would take.

The gray and gloomy weather alternated with rain and the occasional clearing. "Anza is ill," writes Font. "Since we arrived at the mission, Don Juan cannot keep anything in his stomach. But today he was worse, no doubt from the disgusting fare we are served. The cooks, filthy young men, prepare [the most] tasteless food as vile and dirty as themselves. And it doesn't help that we eat without a tablecloth on an old door used as a table, so encrusted with grease that one can scrape the filth with a knife. But personally, I attribute his vomiting to the shock and sadness he felt at the news of the desertions and seeing the people of the expedition so unhappy. He also is disturbed by the 150 percent markup on goods (especially as he had understood that they would be paid in currency) as well as by the people asking constantly for something to eat and trying to sell their meager possessions to the mission for food. He is extremely upset that he is unable to help. These, I believe, are the reasons he has been so unhappy and depressed these last few days, even when I tried to distract him with conversation or playing my psaltery."

As the days went by without any word from the search party, the situation became untenable. In pursuit of the fugitives, Moraga "may be on his way to the Colorado River," and with their supplies dwindling, the expedition could no longer wait at San Gabriel. On Tuesday, February 20, the decision was made to start the following day for Monterey.

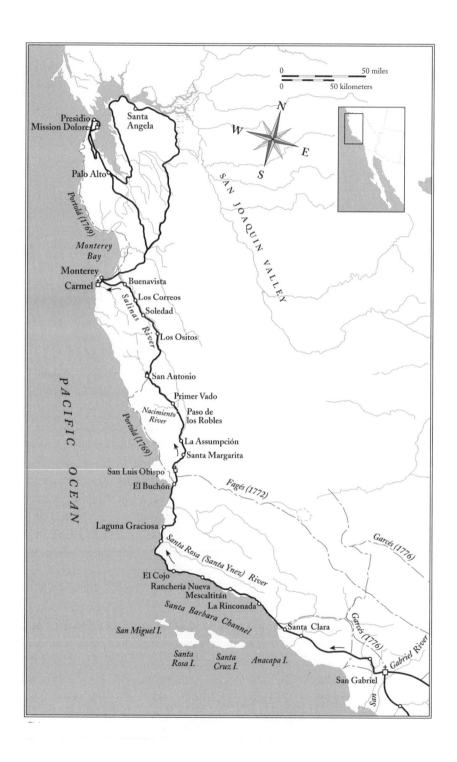

CHAPTER 12

Mission Accomplished: From San Gabriel to the Monterey Peninsula

February 21 to March 11, 1776

Day 146
Wednesday, February 21, 1776

It was Ash Wednesday, the first day of Lent, and Font's sermon that morning repeated the themes he had often preached before: "they had come [to this expedition as to this earth] to suffer, to teach the gentiles Christianity through their example, to endure their labors with patience…as penance for their sins, etc." Making a sign with the ashes he had just blessed, he left on each forehead the imprint of the cross, reminding them that "from ash we come and to ash we shall return."

The joy of finally moving again was mixed with the sorrow of separation. The bulk of the expedition would proceed north with Anza, but Sergeant Grijalba and eight soldiers would remain at San Gabriel with their families and those of the men currently in pursuit of the deserters. Anza had written to Rivera updating him on the desertions and the change of plan and requesting whatever additional supplies, if any, could be spared for those remaining. While waiting for Moraga's return Grijalba's men would take a mule train to San Diego.

It was 11:30 when they finally mounted; "seventeen soldiers, of those to remain in this California, and their families, plus six from my detachment," writes Anza. The animals were set in motion. Font intoned the Alabado and, with tears of uncertainty in many eyes, the travelers joined their voices in the familiar tune. "The earth is very green and covered with flowers," writes Font. "There are many miry places due to the rains, and the pack animals soon lag behind." They traveled west and northwest, covering six leagues to camp at "a site with permanent water and adequate firewood." Pasture had become so commonplace that it was no longer worth mentioning in the journals.

Days 147 to 149
Thursday, February 22, to Saturday, February 24, 1776

They had lifted camp (east of Cahuenga Peak in present-day Glendale) by 8:00 in the morning and continued west (essentially along the corridor of US 101) with the Santa Monica Mountains on their left. The day was clear and the wide, green valley was spotted with walnut and oak trees. With a firm underfoot and ideal conditions, they covered seven leagues according to Anza (ten according to Font) before camping by mid-afternoon. Being on the move again and the lull in the rains had renewed their optimism.

Leaving early the following morning, it was a harder day across the hills before finally entering the valley of Santa Clara. "Most of the women walked [instead of riding] down the last descent," writes Anza, "which is very dangerous, and we continued for another five leagues, which made for a total of ten hours, before arriving at 6:00 that afternoon at the Santa Clara River, where we spent the night."

"From the highest hill we were able to see the ocean," writes Font, "and the first islands of the Santa Barbara Channel....In the plain...an endless herd of deer ran like the wind after having spotted us, a low-flying dust cloud moving over the earth. Geese, ducks, cranes, and other birds crowded the river. During the day, we saw several [male] Indians, all unarmed and completely naked, but the women did not let themselves be seen. Hardly any left their huts. The soldiers from Monterey, being single, had scared them with...their unrestrained passions. This reserved attitude was evident in all the rancherías along the channel."

After sunset the fog rolled in from the ocean, wrapping the camp in a thick blanket of restful sleep. "It appears this is very frequent along the coast…but not harmful." It was still with them the following morning when they lifted camp to move west along the ocean. Following the Santa Barbara Channel, they passed Carpintería and Los Pitos before camping near La Rinconada, all rancherías named by Portolá in 1769. There was a high density of them along the coast with large and prosperous populations. "The entire route is on the beach, almost stepping on the waves," writes Font, "which makes it very amusing and would have been even more so if it had been clear instead of such a foggy day. The people of the expedition, some of whom had never seen the ocean, had much to admire. The Santa Barbara Channel owes its name to several islands about six to eight leagues offshore that form a sort of channel with the mainland.…But one could also think of the trail along the beach as 'channeled' between the sea and the land, which here consists of mountains, as if cut in half and impossible to climb, so steep and abrupt they are, even when covered with green, hard-packed earth rather than rocks. Often there is no way out but along the beach even though sometimes a trail, which they call the high road, runs along the very edge of the cliff tops with a long drop to the sea below.

"The Indians of the channel…trade with those of the Colorado River using [for currency] flat round shells they find on the beach. These are strung together in bundles and hung around their necks or worn on their heads. The men, completely naked, sometimes wear a string or something else around their waist (which covers nothing) and bundle their hair to hold a stick or feather or more often a 'knife' consisting of a flat piece of wood about two fingers wide, on which they attach by means of resin a sharp-edged stone, or, when they can get it, a blade or a piece of iron. This 'knife' is carried across the top of their head and held in place by the hair. They frequently also carry a 'sweat remover,' a long bone used to wipe off perspiration, which they claim is good to remove fatigue. Almost all carry horn-like tubes the size of a small finger inserted through the lobe of their ears, and some have also perforated the cartilage in their nose.

"The women wear deerskin around their waists and sometimes otter furs on their backs, but I didn't see many because as soon as they heard us coming, the young ones especially would hide in their huts while the men remained outside...to ensure nobody entered....The huts are the best I have seen on the entire route. They are large, high, and round, shaped like a half orange with an opening in the top center for light and to vent the fire in the center of the wigwam. They also have two or three holes on the sides for windows. The structure, consisting of solid, arched poles, supports walls of thick woven grass. The door consists of a straw mat that they hold shut from either side with a long pole or a whale bone. Once, to study their construction, I approached one that was open. Coming to the door, which I did not plan to enter..., I was not there two minutes when it was closed [in my face] from the inside and I withdrew offended. This is the result of the violence and extortion displayed by the soldiers on their passage through the area.

"All the villages along the channel have a large, smooth, and flat area surrounded by low walls where they play a game running after balls with a curved stick. Near the village they also have a piece of land where, marked with poles and boards, they bury the dead. The signs, painted white, black, or red, stand upright and can be seen from a distance....On them are hung articles belonging to...the deceased such as baskets, arrows, shells, etc., while the grave is marked with the ribs or other large bones of the whales that occasionally wash up on the beach. All the villages also have a common *temescal* or sweathouse, a partially buried, very solid structure of wood and earth, kept very hot. The Indians sit inside around the fire until their perspiration soaks the ground and then, overheated, run out to bathe in the nearby ocean.

"Although not very robust, these Indians are attractive and have a well-shaped body. The women are pleasant in appearance with their front hair arranged as a toupee and the rest flowing down their back. As with all the other natives, their weapons are the bow and arrow, but unlike the Apache and Pima reed arrows, these are made of wood. The bows are small, about a yard long, graceful and high-strung. Their lifestyle, without laws or king or any special knowledge of God, is similar to that of other tribes. Being skilled fishermen, they live on a diet of seafood and grain seeds, rarely experiencing the misery of hunger. They are, it seems to me, very clever and quick to learn. We understood each other easily through sign language even without an interpreter. But like all Indians, they are very prone to steal everything.

"Everywhere they appeared docile and peaceful...but I don't believe it will be easy to convert them. Not only are they fed up with the Spaniards' conduct, taking their fish and their food, stocking up with supplies when they pass the channel, taking their women and raping them, but also they are much attached to their location, where there is no adequate site for a proper mission. The streams carry little water and many don't flow at all during the dry season but, most important, even though timber and pasture are plentiful, there is not enough land suitable for planting. And [furthermore], the population is extremely large, the most densely populated nation of all I have seen.

"Among the Indians that came to camp I noticed one with a Pima cotton blanket, obviously obtained through commerce with them, despite the distance. There was another Indian with reddish hair who, I was told, was visiting from the island of Santa Cruz. This island, which seems to be triangular, although it was just barely visible in the fog, is about twenty leagues long, very fertile, and densely populated. It is really marvelous to see how skillful they are in navigating these seas."

Although his Eurocentric perspective remains strong, Font has, for the first time, recognized positive traits in a native group: social habits (games, saunas, cemeteries); practical skills (construction, navigation, commerce); attractive physique ("well-shaped" bodies); and intellectual ability ("very clever and quick to learn"). He has also realized that they have a functioning society with compatible values (justified outrage at the soldiers taking their goods and their women) and an attachment to their community. Their diet and standard of living are so good that, with the terrain unsuitable for agriculture, the missionaries could hardly improve upon them, and thus "they would be difficult to convert." Although unable to openly admit it, Font has recognized a native society that he considers worthy of respect.

Days 150 to 152
Sunday, February 25, to Tuesday, February 27, 1776

After an early Sunday mass the expedition continued west, following the coast along the beach. They passed the ranchería at San Buenaventura, where a mission had been authorized but was, for lack of supplies, still pending. At about noon they arrived at La Laguna, where they traded glass beads for baskets and a good supply of fish. "A boat was just coming to land…with many and different types of fish that I did not recognize," writes Font, "and I was able to see how they take a boat out of the water. Ten or twelve men approach and, lifting it together with its catch, carry the boat on their shoulders to the captain's (or the owner's) house. Their fishing instruments are large cylindrical reed traps, hooks made from seashells, and some small nets made with hemp string."

Covering a total of nine leagues, the expedition camped for the night in the vicinity of Mescaltitán. In a thick fog, soaked as if from rain, they left at 8:30 the following morning. They passed rancherías at Mescaltitán and San Pedro y San Pablo, purchasing additional baskets and other objects including stone cups and wooden bowls, which Font found surprisingly well made: "These Indians are so dexterous and meticulous in their work that, judging from what they do in their ignorance and with only stone instruments, given training and the right tools, they could really achieve beautiful things."

The fog, alternating between light and very heavy, was their constant companion as they rode along the beach that day. They noted the bits of sticky black tar cast up by the sea "stuck to the stones…or in small, fresh balls on the sand," an indispensable ingredient for caulking boats. They crossed streams flowing from the hills scattered with pine, "whose cones are so large and soft-skinned they break between your fingers." The smell of tar, sometimes "as strong as on a ship," masked the scent of the seaweed around them. "Toward noon the fog appeared to rise as smoke from between our feet…and it became so thick we couldn't see the people following behind us." By mid-afternoon, having covered almost ten leagues, they set up camp on high ground right next to the ocean and not far from the Ranchería Nueva.

Still in the fog the next morning, they followed the high trail on the ridge, "all ups and downs," until noon, when they descended to the beach near La Gaviota. By early afternoon, they passed El Bulillo just when the fishing boats were coming in. "Everyone supplied themselves with such abundance of sardines that a portion of what Captain Anza had procured…had to be left behind as nobody wanted to carry [any more of] it." After ten leagues they came to camp near El Cojo, having passed five rancherías, including two abandoned ones.

Days 153 to 155
Wednesday, February 28, to Friday, March 1, 1776

Driving against a cold wind, they left El Cojo at 8:00, heading west and around the point at La Concepción, which Font identified as the limit of the channel region. Bearing north-northwest they met the full force of the wind, "which caused us a cold and unpleasant afternoon." Beyond two small rancherías (named La Espada and Los Pedernales by Portolá), the beach became impassable, forcing them onto the high trail close to the fast-moving clouds before descending to a beach through large sand dunes. "The sierra that had been keeping us company on the right [the Santa Ynez] end at La Concepción, and from there the terrain is different: very green and covered with many varieties of grass, flowers, good pasture, and aromatic and medicinal herbs. Today…I saw a lot of samphire [a plant of the carrot family], very similar to that found along the coast of Catalonia except that the stem is taller and the leaves narrower. It was blooming in such abundance of yellow flowers, like small sunflowers, that it was a beautiful sight."

Covering the last leagues at sea level they came to camp near the Santa Rosa (today the Santa Ynez) River, which was difficult to ford except at the mouth during low tide. "After covering twelve leagues in eight hours, we arrived at the Santa Rosa at four in the afternoon," writes Anza, "but we were unable to cross over because the tide was coming in, so we halted to spend the night." And with the tidal water too salty to drink and little firewood available, they spent a cold night on the windswept beach.

"Daylight broke in a fog, which failed to burn out during the morning and by noon had turned so thick that standing next to the ocean we couldn't see it." During low tide they were able to ford the river and in the afternoon they covered some three leagues to camp at Laguna Graciosa. The following morning, March 1, a cold, damp fog continued to drift from the ocean, "causing us a distressing day."

Breaking camp early, they traveled inland toward the northeast and, "after climbing up and down sand dunes for three leagues, [came] down a long slope to a large lake, which seemed to me fed by the tide," writes Anza. The terrain changed from low-lying coastline with stagnant rainwater ponds to "shifting sand dunes that covered all traces of our trail and led us to a high and rugged sierra, the Santa Lucía, which begins here and runs all the way to the Mission of Carmel near Monterey." Entering the hills toward the north, away from the coast, they camped the night at the Ranchería del Buchón after an almost ten-hour day. The location, "with excellent water and abundant firewood," had been named El Buchón (Big Throat) by Portolá's soldiers for a large tumor on the throat of the local chief.

Days 156 and 157
Saturday, March 2, and Sunday, March 3, 1776

Before dawn Anza had dispatched a courier to inform the mission at San Luis Obispo (only two leagues away) of their impending arrival, and by 8:00 the expedition was on the move. The terrain southeast of San Luis Obispo was so swampy the cargo had to be unloaded and hand-carried to unburden the mules stuck in the marsh. The families were also forced to dismount, "causing some distress especially among the women, who had dressed their best for the arrival. But it was worse for those who hoped they could ride it out without getting their feet wet," writes Anza, "as they ended up getting soaked." The delay enabled their hosts to meet them on the road and guide them to a welcoming salvo and tolling bells at the mission.

"Our reception was commensurate with the joy felt by people who spend years without seeing [any] other faces than the twelve or thirteen priests and soldiers of the mission…during their long and difficult exile from the world," writes Anza. "And more so in this case, as they were very concerned with the events in San Diego, fearing another uprising might have happened or be about to happen elsewhere, as the rebels threatened."

The community had for some time lived in fear, suffering from isolation, lack of information, and limited defenses in the face of outside threats. Since Rivera's passage on his way south ten weeks before, San Luis Obispo had lived in ignorance. Had all the Spaniards in San Diego been killed? Had the natives revolted at San Gabriel? Had Anza perished crossing the Colorado? Receiving answers to some of these questions "dissolved their pessimism and turned them instead to thanking Divine Providence for such a timely gift of these auxiliary troops," writes Anza. "Dressed for mass, Father Figuer greeted us in front of the church with smoking incense and, as bells tolled and guns fired, we entered the temple singing the Te Deum," writes Font. "Our arrival was the source of much and reciprocal happiness."

Font goes on to describe the settlement. "The San Luis Mission is located on a beautiful site, a small elevation by a stream of excellent water, surrounded by fertile fields, three leagues from the sea and near the Santa Lucía Mountains. The mission complex consists of a large rectangular structure with a square hall in the middle and rooms in each of the four corners. Two doors, one opening to the center hall, the other to a yard with kitchen and pens, bring light to the building. A separate structure serves as the church, and a smaller one beside it, to house the young female neophytes…under the care and instruction of an older woman, the wife of a soldier, who teaches them personal hygiene and sewing. They are learning so well they [already] behave as Spanish young women. In front of the main building are the guard house and the Christian Indian dwellings, a ranchería arranged around a central plaza. The entire complex, neat as it is, is built of planks, reeds, thatch, and some adobe, for lack of other supplies, and [is] thus very vulnerable to fire.

"The [male] Indians of this mission are cleaner, neater, better looking, and with more attractive features than any other nation I have seen," continues Font. "The women cut the front of their hair to form a toupee while keeping the rest long, tied, or flowing freely down their back, as they do along the Channel. But the [San Luis] women have a more pleasant face, are cleaner, and have large, sparkling, black, and very lively eyes. Their [skin] color is pleasant, between pale and dark, and their face as attractive as that of a Spanish lady. Their personal hygiene and cleanliness is such, in both male and female, that they do not smell as other Indians. In addition, the women find Spanish men attractive and are friendly toward them. No wonder the soldiers were so disorderly [in their conduct] toward them when they were here hunting bears," writes Font, displaying his chauvinistic fiber.

After saying mass and pronouncing a brief sermon, Font baptized a seven-year-old child, with Anza as his godfather, and the expedition enjoyed a Sunday of rest. Font found the latitude of San Luis

Obispo to be 35°:17.5' N, within a minute of its correct location.

Days 158 to 160
Monday, March 4, to Wednesday, March 6, 1776

Having left San Luis Obispo by 9:00, they followed a stream along a wooded canyon across the Santa Lucía Range into the upper Salinas Valley. The sky was clear and the sun warm, the hills spotted with oak and laurel, the fields with flowers. Font identified the flora in terms of his European experience: spruce, alder, oak, pine, etc., but some of the American fauna was new to him. "There are some birds they call carpenters," he writes, "who bore circular holes on the trunks of the oak tree and introduce in each an acorn, so neatly packed that they are hard to remove. Some oak trees have the trunk stuffed full of acorns. It's the [carpenter's] way of...stocking up provisions."

They entered the valley following the Santa Margarita Creek (near the present-day town of the same name) and continued downstream to camp near the Monterey (now the Salinas) River at La Assumpcion [sic], just north of Atascadero. Anza, equating an hour's march with one league, estimated the distance at seven leagues, whereas Font wrote that they covered ten. While both overestimated, given the hills between the mission and Santa Margarita, Anza's number was probably more accurate.

Daybreak brought a courier who had ridden through the night from San Luis Obispo with letters for the priests at Carmel. "They did not write them the day we were there," notes Font, "because they did not wish to miss the opportunity of talking with us. They are so alone, the distances [between establishments] being so large, that it is a special day when they see people."

Sunshine flooded the valley the next morning as they lifted camp, forded the river without difficulty, and headed north. Turning northwest after three leagues, they left the flood plain and entered a rolling meadow spotted with oak trees that led into the Nacimiento basin. They named the meadow El Paso de los Robles (Pass of the Oak Trees, today's Paso Robles). One league beyond the Nacimiento, they came to another river, where they camped for the night.

"Our camp was on the banks of the San Antonio River, which follows a long glen from the Sierra de Santa Lucía, where...it originates," writes Font. "The fleas on this site were especially mortifying. We had already encountered them at the missions, but never as hungry, as numerous, or with such a hard bite. They seem to be a real plague in this land, particularly when the weather warms up, not only in the huts or sheds but in the fields, the trails, or at any stop, they are present!" While Font might have wished to name the site after the fleas, Anza named it Primer Vado, the "first ford" of the San Antonio.

Having left Primer Vado by 8:00, the expedition proceeded upstream along the narrow valley, fording the river two more times in the course of the day. The weather continued to smile on them, and by 4:00 they had arrived at the Mission of San Antonio de la Cañada de los Robles (Saint Anthony of the Oak Glen). The usual welcome ceremony was enhanced by the prompt slaughter of two "acorn-fed" pigs in their honor, "which yielded an abundance of lard," a luxury the settlers had not enjoyed for quite some time.

"The construction of the mission, with solid beams, adobe walls, and sloping roof (they have wood to spare here) is better than the others. There is a [central] hall with two small rooms at one end and [a larger] one at the other that connects [directly] with the church, which is attached. The hall opens to a large patio [where] the kitchen, an oven, and [animal] pens are located. Immediately adjacent is the vegetable garden and [nearby], the fields, which the fathers, with the help of the Indians, have enclosed by a very well made fence of solid posts....It seemed to me, in general, a very attractive and well-balanced mission [complex].

"The Christian Indians, who number about five hundred, are very different from those I have seen so far. They are from a nation in the Santa Lucía Mountains, whose name, if it has one, I didn't learn. Both men and women are small, unkempt, and ugly....They do not look after their hair [as others do]. Several women have stripes in their faces as the Pima. Their language has many shrill and unusual sounds and is difficult to pronounce. With perseverance and a lot of work, Father Buenaventura has learned it and [even] written the doctrine down in it. But since there are not enough letters for all the sounds, he has made use of the letter 'k' and various accents and symbols, which make it as difficult to read as it is to pronounce. The Indians pray in their language once a day but otherwise most of their prayers are said in Castilian."

Day 161
Thursday, March 7, 1776

The warm reception at such a large and prosperous outpost, the attractive and "well-balanced" buildings, the pleasant surprise of fresh pork and lard, in addition to the good weather made the day of rest one of widespread optimism. A solemn high mass of thanksgiving was accompanied by Font on the psaltery. The months of travel, the hardship of desert and mountain, the weeks of uncertainty all receded into their collective memory. Monterey, their last holding station, was only a few days away. Prayers were said for the pending exploration of the River of San Francisco and the successful completion of their resettlement.

And, as icing on the cake of their contentment, in the early afternoon Lieutenant Moraga and three of his men arrived at San Antonio. It had been four weeks since Moraga had left San Gabriel in pursuit of the deserters, and three since he had captured them between Santa Olaya and the Colorado. Returning to San Gabriel he had sent the prisoners on to Rivera at San Diego and rushed north to rejoin the expedition. He had not seen Anza since the beginning of January, so the two men had much to talk about. The search party had recovered most of the booty, including fourteen horses, nine having been lost to exhaustion or killed by natives. In addition, while returning through San Sebastián, Moraga had recovered several of the cattle abandoned in December and driven them to San Gabriel. In the same area, he had been confronted by "more than two hundred armed Indians, including [some] delinquents from San Diego," writes Font "who attempted to block his way." According to Anza, "they noticed…among these…gentiles possessions taken during the looting and destruction of the Mission of San Diego."

From his interrogation of the deserters, Moraga established that the problem had not been one of general discontent, as Anza had feared at first, but an isolated incident of seduction, bribery, and betrayal. "It appears that while we were in San Diego," writes Font, "the corporal of the San Gabriel troop fell in love with one of the women of the expedition." Wishing to gain her favor, he persuaded the mule drivers (by what means is not specified) to provide him with "chocolate and other supplies" from the stock in their charge. Having taken more than could pass unnoticed—including (for their own use) a certain amount of brandy—the mule drivers feared discovery and punishment. It was then that "they agreed with a soldier of the mission troop, who was unhappy and contemplating desertion," to escape together, which they planned for the night he was on sentry duty. While the corporal, the prime mover for the theft, had intended to desert with the group, at the last moment he decided to stay. "He feared the dangers of the journey and the justices of our towns if he left his post without a passport from me," writes Anza, "but [he agreed] that if they wanted to leave, he would hold their secret." Fearing retribution for their still undiscovered crime, the other five put their plan into practice.

On the basis of subsequent information, Font's diary closes the episode with the justice passed by Rivera: "To the soldier, who deserted his post while on duty, he did nothing more than discharge [him] from the military (which saved him from a court-martial), and the corporal, a distant relative of his, who bore the principal guilt, he did not even charge with a crime."

Days 162 to 164
Friday, March 8, to Sunday, March 10, 1776

In clear and cool weather, the expedition wound its way northeast from San Antonio into the Salinas Valley and continued along the "Monterey" (Salinas) River to camp at Los Ositos ("The Little Bears," near today's Greenfield), covering seven leagues in the same number of hours. A slight rain during the night brought a cold and overcast morning, which was spent following the widening valley northwest, past a site Portolá had named Soledad. "During the day several Indians,...different from those of San Antonio, came to our encounter," writes Font. "Some, rather clever, spoke a few words of Castilian and one even asked us where Captain Don Fernando [Rivera] was." The expedition covered some ten leagues that day to camp under threatening skies near the Santa Lucía Mountains, approximately west of present-day Gonzalez. The site, known then as Los Correos, was just the right distance from which to send a courier to alert Monterey of their arrival. "From here we wrote to

Father...Junípero Serra," notes Font, "asking him to send a priest to meet us at the presidio so that we could [together] celebrate a high mass of thanksgiving for our arrival."

Rain began during the night but after Sunday dawn appeared to be abating. "I therefore gave the order to set our convoy in motion," writes Anza in his laconic style. "We started northwest...along the river, turning west-southwest after three leagues to leave both the river and the valley [behind us] and arrived by 4:00 in a heavy rain...at the Presidio de Monte Rey. It has taken us 62 journeys to cover the 316 leagues from my Presidio, somewhat less than I had calculated." It had been 139 days since the expedition had left Tubac in October.

"After leaving [Los Correos]," writes Font, "we followed the Monterey River some four leagues to Buenavista, where we left it on our right hand and continued through hills and dales. Halfway through this section is the site known as El Toro Rabón (the Bull without a Tail), after which one begins to see the pine forests of Monterey. The road, like all the surrounding country, is green, leafy, flowery, fertile, and splendid. In spite of being soaked (we didn't have a dry stitch left on us), everyone arrived at the presidio overjoyed with happiness. The soldiers greeted us firing their muskets and the small artillery pieces they have.

"The Royal Presidio...is on a clearing where the pine-covered sierra ends, not far from the ocean and some distance from the port....It is shaped as a square, with the commander's house and the warehouse on one side; a small chapel and the soldier's quarters on the second; and the dwellings of the families living there on the other two. The construction is earth-covered palisade and some adobe. The presidio square or plaza, which is not very large, is enclosed by a stockade. Everything is rather constrained and, for lack of space, living conditions are very uncomfortable. The commander was lodged at the warehouse and I, in a filthy little room full of lime. The rest set up their tents in the square as best they could.

"The Bay of Monterey is the...area between the Punta de Pinos (Point of Pines), projecting into the ocean some three leagues, and the Punta de Año Nuevo (New Year's Point), extending out about twelve leagues, a long, open, and exposed inlet. The Port of Monterey proper is a sheltered area near the Punta de Pinos, which offers little protection against the predominant northwest wind and is so small that it can barely accommodate two ships in its shallow waters. The Punta de Pinos, about three leagues almost due north of the presidio, is some ten or twelve leagues southeast of the Punta de Año Nuevo."

Day 165
Monday, March 11, 1776

Having left the Carmel Mission before daybreak, Father Junípero Serra and four other priests appeared at the Monterey Presidio by 7:00. "Their arrival resulted in a great and very special joy to all of us," writes Font, "and after exchanging our affectionate greetings, we prepared to jointly celebrate mass." As the expedition chaplain, Font took the leading role in the ceremony. The chapel bells rang, "the priests sang beautifully, and the troops fired salvoes, moving us to tears of joy."

In front of the combined expedition and presidio gathering, Font pronounced a rambling sermon on the themes he had so often preached: "They had been chosen...and God had showered them with His bountiful gifts on such a long voyage, just as he had once done for his chosen, the people of Israel." He went on to correlate the numeral 165 (for the number of days since leaving Horcasitas) to "the Virgin of Guadalupe, the Prince [of angels] San Miguel, and (our father) San Francisco," the patrons whose protection they had initially invoked. "And to what end have we come?" he asked rhetorically. "To gain entry into heaven by enduring hardship in these lands where our good Christian example will contribute to the conversion of gentiles, whose souls are the precious flowers sought by...Jesus Christ."

On and on he developed his theme, moved by the implication of having himself been chosen as the spiritual leader in that great mission. He spoke eloquently, overflowing with emotion and forgiveness. "And so it was with our expedition. The Commander, in the name of the King, cast the net which gathered you in Sinaloa, etc....Let us then give thanks to the Lord, while I, in the name of God and of our King, give thanks to our Commander Don Juan Bautista de Anza for the skill, prudence, and patience with which he led and governed this expedition and promise him that God will reward his good work." Font's diary concludes the description with the following assessment: "God wanted everything to work out so well that I couldn't finish without shedding tears."

After mass, some of the priests returned to the mission while Serra stayed behind to meet the newly arrived soldiers and families. In the afternoon Font and Anza traveled with "the Father President" to accept the hospitality of the Carmel Mission, "not only in response to his insistent invitation, but also because there were no suitable accommodations at the presidio." Lieutenant Moraga was, during Anza's absence, left in charge of the settlers.

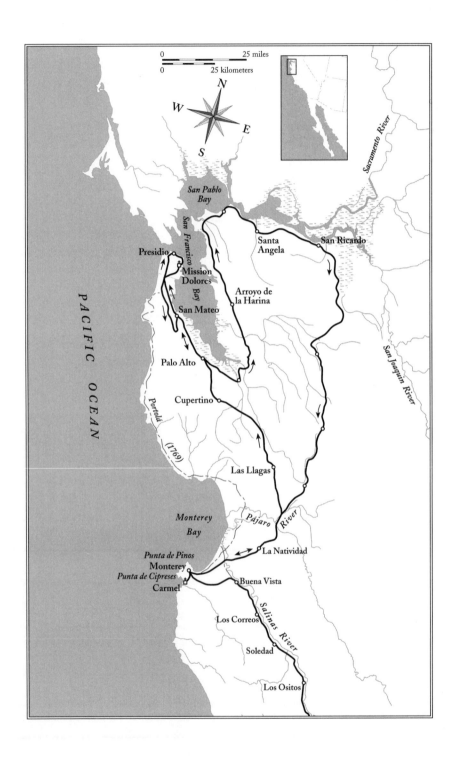

0   25 miles

0   25 kilometers

N
W   *E*
S

Sacramento River

San Pablo Bay

San Francisco Bay

Presidio

Mission Dolores

San Mateo

Palo Alto

Cupertino

PACIFIC OCEAN

Portolá (1769)

Santa Angela

San Ricardo

Arroyo de la Harina

San Joaquin River

Las Llagas

Monterey Bay

Pájaro River

La Natividad

Punta de Pinos
Monterey
Punta de Cipreses
Carmel

Buena Vista

Los Correos

Salinas River

Soledad

Los Ositos

Exploring the
San Francisco Bay Area

March 11 to April 8, 1776

Day 165
Monday, March 11, 1776

"We left the Presidio of Monterey at four in the afternoon," writes Font, "the commander, Father Serra, the comptroller, the doctor [of the presidio], and a few soldiers. Having covered a long league southwest, we arrived at the mission by five. We were received with great joy by the seven priests at San Carlos [del Carmelo], the excellent mission bells (especially a large one brought by sea) tolling, to which the soldiers replied with a salvo. We were then led to the church, where Father Murguía was waiting for us at the door. I gave the commander holy water as we entered in a procession singing the Te Deum with tears of happiness and, after giving thanks to God, we went on to the living quarters.

"The San Carlos Mission is located on a small promontory very near the ocean, adjacent to the Carmel River, which at that point flows into an inlet between the Santa Lucía Mountains and Cypress

---

1 Sebastián Vizcaíno was captain of the vessel that in 1601 explored the California coast. The name Carmel was given to the river and the inlet by the two Carmelite priests who accompanied his expedition.

Point, the location Vizcaíno named the Port of Carmel.[1] It is an excellent site with fertile soil and a healthy, cool climate, although occasionally foggy, as the rest of the coast. The mission has a well-built church (albeit of wood and thatch) adorned with several paintings. A second building, of adobe, has five or six rooms, including the three for the priests, a separate kitchen, and a forge. Surrounded by verdant growth, flower-covered fields, and mountains, it is a marvelous location with a cheerful view of the ocean.

"The Indians of this mission," continues Font, "which include some four hundred Christians, seem to me rather tolerable; neither as ugly nor as smelly as those of San Diego. They are mostly fishermen, and their catch, very diverse and of good quality, is plentiful. Besides an abundance of sardine, easy to harvest because the schools are so large, they also take excellent salmon, which enter the rivers to spawn. I am told that as far inland as San Antonio Mission the Indians harvest this fish from the Monterey River. We ate salmon here almost every day and…dried as much as could be had for the commander to take with him. In short, even though the other missions are good, it seems to me this one is the best of all."

Days 166 to 171
Tuesday, March 12, to Sunday, March 17, 1776
Tuesday dawned in fog followed by a misty rain and the occasional drizzle. It was to be a day of rest for Anza and Font, particularly enjoyable because of their newfound harmony. While Anza began preparations to leave for the Bay Area, Font thrived in the company of his hosts: "I visited fields a stone's throw from the mission and it was a delight to see the vegetable garden, so beautiful and well-tended by Father Palou, who devotes his days to it. It is a square plot surrounded by a band of flowers (already in bloom) and divided into sections of cabbage, lettuce, vegetables, and herbs." With Palou he discussed the Bay Area and borrowed the journal of his trip as well as one by Crespi, who had visited there with Pedro Fagés.

Four of the priests staying at Carmel were particularly pleased with Anza's arrival because they had been waiting two years to take up their assigned duties at San Francisco. While their objective was now within reach, they feared "Rivera's opposition to the new establishments and [that] his absence" would result in further delays, "in which case they were determined to return to their college." Learning of the situation, Font spoke to the commander on their behalf and, in an unusual display of cooperation, Anza "was so cordial as to inform me that he would be writing to Captain Rivera requesting his concurrence to go ahead with the...settlements and that, after writing the letter, he would have me read it."

It was while writing the following day that Anza was suddenly taken with such piercing and extreme pains that "I could barely breathe and thought I would suffocate and die on the spot." Paralyzed, he had to be carried from the table to his bed. "After hours of feverish torment unmitigated by the medicines provided by the presidio doctor, I took an unction made from a root of my province, which diminished half of my pains, although it was still impossible to sleep or even change position."

The letter, however, had been completed and in it, according to Font, "Anza told the governor that he was going on to explore the port...and, if he found a suitable site, on his return [to Monterey] and with Rivera's approval, he would take the settlers there, even if it took him an additional month. He urged Rivera to agree because the Viceroy would be extremely pleased to take possession of that port through a permanent establishment." This was, after all, the whole objective of the expedition Anza had been charged with. "Furthermore," the letter explained, "the people in Monterey...were unhappy with their temporary arrangements and, if the settlements were not established soon, they would lose the priests who [after two years] were no longer prepared to continue waiting and had decided to return [to Mexico] in the first available ship."

"It was this letter," explains Font, "that sealed their enmity, because Rivera realized Anza had taken the position (of Father Serra and the priests) to go ahead with the settlements of which he disapproved and to which he was entirely opposed."

For three days Anza lay feverish and sleepless, unable to leave his bed while the fog, clinging to the coast, sometimes turned to drizzle and the sun was only rarely seen. In the meantime Font, suffering an outbreak of mouth ulcers, "prayed to San Juan de Dios that he should give us health if he saw fit." And that, apparently, the saint did because, "with the good and abundant lettuce I ate there everyday, my mouth was almost entirely healed," and on Sunday, March 17, Anza was able (from bed) to dispatch eight soldiers to deliver his letter and, if needed, remain to assist Rivera in San Diego.

Feeling better, Font traveled that day to Monterey to celebrate mass for the people of the expedition. He was surprised by the crowded conditions at the presidio and, after only a week, the demoralized state of the settlers. "When I arrived many came to see me, complaining about their misery, the bad water (or none at all), the lack of soap, their inability to leave the presidio, etc." Subject to the strict orders of the absent military governor, and with Anza convalescent, Lieutenant Moraga had not been able to improve their situation. Font preached a sermon based on the day's gospel (the five loaves and two fishes Christ shared with those who followed him) and counseled patience and endurance, but upon returning to Carmel he promptly informed Anza of the seriousness of the problems.

Days 172 to 175
Monday, March 18, to Thursday, March 21, 1776

On Tuesday the fog lifted and the day was clear. Anza was feeling well enough to attend a high mass in which Serra sung the sermon and Font accompanied on his psaltery. Both the weather and Anza continued to improve and the decision was made to travel by Friday. "Both he and I," writes Font, "wanted one of the…priests assigned to the new missions to accompany us (which they were eager to do), but the Father President would not agree. He argued that Rivera would not look favorably on the priest's taking part in Anza's exploration and that, given how opposed he was to the whole project, he would use even such a minor excuse for continuing his obstruction.

"I spoke…almost the whole morning with Father Serra, who gave me a number of examples of the problems Rivera has caused…by his opposition to new missions and by withholding assistance to those established, all of which is contrary to the [official] policy of the Viceroy. He told me of Rivera's conservative use of his troops and his disregard for the opinion of others, especially concerning the negative consequences his orders were having on the missions.

"Our conversation...began," continues Font, "when I mentioned to Father Serra that [while] in San Diego, Rivera had stated that the founding of San Juan Capistrano [the mission whose construction was stopped by the uprising] had been poorly planned. 'I have never seen a priest more taken with founding missions than this Father President,' said Rivera. 'He thinks of nothing else than establishing missions in any which way.' He was attributing responsibility for what he saw as an ill-conceived and now abandoned project to Father Serra, and it was the pain of hearing this that triggered our long talk."

It was at this time that Font also learned why Rivera had unfairly attributed responsibility for the uprising to Sergeant Ortega, who was in charge of the escort at San Diego. During 1773, when Serra had traveled to Mexico City to plead the case for more missions, he had also requested the viceroy to replace Fagés, then the military governor of California. An aristocratic officer from Catalonia unhappy with his assignment in Monterey, Fagés constantly displayed favoritism for his Catalonian soldiers, disdain for the mestizo troops, and a despotic rule toward indigenous people, whether Spanish subjects or California gentiles. In addition to this conduct, repugnant to the priest and incompatible with the king's orders, Serra's aversion to Fagés stemmed from his condoning his troop's abuse of native women.

After listening to the case against Fagés, the viceroy had asked Serra whom he would propose as the new governor. At first "the Father President resisted suggesting a candidate but, after the Viceroy insisted..., asking him if he knew of anybody [in Alta California] suitably qualified for the position, Father Serra mentioned Sergeant Ortega, in light of his outstanding conduct during the first expedition."

"Sergeant Ortega," replied the viceroy, "cannot be appointed because he does not have sufficient rank, but Captain Fernando Rivera, presently in Mexico, is available and if Your Reverence approves..."

"To which," continues Font in his diary, "the Father President replied that he would agree to whatever Viceroy Bucareli decided, since, if His Excellency felt Captain Rivera was qualified, surely he would be a suitable candidate."

This, according to Font, was the beginning of Rivera's dislike for Serra and of his hatred of Ortega who, "through no fault of his own," found himself an antagonist to the governor, who saw him as a supporter of Serra and his expansionist plans.

Days 176 to 179
Friday, March 22, to Monday, March 25, 1776

"Having experienced some relief," writes Anza, "and being able to take a few steps, I decided, against the doctor's advice, to get back on a horse so that I could continue with the exploration of the port and river of San Francisco, hoping to recover my health with the exercise. They helped me mount the horse and, not feeling the worse for it, I rode as far as Monte Rey, where I spent the rest of the day and that night."

According to Font, they rode not only to Monterey but, before going to the presidio, followed the coast for a half league toward Punta de Pinos, from where they could identify the Punta de Año Nuevo. "We rode two leagues altogether," records Font, "and Don Juan coped well in spite of the pain in his groin, which hampered his movement and did not permit him to get on and off the horse without help."

In accordance with Anza's orders, Lieutenant Moraga had been preparing their departure and that evening they discussed the details. The explorers, numbering twenty, consisted of Anza, Font, and Moraga, with a corporal, ten soldiers, and six servants. Eight of the troops were Tubac regulars; Corporal Robles and his two men from the Monterey presidio, who had explored the Bay Area before, would serve as guides. During their absence, the comptroller would be in command at the presidio. Provisions had been packed for twenty days, and Anza, satisfied with the preparations, retired soon after dinner. The night was cold, starlit, and still. While Monterey slept, a light breeze repeatedly brought the barking of the sea lions.

After Font's mass on Saturday morning the group left by 9:30, retracing their steps through the same corridor they had used arriving (along present-day California Highway 68). Crossing the Salinas River and continuing northeast, "we stopped at 3:45…on the far side of the valley, on a glen known as La Natividad [or Asunción in Anza's journal], after having covered some eight leagues. The soil is hard, compact, and mostly flat, without trees except for the poplars lining the river. The Valley of Santa Delfina [the Salinas] is long but not very wide as it opens up toward a large cove on the sea, bound at one end by the Punta de Año Nuevo." From Natividad that night they could just hear the sound of the ocean some miles distant.

Leaving camp early the following morning they passed over the end of the Gabilan Range into a wide inland valley. After crossing the San Benito River (a stream, according to Anza), "we turned north-northwest into the spacious San Bernardino plain, where we camped at 3:30 by a creek at Las Llagas after covering eight leagues in as many hours." The "spacious plain of San Bernardino" is today the Santa Clara Valley, where the Llagas Creek still flows near Gilroy.

"There were not many trees along the trail," writes Font, "but by the streams, near the ponds, and on the hills there were plenty of spruce....We saw quite a few deer and [many] white and dark geese. After fording a marshy stream we came to a ranchería, where I counted some twenty huts. Two Indians came to meet us and gave us three freshwater fish, about a foot long and full of bones, the same species as we had eaten at the Colorado. We passed an alder and poplar grove (the soil seemed to be better here) and saw a group of Indians [apparently] fleeing near the hills on our left. At first only one approached us, but, following his example, as many as eighteen came. The rest kept their distance so we couldn't tell if there were women with them. They were obviously hunting and gave us some of their catch. The commander accepted a rabbit and an arrow [as a sign of] peace."

Continuing north the following day just east of the Santa Cruz Mountains (along the plain now occupied by San Jose and Santa Clara), they covered eight leagues according to Anza (twelve according to Font) to camp near the almost dry stream of San Joseph Cupertino. In the course of the day they encountered many natives whose behavior, unlike that of the previous day, was not particularly friendly. "Groups of naked Indians appeared among the oak trees," notes Font, "screaming and running like deer, and without being openly aggressive, gesticulating with their bows and arrows as if to stop us or keep us from going farther....As we paid no attention, some thirty of them ran single file and passed us. When they were well in front again, they began screaming, making signs...as if angry and repeating their gestures for us to stop. They spoke continuously and very loud (although we could not understand them at all) and kept repeating their antics several times over the space of one league.

After a while some drifted gradually away until eventually they left us in peace."

From the high point of Cupertino, Anza for the first time can appreciate the large expanse of the bay and the peninsula on which they were traveling north. "From this site," explains Anza, "we can see on our right the estuary of the port of San Francisco, which we will have to circumvent in order to reach the river of the same name. [For this reason] we will have to return to this place or even farther south."

Days 180 to 182
Tuesday, March 26, to Thursday, March 28, 1776

They left San Joseph Cupertino at 7:30 toward the northwest through a high plain with extensive oak groves. Visible in the distance was "most of the estuary that makes up the southeast of the port, surrounded by smaller, shallow ponds and large areas of salty marsh." Passing a construction unlike any they had seen, "we went to inspect what it was," explains Font, "and found a circular fence made of tightly woven laurel branches about six hands high." After describing some details within the circle—"a bundle of poles about two yards long stuck in the ground, their blunt ends covered with feathers like arrows" and "a fire pit visible in the center"—he concludes that "it was assumed to be a ceremonial site or dance ring."

They passed several streams with little water before coming to a ranchería by the San Francisco Creek, identified as a possible site for a mission by a cross planted the previous year. In spite of the village, good soil, and abundant supply of wood, the location was later considered unsuitable because "the creek would disappear during the dry season."

Continuing west-northwest they passed four more rancherías before coming to camp at 3:30 by the San Mateo Creek, having covered eight leagues. "Near this and all the other streams we crossed today," writes Anza, "we have found large laurel trees with a strong and extraordinary fragrance."

Leaving San Mateo by 7:00 on a sparkling clear morning, they arrived at the mouth of the bay by 11:00 and camped by a pond open to the bay and fed by a spring "with enough water," writes Anza, "to power a mill. After unloading our baggage we proceeded to inspect the area to the west and south as a possible site for a fort. This activity occupied us until 5:00."

Their inspection took them first to a panoramic site where in February Rivera had planted a cross, "which we found on the ground and no longer in the form of a cross, as the Indians had...taken the ropes with which it was tied." It was from this location that Font was able to sketch a chart of the port entrance, including points on both sides and the offshore rocks.

The following morning they replanted the cross on the edge of the cliff where the mouth was narrowest so that the cross "is visible from a great distance and to any vessel entering the port." At its foot they left a written statement claiming possession on behalf of the King of Spain. While maintaining camp, they set out to explore along the port entrance to the east, and Anza was pleased to find an abundance of wood and water, although he did note that "both the green and the dead oaks are bent to the ground by the incessant northwest wind." He also comments on the large and docile native groups, "who often accompany us [but only] within the bounds of their own territories due to the enmity that frequently exists between neighbors."

Days 183 to 185
Friday, March 29, to Sunday, March 31, 1776

They lifted camp at 7:15 and most of the group started south while Anza led a small group east. "I gave orders that they should wait for me at the San Mateo Creek [near where they had camped on Tuesday] while I went with the chaplain and five soldiers to explore what we had not yet seen near the bay." Anza's party continued east and southeast over wooded hills and fertile lands with ponds and springs, noting that there was no shortage of good sites for a settlement. "We came to a beautiful creek," writes Font, "surrounded by chamomile, lavender, and other aromatic herbs and, being [almost] Good Friday, we named it Arroyo de los Dolores.[2] To test the soil, which seemed very good to us, the lieutenant planted some corn and chickpeas. I felt the location was beautiful, the best in which to site one of the two missions."

---

[2] The Friday of Christ's crucifixion is called in Spanish the Friday of Pain, i.e., Viernes de Dolores. Font's journal erroneously identifies Good Friday of that year as March 29, instead the correct date of April 5.

As on the previous day, the area was populated by friendly natives and well supplied with lumber and water. The exploration, covering some fifteen leagues, took all the daylight hours. "In the afternoon," writes Anza, "during a light rain that lasted about an hour and a half, we were surprised by a bear. After we managed to kill it with several shots, some of the men who are fond of bear meat butchered it. By 6:30, already in darkness, we arrived at San Mateo…, where I found our camp hosting the men from a nearby ranchería, the most contented and obliging people [we have seen] since the Colorado River."

"The Indians of this ranchería," writes Font, "were attentive and polite, although invasive to the point of being annoying. Later that night we had to expel them from camp in order to sleep. I feel they would be easy to convert if a mission were established nearby."

In spite of the downpour during the night, they lifted camp by 7:15 and retraced their steps to the "high pine tree" near the San Francisco Creek. Font was so taken by the straight and tall *palo alto* (meaning "high pole") that with the help of a graphometer he measured its height to be about fifty yards and its "circumference at the base five and a half yards."[3]

Leaving Palo Alto in the rain, they veered southeast away from their own northbound trail. The flat terrain of the South Bay area was crisscrossed with streams flowing through increasingly marshy land near the estuary. The Monterey soldiers believed the area to be impassable except far south in the valley (perhaps as far as Las Llagas, according to one of them), but Anza would not heed their advice. Proceeding east-southeast they encountered "a large stream or reasonable river," according to Anza, "which we managed to ford only with difficulty. It had been raining quite a bit and was threatening to turn even heavier so, having crossed, we decided to halt for the night at 4:00." The river they named Guadalupe and their camp was somewhere within today's city of Santa Clara.

During the night the clouds cleared, leaving a layer of frost on the wet landscape. After Sunday mass the small party zigzagged its way through the marsh, eventually reaching higher and well-drained land. Following the contour of the bay at a distance, they continued north-

---

3 The graphometer was an instrument that enabled a user to establish the angle between a measurable horizontal reference line and a line of sight to a distant point, thereby allowing him to calculate the height of faraway objects.

west, crossing five streams and six rancherías. They camped, after seven hours, by the Arroyo de la Harina, today's San Lorenzo Creek.

Days 186 and 187
Monday, April 1, and Tuesday, April 2, 1776

Leaving camp by 7:00 on the same course, they covered several leagues with sierra on their right and, after passing a redwood forest, found themselves facing the mouth of the bay, "framed by two points that we could clearly see from here." Font estimated the opening to be four leagues away. The area showed tracks of large deer "whose hoofs resemble those of cattle. The soldiers set out to find the herd but, having caught up with one animal, failed to kill it."

Bearing northeast, they climbed a small range from which they could see "the interior islands and a large expanse of bay to the north" before descending again to the coast. After passing two rancherías and covering a league along the water, they set up camp near a stagnant stream, "not far," according to Anza, "from where the San Francisco River flows into the bay of the same name."

The night was clear and still; the morning splendid with no trace of the mosquitoes that had plagued them the previous day. As the sun warmed the air, a mild breeze from the Bahía Grande (San Pablo Bay) kept temperatures pleasant.

Camp was surprised at daybreak by "ten gentiles wearing feathers and garlands of flowers" singing and dancing and bearing gifts. Responding to the invitation, the group left camp by 7:00 and followed the festive natives to their ranchería, where they enjoyed a celebration of dancing, music, and food. The visitors were glad to participate for some time, but after a while "the commander said it was enough. He distributed glass beads to all the women, accepted their gifts of food, and we said our good-byes. I was touched by the...joy with which these poor Indians had received us and how sad they appeared to be seeing us leave."

The hills were higher and closer together as they continued for another league. "We descended to the shore at the opening, where the river meets the bay, and halted to take a latitude reading" (38°:5.5'N, which is essentially correct). The view was splendid. They felt the location was ideal for establishing whether the back of the bay was fed, as some believed, by a mighty river (the one they referred to as the River of San Francisco) or if it was the beginning of an enormous marsh. Some "very well-made reed boats" were tied nearby. At the opening of the bay (or river), "about a quarter of a league wide," two natives were fishing from a similar boat tied to a long, thin pole; Font observed that the boat was facing the ocean. "The mouth does not appear to have any current," he records. Anza looked for signs of floods, debris on branches, or any high-water marks, but he could find none. They recorded that the water was too salty to drink, although "less than the ocean." They observed "five reed boats cross from one shore to the other in less than fifteen minutes" and experience no side drift. From all this they were led to believe that the "River of San Francisco" was probably a freshwater port "enclosed," according to Font, "within a basin of low-lying hills on both sides and extending east for six leagues to open over an enormous plain."

Continuing southeast along the coast until 5:00 in the afternoon, they camped by the brackish pool of a stream known as Santa Angela.

Days 188 and 189
Wednesday, April 3, and Thursday, April 4, 1776

Moving east the following morning they covered three leagues across a plain before climbing some hills from which they could see the changing nature of the bay. The expanse of open water to the east (which Font called the Fresh Water Port) appeared as three estuaries surrounded by low-lying islands. While the priest was steadfast in his bay theory, Corporal Robles and the soldier Soberanes, who had explored the area with Fagés, believed it was a river. Trying to reconcile opinions and observations, Anza was unable to reach a conclusion himself. The river-versus-bay theories quickly turned into absolute positions, with Font devoting pages of his journal to adamantly defending his view.

With all the Spanish settlements located on or close to the ocean at the time and only limited knowledge of the inland areas, it was believed (as shown by Font's map) that the basin between the coastal sierra and the high mountains (the Central Valley) was an impassable marshland extending perhaps as far south as San Antonio or San Luis Obispo. This implied that the route from the Colorado River to

Monterey (and eventually to San Francisco) on the east side of the coastal sierra—the route the authorities wanted Anza to investigate—would not be feasible. If, however, that basin drained to the bay through a river, the marsh might not be as formidable as assumed. Based on secondhand information from a priest who asserted the marsh was impassable, Font clung to his theory of a stagnant basin, which implied there was no river. Such was the state of their deliberations.

While descending toward the east, they passed a herd of deer, which the soldiers pursued again without success. Shortly after, they encountered a hunting party of "several Indians from the sierra, one of them with his skin dyed the same color as the head of a deer he is carrying." Later they crossed a group of natives carrying four or five salmons each; "We have noticed," writes Anza, "that since the mouth of the bay the most abundant fish is salmon—deep red, tender, and large. Of the ones we have seen none was less than five hands."

After covering six leagues, they camped on the edge of the water at an abandoned ranchería, which Anza named San Ricardo. "Immediately after stopping we went to the side of the water, where we threw sticks as far as possible and, instead of flowing away, they drifted back to us." In the absence of a current, Anza assigned the lieutenant to mark the high and low points of the tide, which, during the night, was found to be considerable. Although the evidence suggested they had found a tidal estuary, it did not preclude the possibility of its also being fed by a river. "I have therefore decided," writes Anza, "given that we are here, to follow this river (or bay) upstream in order to clarify the situation for the authorities."

Therefore, at 7:00 the following morning they left San Ricardo toward the east along the shore. "It wasn't long before we were separated from the coast by an arm of water…that, blocking our way, forced us to leave it on our left. After three leagues of water and swamp that we could not traverse in spite of repeated efforts on foot and on horseback, we had to turn southeast. This direction we maintained for about five leagues, at which point we encountered a larger body of water flowing north." Looking east and north as far as the eye could see they faced an endless expanse of reed-covered marshland. "The soldiers from Monterey assure me that this is the same marsh found twenty-five or thirty leagues from the missions of San

Antonio and San Luis, which, even in the dry season, has been found to be impassable. Coupled with my own observations, this opinion led me to conclude that what we believed to be a river is really a large lake fed by the water from the marsh and the Sierra Nevada."

Satisfied with his conclusion and "having decided to return [to Monterey], we took a southwest direction over a flat and sterile plain, after which we began to climb the sierra that we had on our right yesterday." Intending to find a short route to the Santa Clara Valley, they encountered such difficulties they named it the Sierra del Chasco (the Mountains of Disappointment), today's Diablo Range. After a long and arduous day of more than twelve leagues, they camped on the hills near water and firewood.

Days 190 to 193
Friday, April 5, to Monday, April 8, 1776

Good Friday dawned clear and still, without trace of the strong winds of the previous day. The air warmed to a pleasant spring temperature. Leaving camp before 7:00 "to cross the sierra in front of us that [have] not yet been explored on this side," they were surprised to come upon a labyrinth of narrow canyons and abrupt hills. Only the occasional crest rewarded them with a vista over the large marsh to the east and the many obstacles in their path to the southwest.

Unlike the vicinity of the bay, this area was almost devoid of people, the only trace being a "miserable abandoned shed" and a single native "running in the distance." There was, however, evidence of a large bear population. After many hours of difficult march, Anza estimated they had covered just seven leagues when they made camp in a high valley they named after the saint of the day, San Vicente. In the glow of infinite stars, the temperature that night dropped below freezing.

Saturday proved to be even more frustrating, with "impenetrable canyons and precipitous cliff sides" causing much backtracking and detouring. "Nobody could have imagined how wide and difficult these mountains were, even now when we know we are not far from our northbound route." To which must be added, according to Font, "the discomfort caused by the numerous brown ticks that have plagued us…, especially today when I removed fourteen from myself over a short time."

On the move after a sunrise Easter service, they descended Coyote Creek past some hot springs (near Gilroy) into what they called the San Bernardino (today's Santa Clara) Valley, where they crossed the Pájaro River and came to camp in the late afternoon, once again "within the sound of the ocean." By 10:30 on Monday they were "greeted with much joy by the people of the expedition at Monterey, who were delighted with the…news of the beautiful sites that we had marked out for the mission and the presidio of San Francisco."

While the lieutenant remained in Monterey, the commander and his chaplain stayed only a short time, continuing on to Carmel, "where I hope to find some cure for my leg," writes Anza, "which is still causing me great discomfort." It was mid-afternoon when they were received at San Carlos with the usual fanfare and the warm welcome of Father Serra.

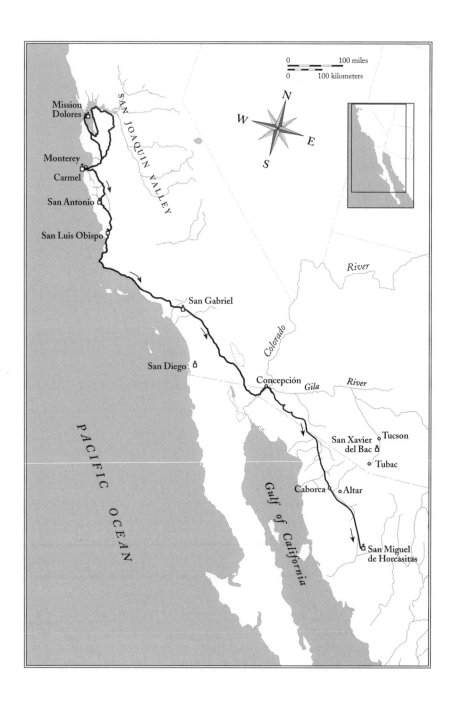

0 100 miles
0 100 kilometers

N
W *E*
S

Mission Dolores

SAN JOAQUIN VALLEY

Monterey
Carmel
San Antonio
San Luis Obispo

San Gabriel

San Diego

Concepción

River

Colorado

Gila *River*

San Xavier del Bac
Tucson
Tubac

Caborca
Altar

PACIFIC OCEAN

Gulf of California

San Miguel de Horcasitas

Return to Sonora

April 9 to June 1, 1776

Days 194 to 197
Tuesday, April 9, to Friday, April 12, 1776

Four days of grilled fish, fresh vegetables, and quiet rest in the relative comfort of the mission alleviated the pain in Anza's groin. The good food and company worked wonders on the ailing explorers, whose exchange of impressions about the Bay Area continued endlessly, in spite of Font's mouth ulcers. When unable to converse, he prepared a map of their sixteen-day exploration that was so well received he was asked to make copies for both Serra and Anza.

On Wednesday "a school of sardines stranded on the sand turns the beach flickering silver, and the commander walked down…to see this wonder in the afternoon, but on account of the burning in my mouth I wasn't feeling well enough to join them," writes Font. "During these days we ate an abundance of fresh green salads, which gave me some relief." On his departure a few days later, Font was still talking about the food: "The priests were so generous that they packed an abundance of greens to take with us: lettuce, cabbage, and spring beans for the trip as well as dried salmon, although the latter I did not get to taste or even see again as the commander kept it all."

The letter dispatched to Rivera at San Diego four weeks before had not yet been answered, and since the governor was the highest authority in California, Anza would not take the next step without his concurrence. His task had been to recruit settlers and deliver them to Monterey, and he had done so; although exploring the bay could be justified as laying the groundwork, establishing the settlements would exceed his orders. Therefore, having accomplished his mission, on Friday, April 12, he determined to return to Sonora. Meticulous in following procedure, especially given the governor's contrary position, he planned to meet Rivera to transfer his charges. "To this end," he writes, "I dispatched five soldiers [to San Diego] with a message to the governor [asking him] to come to San Gabriel on the 25 and 26 of this month to discuss and resolve the subjects we have both been entrusted with."

Days 198 and 199
Saturday, April 13, and Sunday, April 14, 1776

With Anza better, they left the mission after mass and spent the day at the presidio busy with preparations. Lieutenant Moraga, the highest-ranking officer, would assume responsibility for the 190 settlers remaining at Monterey; Font's journal lists all of the expedition members by name, including the status of each man as a veteran, new recruit, or settler. In Rivera's absence, Moraga would also assume command of the presidio. Although the conversations between Anza and Moraga were not recorded, the journals convey the anxiety of the latent conflict between Anza and Rivera that the lieutenant would inherit regarding the settlements.

The small group returning with Anza, unburdened of families and cattle, was a detachment of twenty-seven men, including Font, and a mule train. At the last moment, a soldier and his wife, regretting their decision to emigrate, were granted their request to return to Sonora, bringing the total to twenty-nine.

The Sunday of their departure dawned clear and warm. By mid-morning, the mission priests, including Serra and Prieras, a minister returning to San Antonio, joined them at the presidio, and while a large crowd gathered in silence, they ate lunch together. The cargo was packed and the animals loaded; it was time for good-byes. Even laconic Anza was moved to record his emotions:

"This has been," he writes, "the saddest day this presidio has ever known. As I mounted my horse on the plaza, the people whom I led from the country to which I am now returning gathered there as if by common accord. Whether they received bad or good treatment under my command, most of them, but especially the women, came with tears in their eyes, more for my departure than for their own exile. I was overwhelmed by their show of affection, embraces, wishes for my happiness, and praise that I do not deserve. For, since the time I recruited them, I have experienced only their loyalty and to this day no thought of desertion from any that I brought to this distant outpost. This I must record here in honor of the people who will perform a great service to the Crown and for which they have willingly left behind their parents and country, which is the most a person can sacrifice."

At 2:00 Anza gave the order to march. The sadness was broken by one of the priest's intoning a verse that the crowd immediately recognized, and hundreds of voices burst into the Alabado as the train slowly moved out of the presidio.

Afterward it was a quiet and uneventful ride east along the well-known trail to the Salinas Valley. The party was accompanied by Moraga as far as Buenavista, where they set up camp for the night.

Day 200
Monday, April 15, 1776

The small camp was up before dawn. By 6:30 the lieutenant was headed west back to the presidio while Anza's group followed the river southeast. The spring morning was cool and dry. They had not covered two leagues when they encountered the five soldiers dispatched to Rivera on Friday, who, having met the governor near San Antonio Mission, were on their way back to Anza. Sergeant Góngora, extremely disturbed, requested to speak to the commander in private.

"Once alone," writes Anza, "he said to me: 'Sir, Captain [Rivera] is out of his senses or gone mad in [my opinion] and that of his men, who also say he has been excommunicated for taking the Indian

Carlos from the church where he had sought refuge [to avoid being punished for the attack on the San Diego mission]. I myself have witnessed his unreasonable behavior…, having even been demoted from sergeant.…In reply to his questions when we met Saturday afternoon, I told him I had letters for him. Without requesting them he said to me: "Very well, you may withdraw." That evening he did not call me to his presence at all but on Sunday morning, when we were preparing to leave, he called out: "The letters from Don Juan! Let me have them!" Doing so, I said to him: "This one is from the Lieutenant Colonel and this other one, from Lieutenant Moraga." He put them in his sack without opening them and at the same time gave me [these] two, to be delivered to you wherever I found you.'"

Anza continues: "After this conversation I opened the letters (replying to mine of the thirteenth of March) [in which] he opposes establishing the presidio at San Francisco in spite of my offer to do so with a smaller number of troops than originally planned for this purpose." Any hopes that Rivera had changed his mind on the matter were shattered.

According to Font, Góngora's report was particularly disturbing because even though the sergeant, like most of Rivera's men, was known to have a good rapport with his commanding officer, during the course of their meeting he requested to be transferred under Anza's orders. This being impossible, of course, the detachment continued without him to Monterey while Anza and Font pondered the consequences of what they had just learned.

It was still early morning and barely a league farther when they met the returning governor's party. Rivera, beard unkempt, wrapped in blue blankets, the cap on his head leaving only his left eye show-ing, was riding a mule. Anza brought his horse close and for a few minutes the commanders stood face to face.

"I respectfully inquired about his health," writes Anza, "to which he answered he had a bad leg. I had no sooner expressed my regrets than he spurred his mule and, saying, 'Good-bye, Don Juan,' rode on.

"'Good-bye, Don Fernando,' said I, loud enough to be heard, 'and I look forward to your lordship's reply to my letter…in Mexico [City] or elsewhere.'

"'Very well,' he called out from the distance."

"At which point," writes Anza, "I asked the priests…to certify in writing what they had witnessed so that I could formally present the facts to His Excellency. Feeling more embarrassed by his disregard for the Viceroy's orders than by his personal rudeness in the brief time we faced each other, rather than the madness noted by the sergeant, I saw a complete unwillingness to deal with the subjects he is responsible for and which he had previously agreed to discuss with me. There were other things I wanted to tell him, but since this conflict may damage both our careers, even though I have fulfilled my… orders, I refrained."

The short meeting was over before it had begun, so abruptly that there was no time to learn from the soldiers about the events at San Diego or San Gabriel, or even to confirm Sergeant Góngora's information. Standing on the banks of the river, Font and Prieras looked at each other and at Anza in disbelief as the governor and his troops disappeared in the distance.

After covering some sixteen leagues into the long valley, they set up camp toward nightfall at San Bernabé, not far from present-day King City. Earlier in the afternoon the ailing Rivera had arrived at the Monterey presidio.

Days 201 to 203
Tuesday, April 16, to Thursday, April 18, 1776

Following San Bernabé (today's Quinado) Canyon just after dawn, the party arrived at San Antonio Mission by mid-morning. "We were welcomed with joy by the priests," writes Font, "surprised to see us so soon after Rivera's visit. But they were even more surprised to hear…about our encounter [with him] the previous day. Father Dumets stated that Rivera's excommunication would be reasonable had he violated ecclesiastical jurisdiction but, not knowing the details, refrained from passing judgment. He did mention we might find Father Garcés at San Luis [Obispo], which he apparently intended to visit."

Even though it was only morning, they decided to halt for the day. Their early arrival enabled the mission to show their best hospitality, particularly with "a very correct table," writes Font, which included "sausage made to order that day and a roasted pig."

Leaving San Antonio the following afternoon with enough roast "for the road" they covered five leagues to camp by the San Antonio River.

The days started early in April and as the first light marked the wrinkles on the faces of the mountains, the small group was packing camp. By 6:00 they were moving southeast along the river, their voices joined in the Alabado. It was a long day along the Paso de los Robles southeast to the Monterey (Salinas) River and upstream to the Santa Margarita, fourteen uneventful leagues in eleven hours.

While Anza was making rapid progress on his return, Rivera's arrival at Monterey had alerted Serra to the open conflict between Rivera and the priests at San Diego. Coupled with word of the governor's strange behavior during his encounter with Anza, the news made Serra aware that Rivera's judgment could not be trusted. That day Lieutenant Moraga also felt it necessary to write to Anza from Monterey, giving his opinion that Rivera "has lost his mind." All this, however, was not yet known to Anza and Font that night as they enjoyed the last of the roast pork in Santa Margarita.

Days 204 to 206
Friday, April 19, to Sunday, April 21, 1776

The hills were bathed in sunshine when they started that Friday morning, and the party reached San Luis Obispo by noon. The missionaries' surprise at the group's arrival and their reaction upon learning of Rivera's behavior echoed those of San Antonio. The conversation that afternoon recalled the former clash between the Church and the military, as personified, respectively, by Serra and Fagés, the previous governor, who would then have appeared reasonable compared to Rivera. A feeling of pending crisis loomed over the gathering.

"That afternoon," writes Anza, "one of the priests from Carmel Mission [acting as courier] caught up with me here. He had a letter from the Father President for me to deliver to His Excellency [the viceroy]." But the priest also had a personal message from Serra: "He asks me, through his envoy, to wait for him somewhere between here and San Gabriel. If permitted to do so, he will come with Rivera, who is setting out to meet me. The motive of the Father Superior for this trip is to attempt to mend relations between the governor and the priests at San Diego following the forcible removal of the Indian who had sought refuge at the church. He also intends to intervene on behalf of the Indians who wish to negotiate peace with the governor, who is set only on severe punishment.

"The courier gave me [two other] letters (which I will also share with His Excellency): one from Rivera, where he apologizes for leaving [the other day] due to his illness, without explanation, and requests that I wait for his arrival to discuss official matters; the other from Lieutenant Moraga, informing me of Rivera's arrival at Monterey and expressing his [concerned] opinion that the commander has gone mad."

Exceptional circumstances had brought the six priests together at San Luis Obispo, and they were enjoying each other's company; they shared in the work, they sang, they prayed as a group. Font especially thrived in the presence of his fellow countrymen. On Sunday, with Anza as godfather, they baptized five adults who had completed their religious education, and they celebrated two weddings, including that of a woman just baptized. The rain that day could not dampen the joy of the community, whose festivities included the participation of the usually secluded native maidens and Font providing music on his psaltery.

It was late afternoon when four soldiers arrived with the news that Rivera, "due to fatigue," had stopped one league from the mission. He had left Monterey a day early (on Thursday, April 18) ostensibly to catch up with Anza, but in reality, according to Font, he had departed ahead of schedule to avoid taking Serra with him to San Diego. His continuing uncooperative behavior prompted Anza to react defensively: "Upon receiving the news I immediately sent a corporal and two of my soldiers with an answer to his letter, in which I…agreed to meet with him [as requested] to discuss our official business…provided it was done in writing, and…I offered to wait for him here if he so advised me."

Days 207 and 208
Monday, April 22, and Tuesday, April 23, 1776

"At noon the following day," writes Anza, "I received an answer…in which he informs me that he considers it more appropriate to discuss our business at the Mission of San Gabriel." There is no explanation for Rivera's request, but the fact that the added distance of some two hundred miles implied a week's delay prompted Anza to assert in his journal that "it is all a question of postponing the establishment of San Francisco, which he opposes." This assessment, however, was not echoed by his own letter to Rivera of April 21 (not copied in his journal), in which it is Anza who informs Rivera that he himself will be leaving San Luis the following day and proposes to hold their meeting at San Gabriel. The same letter also contradicts the claim that he offered to wait for Rivera at San Luis.

These distortions reveal both the bias of a journal Anza used to justify his own actions to the viceroy as well as the degree to which the relations between the two commanders had soured. If Rivera's actions may have been the result of mental unbalance, Anza's reactions that afternoon certainly cast a light of unreasonable behavior on the commander's own conduct.

"Shortly after lunch," writes Font, "as Captain Rivera arrived at the Mission [of San Luis]…the priests went out to meet him but Captain Anza and I chose not to do so because of his behavior during our meeting on the road. Instead we withdrew to our rooms as if we had been napping. Rivera asked to speak to Anza, and the comptroller came to his room with the message. Through him Anza replied that he was at the time taking a nap but that he would be glad to speak to Rivera afterward provided that the only subject of their talk was the expedition and its establishment in the Port of San Francisco. He added that, to avoid arguments, they should only communicate in writing on that subject. Captain Rivera waited for about an hour before he left for San Gabriel, without having seen Anza. He did get to greet me [however] because during that time I had to leave my room and we saw each other in passing."

Rested after four days of enforced delay, the small group left San Luis on the Camino Real early on Tuesday, covering thirteen leagues in just over eleven hours. Accompanying them as far as the Santa Barbara Channel were six local natives on their way to purchase two fishing boats, which they would row back along the coast. Going all the way to Mexico City was Pedro, the illegitimate child of a former captain and "his Indian concubine" who was being rewarded with a two-year educational stay as the ward of the viceroy. The precocious and intelligent ten-year-old could speak and read Spanish and was considered the best interpreter at the mission.

Days 209 to 213
Wednesday, April 24, to Sunday, April 28, 1776

Averaging some twelve leagues per day, they retraced their route along the coast in four days as far as the Santa Clara River, from which they continued inland north of the coastal range. On the fifth day, Anza chose to halt at 5:00 p.m. two leagues west of San Gabriel, sending four soldiers ahead to announce their arrival the following day.

Anza had come to believe that nothing would change Rivera's position and that their discussions would be futile. To what extent he questioned the governor's sanity is hard to tell from his journal, but he was conscious that they were not dissimilar in temperament and feared provoking a confrontation damaging to all, therefore his emphasis on written records and keeping a distance.

"After dispatching the soldiers," writes Font, "Captain Anza told me that he intends to stay in his tent rather than with Rivera in the mission as he does not want to risk another insult from the governor. He did not mean to offend the priests but was only trying to prevent a flare-up, perhaps a crisis, from occurring. Although I tried to dissuade him, due to the negative tone of his action, I was unable to do so. Afterward, I recognized he was right in his decision. Something much worse could have happened."

Days 214 to 216
Monday, April 29, to Wednesday, May 1, 1776

They lifted camp at 6:30, traveling the Camino Real. Intent on appropriate behavior, Font along the way persuaded Anza to reconsider his position of refusing the mission's hospitality and staying in his tent. "We eventually agreed," he writes, "that he would first call at the mission [before setting up his tent] and that if Captain Rivera greeted us correctly, he would forget the past, stay there, and speak [face to face] with the governor."

Arriving at the mission by 8:00 they were received with bells tolling, a welcoming salvo, and the usual expressions of affection from the missionaries who came out to greet them. Rivera, however, was conspicuous by his absence. "In spite of this," writes the priest, "Anza remained at the mission about a half an hour, allowing time for Rivera to make a gesture, but, given that he would not leave his room or let himself be seen, he said to me: 'Father, I am going to do what I planned…as you see what I am exposing myself to by staying here."

With Anza camped a short distance away, over the next three days the commanders exchanged correspondence on every possible detail concerning the transfer of settlers, animals, and goods, as well as information about possible sites for the settlement of San Francisco. But in the entire time at San Gabriel they did not once speak directly to each other or meet face to face. Font, on the other hand, while staying at the mission, had his meals together with Rivera and the priests.

Days 217 to 219
Thursday, May 2, to Saturday, May 4, 1776

Having at last completed the formalities of transfer, Anza had no further business in California. On the afternoon of May 2, his party took leave from the priests, "although not from Captain Rivera, who did not bid us good-bye but remained in his room ostensibly finishing some letters for the commander to take to Mexico." With the addition of the child from San Luis Obispo, the group then numbered thirty persons with eighty-six animals, including a baggage string of twenty mules. They covered only two leagues before camping at the same place they had stopped exactly four months before.

The weather, however, was quite different than it had been before. Friday's march was broken by a three-hour siesta "to pass the hottest hours" by the Stream of the Bears before going on to cover ten leagues for the day. After setting up camp, a courier arrived from Rivera with a letter for the rector of San Fernando (in Mexico City) and a note asking Anza not to wait for his report to the viceroy, as an important document left in San Diego had prevented his completing it. For this reason, Rivera claims, "he will [have to] send it directly" from there. As Font had predicted, in the present circumstances the governor would not trust Anza to carry a letter to the viceroy whose content would probably conflict with Anza's version of events.

During a long candlelit night Anza replied to the governor and wrote to Lieutenant Moraga concerning his recent interaction with Rivera, including the possibility that the governor was incapacitated by insanity, and Font wrote letters to both Serra and Paterna. Considering it inappropriate for the rector of San Fernando to receive news from California before the viceroy, Anza refused to carry Rivera's letter and returned it to the governor. "With this," writes Font, "we finally bolted and locked the door on all the obstacles Rivera had thrown on the expedition's path."

It was under heavy cover just after dawn, thunder pealing in the distance and drops falling nearby, that the courier started back to San Gabriel and the expedition headed east toward the Santa Ana River. A midday siesta and eight leagues later, they camped in a desolate spot short of both grass and water.

Days 220 to 222
Sunday, May 5, to Tuesday, May 7, 1776

Averaging almost twelve leagues a day, they advanced along the Valle de San Josef (Bautista Creek and Cahuilla Valley) and into the Valle del Príncipe (the Terwilliger) within sight of San Carlos. The warm spring weather turned into "overcast skies with occasional showers and a chilling northwester that made us feel colder than last December," records Font. "Feeling frozen, we stopped before the Pass of San Carlos for something to eat and to warm up but the cold lasted all afternoon…and into the night, a farewell from the lands of Monterey and its winds."

Descending Coyote Creek they stopped for the night at Santa Catharina, from which they left at dawn "in the dust of the furious wind blowing through the canyon, especially in the early morning." As they entered the open and cloudless Borrego Valley, the wind dissipated. "The land is barren and sterile, devoid of anything good, all sand and dunes, the hillsides covered with stones." By midday they rested at San Gregorio, "but there was so little water that not all the animals could drink." It was 7:30 p.m. when they set up camp near the marsh at San Sebastián.

Days 223 and 224
Wednesday, May 8, and Thursday, May 9, 1776

As the crow flies, the eighty miles of desert between San Sebastián and Concepción was the most difficult passage of the entire journey. The route via the wells at Santa Rosa and Santa Olaya required an additional forty miles. For Anza and some of his men it would be the fourth crossing of this area, and they were again forced to choose between the shortest and the safest route. Anza favored the shortest, aiming for the Cerro de San Pablo, which he believed to be twenty to twenty-five leagues away (it was actually thirty-two), but the guide—one of the soldiers most familiar with the desert—was reluctant. He felt Anza was underestimating the distance and considered it too risky. Perhaps remembering their brush with disaster during the first crossing, Anza accepted a compromise: they would aim for El Carrizal and Santa Olaya.

Because of the heat, they left San Sebastián in the afternoon, passing San Anselmo, where they watered the animals, and continued east-southeast for twelve leagues. Near midnight they stopped without pasture for a few hour's sleep in the cool night.

An hour before sunrise they were on the march again, covering eight leagues before arriving at El Carrizal (also known as the Wells of Joy) at noon. The water was "as red as colored by cinnabar, very salty, and worse than the last time," writes Font, but the animals drank their fill while they rested during the day. On the move again at 5:00 p.m., their backs to the setting sun, they reached Santa Olaya by midnight, having crossed twenty-five leagues of desert in a day a half.

Days 225 to 227
Friday, May 10, to Sunday, May 12, 1776

Their arrival was not unnoticed by the locals. "Shortly after daybreak," writes Anza, "the natives started coming with gifts of corn, beans, and…pumpkins after spreading the news of our coming to the whole river. Due to the little pasture and poor water of the previous days, I decided to let the animals rest this morning." Starting northeast in the afternoon, they covered four leagues to spend the night by the Cojat village they had stopped at on December 5.

At daybreak they continued following the Colorado upstream "through a winding…trail [different] from the one we knew on account of the swollen river and flooded fields," writes Font. "At every ranchería both male and female Indians would come out expressing great joy at seeing us, some joining us, at times walking alongside, or…running playfully ahead with their poles." It was a celebration that accompanied them all the way to Concepción, where they arrived at 11:00 that morning.

Father Eixarch, the lone missionary on the Colorado since Garcés had left in December, welcomed the party effusively. Font was overjoyed. The separate journals of Garcés and Eixarch during this period provide insight into two worlds—the former's vast exploration of the Southwest accompanied only by Tarabal, and the latter's tranquil and symbolic stay in the midst of the Yuma—but those are chapters for another story.

Although the Spaniards' arrival at the river was no longer a novelty, their welcome as old friends that morning had lost none of its warmth. Indeed, Palma, who joined them the following day, had long been looking forward to Anza's return. Over two years he had nurtured a project to integrate the culture and religion of Spain with that of the Yuma, creating a society as harmonious as that which he perceived between the white leadership of Garcés and Anza and the native soldiers in Spanish uniform. And as he had suggested to the commander on his way north, not having yet received the missionaries and settlers he had requested from the governor of Sonora, he was ready to present his case to the viceroy. He had planned his trip for weeks, and when he met Anza that Sunday all the details were in place.

"Captain Palma," writes Font, "told us that he wanted to come along to Mexico [City] to meet the Viceroy and tell him that both he and his people very much wanted and would be very pleased to have priests and Spaniards come to live with them in their land. So to deal with this question…, Captain Anza, Father Eixarch, Palma, and I, together with three or four elders as witnesses, came together that night inside the house and discussed it extensively. The commander told Palma about the length of the trip and the time it would take and reminded him he would not be able to return to his country for a long time.

"'How many years would it be before I return?' asked Palma.

"'A year at the most,' replied the commander, adding that perhaps he would come back with him personally and settle in his country. (With what authority he was making such a statement I don't know, although on more than one occasion I heard him say that he would gladly come to live on the Colorado, he felt so at home with those Indians.)

"Then Palma said that it was good, and the commander agreed to take him to Mexico [City] but asked that he not go alone but be accompanied [by some from his tribe]. From the many who volunteered, Palma chose one of his brothers and a son of Captain Pablo. In addition, a young Cojat who had wanted to go to Mexico since meeting Garcés in his country was also accepted. The four of them traveled with us as far as the Presidio at San Miguel [de Horcasitas], where I completed my journey and they continued on with Captain Anza."

In preparation for his departure, Palma "transferred his authority to one of the elders, charging him to defend the land from their enemies and take command of the river." He also made arrangements for the planting and care of his fields. It seemed as if the tribe, together with their leader, had thought of everything. "Some two hundred men," writes Anza, "expressed to me their satisfaction that Chief Palma was undertaking his journey with the approval of the whole nation."

Days 228 to 230
Monday, May 13, to Wednesday, May 15, 1776

Due to the spring thaw in the mountains, the Colorado was cresting. The plain north of Concepción was, as far as the eye could see, submerged under the annual flood that nurtured it. Where they had twice crossed, above the Gila junction, the river was now a sea, impossible to ford. At Concepción, it narrowed to a one-hundred-yard channel of swirling eddies and fast current, and it was there that Palma planned to take them across. The chief and his people, having lived by and of the river for generations, had mastered its ways. In preparation, they had gathered logs, which they tied together into rafts and manhandled across the channel. The logs were tied and untied to suit the cargo or to be floated back separately. The women, who, according to Anza, "are better swimmers than the men," shuttled back and forth ferrying small goods in clay pots and waterproof baskets.

"The [first] raft was finished at noon," writes Font, "and a load was taken across with some people. They then disassembled it and made two, which they completed at about 6:00, at which point the commander determined that we should cross. The rafts were loaded with our baggage, and thirteen of us, including Anza, Father Thomas, and myself, went together in one. As we left the bank the logs appeared to sink, which caused two of our group to jump ashore in fear, abandoning the rest of us to great danger. The overloaded raft, deep in the water, was difficult to control, and as we began to float freely, a strong eddy almost sank it. At this point the Indians indicated that we should all jump to land, but Captain Pablo, who was in charge, stopped us. The thought of turning back offended him and his expressions emphatically conveyed that he was capable, on his own, of taking us across. His leadership prevailed and the crew [of some forty in the water] pushed us farther into the stream. At the same time, most of the two hundred men and women on shore, realizing [the danger of] the situation, jumped in to help and quickly surrounded the raft. In the midst of shouting and cheering—especially when, halfway across, a soldier fired his musket, which they love—it took them twelve minutes to push it to the other side. Besides getting somewhat wet, the only inconvenience was that we landed [a quarter league] farther downstream than the [other rafts], which had not been so heavily loaded.[1]

"One cannot deny that these Indians, excellent swimmers and the best friends of Spain, are truly deserving of our gratitude and respect for their loyal services. Our lives and possessions were in their hands, and of all the cargo that the women ferried, the only loss was a basket of horseshoes that began to take water and the swimmer was unable to save from sinking."

It took them until Wednesday to complete the crossing, which Anza describes as part of "the most exhausting four days I have experienced in the entire trip." He goes on to add that "I can now confirm what I have said on a previous occasion: with the nations that inhabit this great river as friends, we will be able to cross it without

---

[1] From the measurements given, which imply a downstream drift of more than ten times the width of the river at that point, it is possible to visualize the strength of the current and to understand the need for disassembling the raft to bring the individual logs upriver before swimming them back to the west bank.

much trouble, but with them as our enemies, it would be almost impossible. It is only where the Gila joins the Colorado that during [the winter] it is possible to ford the two rivers. The rest of the year, when the Colorado is too high to ford, the best location for cross-ing…is right here. Above and below [Concepción] the waters spread as much as five leagues in width and it becomes impassable due to the mud."

The river forded and the expedition preparing to continue, Anza received late word that a Spaniard had arrived on the opposite bank. When the Yumas brought him across on Wednesday afternoon, he was identified as one of the deserters captured by Moraga who had since escaped from San Diego and crossed directly to Santa Olaya. After questioning, Anza took him into custody and assigned him to work as a mule driver.[2]

It was 5:00 in the evening by the time they took leave of the crowd that had gathered to see Palma off to Mexico. With the addition of the Yumas, Eixarch, two servants, two interpreters, and the deserter, the group now totaled forty. Following their lengthening shadows, they rode east along the Gila into the night while Anza and some soldiers scouted ahead for the campsite of November 27.

"Recognizing it was almost 10:00," writes Font, "I stopped, lit some fires, and had the path checked. Finding no fresh tracks I real-ized we had left Captain Anza behind and, knowing that the site could not be far, determined to stop there for the night so that we could find each other in daylight. While there was some pasture for the animals,…we spent the night without any supplies."

Days 231 to 233
Thursday, May 16, to Saturday, May 18, 1776

"We saddled up at dawn," writes Font, "and I sent two men back to look for Anza, who arrived at our camp by 6:15. Happy at having found each other, we continued for two leagues and stopped by the

---

[2] The fugitive's direct east-west crossing of about 175 miles in ten days over mountains and desert was the first by a European and a remarkable accomplishment in itself. Anza was cog-nizant of the usefulness of the man's experience and, as he had once been with Sebastián Tarabal, was lenient with the deserter.

Gila, where we built a shelter with branches [in which to spend the heat of the day] and waited for the mules to catch up. It being Ascension Day, I said mass.

"Some Indians who had followed us on foot…had to be persuaded to turn back. They were so set on accompanying Palma that we really had to insist, and eventually all but one obeyed us. The one exception, a Cojat, asked to stay…, promising he would start back the following day.

"As we were preparing to leave that afternoon, the lead mule driver noticed that his machete was missing and, suspecting one of the Indians, we informed Palma. An angry chief immediately spoke to his companions, one of which (the Cojat among them) stated that the Indian who had asked to remain with us another night had hidden it." In the ensuing questioning, the suspect denied his guilt, but Palma's brother saw in the movement of his eyes where he had buried the machete and, digging there, found it.

"I then took the thief by the hand," writes Font, "called Palma over, gave him my whip, and asked him to punish the man. No sooner had I done this than he began to whip the Indian with such force that on the third lashing he drew blood. Seeing the anger with which Palma had begun, I had to stop him for fear he might kill the thief."

Leaving camp by 4:00 they covered three leagues to stop for the night at Laguna Salobre, not far from the Gila, where, due to the intense heat, they spent most of the next day. "Between the hours of 11:00 and 3:00," notes Anza, "the sun is so extremely hot it paralyzes both animals and people."

It was mid-afternoon when they left Laguna Salobre, traveling southeast away from the river. Since Anza's ultimate destination was now Mexico City, he chose to take the route via Caborca and San Miguel de Horcasitas, which was significantly shorter than that along the Gila and via Tubac. In spite of avoiding the worst of the heat, that day they lost three animals to exhaustion before stopping at midnight. Marching four hours on Saturday morning, they rested at Tinajas de la Candelaria between 9:00 a.m. and 6:00 p.m. and continued through the evening and into the night until 1:45 a.m., when they stopped at Llano del Tuzal, having covered fourteen leagues.

Days 234 to 236
Sunday, May 19, to Tuesday, May 21, 1776

"We stopped," writes Font, "to lie down for a while without unsaddling the horses and to wait for the mules to catch up. The string arrived at 4:00 a.m. and went on without stopping. After eating breakfast, we changed [horses] and left Llano del Tuzal by 5:00 a.m., arriving at El Carrizal de Sonoita at 11:30 that morning."

Although the water was slightly brackish, the creek was flowing, and the site where they spent the rest of the day had "reasonable" pasture. The animals arrived at 1:00 p.m., having gone with little food and water and no rest for nineteen hours; the cost was another three horses and a mule lost to exhaustion. The oppressive daytime heat had also worn down the men, but they were better able to recover sleeping under blankets in the cold desert nights.

At 5:15 the following morning they lifted camp and continued east along the creek as far as the ruined mission at San Marcelo de Sonoitac, where "we saw some twenty [Papago] families and their governor," writes Font. "The stream here has a permanent supply of adequate water to support a village and some crops, but it lacks wood; there are only a few small willow trees and some shrubs bordering the water." Leaving the village after a six-hour rest, they passed a cross marking the site "where the Indians [many years before] had killed their Jesuit missionary," and from there they continued southeast to camp at the foot of some hills with good pasture. Starting before dawn on Tuesday, they stopped at Quitobac during the warmest hours before covering another fourteen leagues to camp at San Juan de la Mata.

Days 237 to 239
Wednesday, May 22, to Friday, May 24, 1776

The route between Caborca and the River Junction, never as traveled as a Camino Real, was at that time a well-known trail between the Yuma nation and New Spain. It had been opened in the 1760s by the Jesuits, who were probably responsible for the name (not used by Anza) that it acquired in later years: El Camino del Diablo, the Road of the Devil. Palma had traveled on it to deliver Tarabal in 1873 and to petition the governor of Sonora in 1874 or 1875; Anza had taken the first expedition through it in 1874; and Eixarch just the previous month had used it to visit the Altar Valley. Because the route was familiar, it was not surprising that the group was able to maintain their pace by covering long stretches in the dark to take advantage of the cool nights.

Leaving San Juan de la Mata at 5:30 a.m. on Wednesday, they arrived at San Ildefonso by 11:00 p.m., traveling partly at night and allowing for a siesta at San Eduardo de Aribaipia. An exception to their midday break was made on Thursday when the six-league trek from San Ildefonso to Caborca was completed before noon. "We were received with joy and the affection of a brother by the minister of that mission, Father Calzada," writes Font, "and, in the afternoon, by Father Moreno [when he] returned from Pitic, a parish visit two leagues [to the east]."

Taking advantage of Altar being only eight leagues away, Anza dispatched four soldiers with a request for fresh mounts from the presidio. Accompanied by "Lieutenant Felipe Velderraín" [sic] and several soldiers from Tubac, they returned the following day after dark, bringing with them a dozen fresh horses. The lieutenant also brought news of a disastrous raid on the Tumacacori Mission and increased Apache activity throughout the region; this was the reason for the presence of a Tubac detachment in the Altar Valley. "The priests at Caborca," writes Anza, "have also confirmed what we had already heard from the Papagos: [there have been] Apache robberies and killings in this area, as well as a raid [on the mines] at Cieneguilla (where we will be passing through)."

Days 240 to 243
Saturday, May 25, to Tuesday, May 28, 1776

Valderraín and the soldiers from Tubac left Caborca on Saturday together with Eixarch, who was on his way back to his mission at Tumacacori. In the afternoon, the expedition started on the road toward Horcasitas. As the sun set, the temperatures became bearable, and they traveled over flat terrain for eight leagues before stopping toward midnight for a few hours of rest. In the cool of the breaking day they continued for five hours and arrived at El Real de la Cieneguilla by 9:00 a.m.

The Royal Camp at Cieneguilla was an established mining village, producing, according to Anza, "between seventy and seventy-five gold marks per week." The "Spanish" population included miners, merchants, a priest, and a garrison, while natives provided the labor force. The expedition members were invited to stay in private residences during their stop. "We were received," writes Font, "by Lieutenant Tueros (who provided a house for our stay) and the rest of the community." Palma and his companions were the guests of Don Antonio and Doña Ignacia de Castro, who later hosted a party for them before they left. "After the formalities," continues Font, "I said mass, and in the afternoon, invited by Don Francisco de Guizarnotegui, visited the placers, distant about a league from town, and saw how the Indians extract the gold. We returned at dusk."

Anza comments on the precarious situation of Cieneguilla, where the constant threat of Apache attack on labor and supplies was discouraging the settlers, adding costs, and affecting production to the point of endangering the survival of the mine. "This morning," he writes on May 27, "we received word...that a party of over one hundred mounted Apaches was seen heading in this direction, for which reason I decided to spend the day here." As a precaution, the following morning he dispatched ten soldiers to reconnoiter a league in every direction around town, but they found no trace of the enemy.

Days 244 to 247
Wednesday, May 29, to Saturday, June 1, 1776

They left, as had become their practice, in the late afternoon. Two mule trains heading in the same direction joined them for protection, doubling the size of the group. Having covered seven leagues for the day, they stopped at midnight for a rest at Cerro Prieto until 5:00 a.m. In the late morning they reached the pond at Tecolote, where fresh tracks revealed the recent presence of presumed enemies. Because of the potential threat, after watering the animals (which took until 2:00 p.m.) they continued on rather than stopping for the usual midday rest. Heat rays shimmered in the distance and the light was blinding, but the Apaches, if still in the area, remained invisible.

Setting up a defensive perimeter, they camped in the late afternoon near La Tortuga.

"Shortly before 5:00 a.m.," writes Anza, "we lifted camp and rode five leagues to the Pozo de Crisanto, where we rested until 3:00 in the afternoon before riding the same again for the day. As we were setting up at La Mesa, already dark, the rearguard reported having seen...a large number of enemies, who silently rode across our tracks in the distance and disappeared....Anticipating an attack, we [took our positions and] remained on guard through the night.

"As soon as it was daylight I left camp with four soldiers to reconnoiter the area but found only the tracks of some thirty warriors who had taken the opposite direction to ours. After rejoining the group and riding for two leagues, we came to the Presidio at San Miguel de Horcasitas, from where I will begin my trip to Mexico [City] as ordered by the Viceroy, and where I now conclude this diary on the first of June of 1776."

And thus with his usual laconic simplicity, Anza concluded his report of the expedition that established the Californio society—not the resettlement of another European group in the New World, but the transplanting of a Native American people who, together with the language, culture, and religion of Spain, also carried a good deal of Spanish and some African blood. Separated by a distance of months from the mainstream of power, these subjects of Carlos III of Spain exchanged their status as second-class citizens at home to become the ruling class of California. And in their protected isolation, whether indigenous, mestizo, mulatto, criollo, or peninsular-born, they continued to intermarry with local natives who, by virtue of acquiring their language and religion, also became "people of reason." During the next three generations, while the Spanish Empire was reduced to a few scattered islands and the young United States grew ominously in power, the Monterey Californios created a uniquely integrated society that thrived for seventy years from San Diego to San Francisco.

About the Author

Vladimir Guerrero, professor of Spanish language and literature, has taught at the University of California, Davis; the University of Pennsylvania; Michigan State University; and the University of Oslo, Norway. He holds a PhD in medieval Spanish literature from UC Davis. Besides academic articles in his field, he has published short fiction in Spanish. While living in California his interest in the early Spanish period led to the study of the Anza expeditions and resulted in *The Anza Trail and the Settling of California*, his first book.

A California Legacy Book

Santa Clara University and Heyday Books are pleased to publish the California Legacy series, vibrant and relevant writings drawn from California's past and present.

Santa Clara University—founded in 1851 on the site of the eighth of California's original twenty-one missions—is the oldest institution of higher learning in the state. A Jesuit institution, it is particularly aware of its contribution to California's cultural heritage and its responsibility to preserve and celebrate that heritage.

Heyday Books, founded in 1974, specializes in critically acclaimed books on California literature, history, natural history, and ethnic studies.

Books in the California Legacy series appear as anthologies, single author collections, reprints of important books, and original works. Taken together, these volumes bring readers a new perspective on California's cultural life, a perspective that honors diversity and finds great pleasure in the eloquence of human expression.

Series editor: Terry Beers
Publisher: Malcolm Margolin
Advisory committee: Stephen Becker, William Deverell, Charles Faulhaber, David Fine, Steven Gilbar, Ron Hansen, Gerald Haslam, Robert Hass, Jack Hicks, Timothy Hodson, James Houston, Jeanne Wakatsuki Houston, Maxine Hong Kingston, Frank LaPena, Ursula K. Le Guin, Jeff Lustig, Tillie Olsen, Ishmael Reed, Alan Rosenus, Robert Senkewicz, Gary Snyder, Kevin Starr, Richard Walker, Alice Waters, Jennifer Watts, Al Young.

Thanks to the English Department at Santa Clara University and to Regis McKenna for their support of the California Legacy series.

SCU

CALIFORNIA
LEGACY

Other California Legacy Books

Unsettling the West: Eliza Farnham and Georgiana Bruce Kirby in Frontier California
JoAnn Levy

Indian Tales
Jaime de Angulo

Under the Fifth Sun: Latino Literature in California
Edited by Rick Heide

The Journey of the Flame
Walter Nordhoff

California: A Study of American Character
Josiah Royce

Death Valley in '49
William Lewis Manly

Eldorado: Adventures in the Path of Empire
Bayard Taylor

Lands of Promise and Despair: Chronicles of
Early California, 1535-1846
Edited by Rose Marie Beebe and Robert M. Senkewicz

Unfolding Beauty: Celebrating California's Landscapes
Edited with an Introduction by Terry Beers

The Maidu Indian Myths and Stories of Hanc'ibyjim
Edited and Translated by William Shipley

And many more!

If you would like to be added to the California Legacy mailing list, please send your name, address, phone number, and email address to:

California Legacy Project
English Department
Santa Clara University
Santa Clara, CA 95053

For more on California Legacy titles, events, or other information, please visit www.californialegacy.org.